AF352722

# The *Emotions* of Justice

GENDER,

STATUS,

*and*

LEGAL

PERFORMANCE

*in*

CHOSŎN

KOREA

## Jisoo M. Kim

UNIVERSITY OF WASHINGTON PRESS

*Seattle and London*

This publication was supported in part by the Korea Studies Program of the Jackson School of International Studies through the Core University Program for Korean Studies through the Ministry of Education of the Republic of Korea and the Korean Studies Promotion Service of the Academy of Korean Studies (AKS-2011-BAA-2101).

이 저서는 2011 년 대한민국 교육부와 한국학중앙연구원(한국학진흥사업단)을 통해 해외한국학중핵대학육성사업의 지원을 받아 수행된연구임 (AKS-2011-BAA-2101)



UNIVERSITY OF WASHINGTON PRESS
*www.washington.edu/uwpress*

Cataloging-in-Publication Data is on file with the Library of Congress
ISBN 978-0-295-99503-8

The paper used in this publication is acid-free and meets the minimum requirements of American National Standard for Information Sciences—Permanence of Paper for Printed Library Materials, ANSI Z39.48–1984.∞

In Memory of JaHyun Kim Haboush

*Contents*

*Acknowledgments*

Since I began my academic and intellectual journey at Columbia University, I have received incredible support and encouragement. To begin, my greatest scholarly debt is to the late JaHyun Kim Haboush who introduced me to the world of female petitioners during Chosŏn Korea. She has been my source of inspiration for studying Korean history, and from her I learned how interesting premodern Korean history could be. Through her writings, she will continue to inspire students studying Korean history. I am also indebted to Dorothy Ko for my understanding of Chinese women's and gender history and Madeleine Zelin for my knowledge of Chinese legal history. Their teaching and valuable guidance led me to place my work within the broader East Asian context. My thanks also to Charles Armstrong, Ted Hughes, and Eugenia Lean for providing critical advice and insightful comments.

I am grateful to all colleagues and friends who have provided valuable feedback and support at various venues during my research and writing process. Although it is impossible to mention everyone, I would like to recognize in particular Boudewijn Walraven, Donald Baker, John Duncan, Sun Joo Kim, Eugene Park, Anders Karlsson, Michael Pettid, Marion Eggert, Martina Deuchler, Hyaeweol Choi, Se-Mi Oh, George Kallander, and Jungwon Kim. I would also like to thank Tamara Loos, Janet Theiss, Anne Walthall, and Susan Burns, whose invaluable comments as discussants on my presentations at conferences have sharpened and refined my argument.

My special thanks also go to Kim Young-shik, Pak Tae-gyun, and Sem Vermeersch for their warm hospitality while I was at Seoul National University's Kyujanggak Institute for Korean Studies. I would like to echo my gratitude to Paik Young-suh, Michael Kim, and Choe Key-sook for generously helping me with my needs while I was at Kukhak Institute of Yonsei University. I have learned and benefitted from many discussions I had with colleagues in Korea.

I am grateful especially toward Chung Kung-shik, Kim Ho, Han Sang-gwon, Oh Soo-chang, Kim Sun-kyung, and Chung Ho-hun.

My colleagues in the Department of History and the Elliott School of International Affairs at the George Washington University have given me much support to finish this book. In particular, I would like to thank Bill Becker, Ed McCord, Shawn McHale, Ronald Spector, Gregg Brazinsky, Daqing Yang, and Young-Key Kim-Renaud for giving me their help and critical advice whenever I needed.

I could not have finished the book without receiving financial support from various organizations. Most graciously, the Advanced Research Grant from the Korea Foundation allowed me to go on leave and focus on completing the book. Earlier research and writing were also supported by the Sigur Center for Asian Studies at the George Washington University, Whiting Dissertation Completion Fellowship, AAS Travel Grants for Korean Studies Graduate Students, and Kyujanggak Archives Travel Grants from the International Center for Korean Studies at Seoul National University. I also thank Kyujanggak Library, the Central Library of Seoul National University, and the National Museum of Korea for granting me photographic permissions.

I would like to thank Clark Sorensen, the editor of the Korean Studies Series at University of Washington Press, as well as two anonymous readers of my manuscript for their detailed and insightful comments. Their suggestions vastly improved the quality of the manuscript. In this vein, I am also deeply grateful to outstanding editors and staff members at the University of Washington Press, including Lorri Hagman, Mary C. Ribesky, Beth Fuget, Rachael Levay, and freelance copyeditor Charles Wheeler, for their professionalism. I am most grateful for their help in seeing my first book come to fruition. I am, of course, solely responsible for any errors, omissions, and mistakes that remain.

The vernacular petition of Madam Yi in chapter 2 and commoner woman Chŏng's petition in chapter 3 of this book originally appeared in "Women's Legal Voice: Language, Power, and Gender Performativity in Late Chosŏn Korea," *Journal of Asian Studies* vol. 74, no. 3 (2015). I would like to acknowledge permission to republish materials used in this article.

Finally, but not least, I thank my family for their support. Although my father passed away before I graduated from college, he has always been and continues to be with me in spirit. My mother, Soon Nam Cho, has provided me with unlimited love and care throughout my life. She has been my source of inspiration in many ways and always encouraged me not to settle for less. I would like to also express my gratitude to my sister, Ji-Hyun Kim and her family for their comfort and support. I owe the most to my husband, Daewoo Cho, for his incredible patience and understanding. His endless loving support has been indispensable in pursuing my academic journey. My son, Justin M. Cho, was born in July 2006 and is truly a blessing. He has made our life immeasurably sweeter. He is now old enough to ask me about the book I am writing. I hope that he will one day read it on his own.

For the romanization of Korean terms and names, I have used the McCune-Reischauer system. When referring to Korean historical figures and Korean authors in this book, I have kept their family name first without using a comma, as is the standard practice in Korean. For authors who have published in English, I have followed the sequence of given name followed by family name.

To minimize confusion for English readers when referring to women of different status who appear in petition sources, instead of using the title "*ssi*," which refers to elite yangban women's status, I use "madam" after their natal surname (e.g., Madam Kim). For commoner women, I do not use the title "*sosa*" (or "*choi*," which is the colloquial pronunciation of *sosa*), which refers to their commoner status, but instead I refer to them by their natal surname as shown in the sources and specify their status when their name first appears (e.g., commoner woman Hwang). Finally I refer to slaves by their first name as shown in their petitions (e.g., Malgŭm).

In Chosŏn Korea, dates were recorded using the sixty-year cycle that was developed in ancient China. The years specified in petitions use a name comprised of two Chinese characters. In many petitions, it is difficult to know the exact date because, for example, the year *kabo* could refer to 1714, 1774, 1834, or 1894. Taking into consideration that petition sources collected by the Kyujanggak and Changsŏgak archives are mainly from the late Chosŏn period, scholars project that they were written in either the eighteenth or nineteenth century. Accordingly, the possible dates I provide in notes are from these two centuries.

For the *Veritable Records of the Kings of the Chosŏn Dynasty* (Chosŏn wangjo sillok), I used the online source provided by the Kuksa P'yŏnch'an Wiwŏnhoe (National Institute of Korean History) at http://sillok.history.

go.kr/main/main.jsp. Citations from this record include, in sequence: the *Sillok* of each king; volume number; and reign year, month, and day (e.g., *T'aejo sillok*, 1 [1/7/28]).

All translations are mine unless otherwise indicated.

*Kings of the Chosŏn Dynasty*

| | | |
|---|---|---|
| T'aejo | 太祖 | 1392–98 |
| Chŏngjong | 定宗 | 1398–1400 |
| T'aejong | 太宗 | 1400–18 |
| Sejong | 世宗 | 1418–50 |
| Munjong | 文宗 | 1450–52 |
| Tanjong | 端宗 | 1452–55 |
| Sejo | 世祖 | 1455–68 |
| Yejong | 睿宗 | 1468–69 |
| Sŏngjong | 成宗 | 1469–94 |
| Yŏnsan-gun | 燕山君 | 1494–1506 |
| Chungjong | 中宗 | 1506–44 |
| Injong | 仁宗 | 1544–45 |
| Myŏngjong | 明宗 | 1545–67 |
| Sŏnjo | 宣祖 | 1567–1608 |
| Kwanghae-gun | 光海君 | 1608–23 |
| Injo | 仁祖 | 1623–49 |
| Hyojong | 孝宗 | 1649–59 |
| Hyŏnjong | 顯宗 | 1659–74 |
| Sukchong | 肅宗 | 1674–1720 |
| Kyŏngjong | 景宗 | 1720–24 |
| Yŏngjo | 英祖 | 1724–76 |
| Chŏngjo | 正祖 | 1776–1800 |
| Sunjo | 純祖 | 1800–34 |
| Hŏnjong | 憲宗 | 1834–49 |
| Ch'ŏlchong | 哲宗 | 1849–63 |
| Kojong | 高宗 | 1863–1907 |
| Sunjong | 純宗 | 1907–10 |

*The*
# Emotions
*of*
# Justice

# INTRODUCTION

So we learn about justice by being cheated or treated unfairly as inferiors, by being punished when we expect to be rewarded, by having something that we think is indisputably ours taken away from us, by being hurt—and, in some primal sense, wanting to get even. . . . Our sense of justice, in other words, has its origins in revenge as well as in care and compassion.

—Robert Solomon, *A Passion for Justice*

IN THE SECOND MONTH OF THE YEAR *KYŎNGO*,[1] A FEMALE SLAVE named Malgŭm filed a plaint with a magistrate against Sŭngŭn, her husband's male relative.[2] Malgŭm's husband, also a slave, had inherited land from his father that his great-grandfather had bought from a male slave named Ŏsŏn. When Malgŭm's husband was alive, he had sold two parcels of land and had kept the remaining land. But after her husband's death, Sŭngŭn filed suit against Malgŭm to dispossess her property. In order to preserve her land, Malgŭm filed a counter plaint against Sŭngŭn claiming her ownership over her husband's land and stating that Sŭngŭn had attempted to take away her land by forging a document. The kernel of the case was that Sŭngŭn and Malgŭm were claiming ownership over the same fields.

Malgŭm in her petition stated:

I, the humble petitioner, address my grievous situation [*wŏnjŏng*] that occurred in this world. . . . In the year *kapcha* when my husband passed away, Myŏngbok's cousin Sŭngŭn, who is by nature a cunning man, stole the deed when he visited us several times during my husband's funeral. . . . While my husband and father-in-law had cultivated the fields for two generations, he [Sŭngŭn] had remained silent. How could he attempt to deprive me of my land now? When my husband, Myŏngbok, was alive, he did not say a word to stop him from selling the fields. Now that my husband is dead, how could

he file suit? . . . Please restrict Sŭngŭn from selfishly scheming to dispossess
my land and help save this widow by clearing a false charge made against me
so that I can relieve my grievance [wŏn]. I address Your Honor and sincerely
wish you to settle the case by giving an order [see fig. I.1].[3]

On the ninth day of the second month, the magistrate stated in his written
judgment that Sŭngŭn should be arrested if the petitioner's case were verified. After conducting an investigation, the county office found that Sŭngŭn's
document did not match the government's land register and concluded that
he had failed to provide evidence to support his possession of the land. On
the sixteenth day of that month, the magistrate ordered to endorse Malgŭm's
possession of the fields.[4]

Malgŭm's petition demonstrates a female slave's legal capacity to lodge a
complaint against a male relative concerning ownership of land. This example
corroborates the observations in an article authored by W. Woodville Rockhill, the United States chargé d'affaires in Korea from 1886 to 1887. In 1891,
Rockhill wrote, in an article containing a brief survey of Korean society based
on his experience in Seoul, "The rights of owners over their slaves are limited by law. Thus one may not be put to death by his owner before the latter
has obtained the permission of the Board of Punishments if he resides within
Seoul, or of the high provincial authorities if living elsewhere. Slaves, moreover, enjoy certain civil rights. Thus one slave may bring an action against
another to obtain damages or recover debts."[5] In this article, Rockhill pointed
to slaves' legal capacity as one of the characteristics of the judiciary practice in
the Chosŏn period (1392–1910).

Like other chattel slaves, Chosŏn slaves were recognized as both property
and human beings. The humanity of slaves seems to have been acknowledged
in law in a number of ways: they were individually held responsible for their
actions; they were protected by law against arbitrary murder by masters as
well as third parties; and they owned property in the form of land, cash, and
even other slaves.[6] Although slavery is often characterized as a form of brutal
domination and asymmetrical power, Chosŏn slaves' ability to engage in legal
activities complicates our understanding of their subjectivity.

My aim in this study is neither to explore the subjectivity of slaves nor
the slavery system in the Chosŏn.[7] The preceding anecdote shows how the
complexity of the society emerges when we take into consideration that even
a female slave such as Malgŭm had the legal capacity to lodge a complaint
against a male relative. The Chosŏn state is often portrayed as a rigid soci-

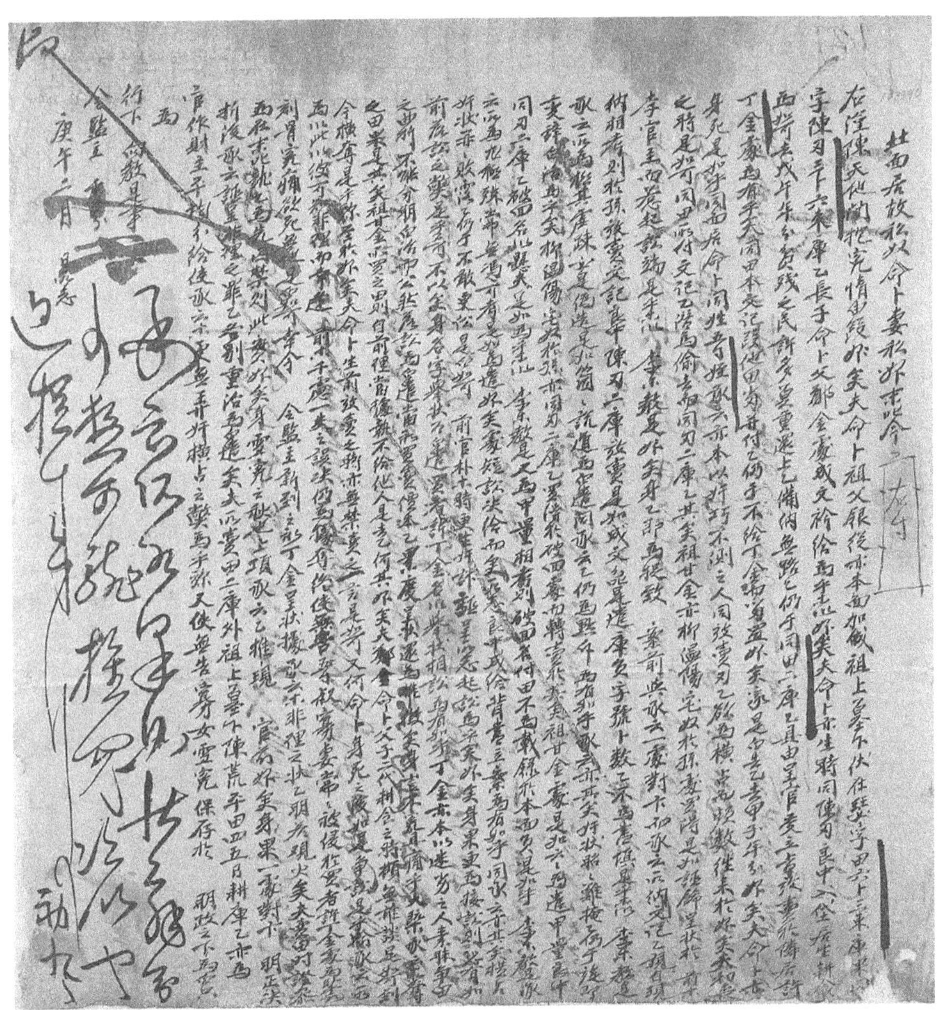

FIGURE I.1. Malgŭm's petition (land dispute) submitted to county office. The text in the left margin is the magistrate's written response with his official red seal. The first line in the right margin is the title written in the order of petitioner's residence, her dead husband's name, and her social status followed by her first name. Below the title is a diagram showing the length of her index finger, which was drawn to verify that Malgŭm was the petitioner. Slaves had to draw the shape of their finger, as they did not have a name seal. *Komunsŏ* 183390–2. Courtesy of Kyujanggak Archives, Seoul National University.

ety due to its hereditary status system, which included a slave status, and its gender division based on Confucian concepts. This book presents a different, more complex picture of how subjects of different genders and statuses interacted as equally recognized legal subjects in this society.[8] During the Chosŏn, women, irrespective of their status, were recognized as legal subjects equal to their male counterparts and able to air grievances to the state on their behalf. "Legal subjects" here are those who had the capacity to engage in legal actions such as filing petitions, buying and selling, entering into contracts, borrowing and lending, and making bequests.

In a hierarchically structured and gender-segregated society such as the Chosŏn, which had a hereditary status system that was largely divided into elite aristocrats, middle people, commoners, and the lowborn, how was it possible that even female slaves were allowed to express negative emotions or the sense of injustice in public by exercising their legal capacity to address grievances to the state?[9] What was the reason for conferring legal capacity to every subject regardless of gender or status? What were the modes of petitioning and the narrative strategies utilized to pursue petitioners' interests? To investigate these inquiries, I draw on a wide array of sources, including petitions, official documents, criminal records, legal codes, and didactic texts.

The petitioning activity of multiple subjects in the Chosŏn involves three discursive fields of law: the role of emotions in administering justice; the construction of legal culture through the performative aspect of petitioning activity; and the formation of legal subjectivities. This is a multifaceted and multilayered history in its treatment of legal institutions in which emotions played a significant role in administering justice; legal practice where ordinary people, both elites and nonelites, sought rectification through expressing negative emotions in court, which ultimately aided in shaping legal discourse and institutional development; and legal performance in which the narrative, display of emotions, and mode of petitioning shifted in different time periods.

In this book, the meanings of emotional words are understood in the context of local cultures, the value systems that they signal, and the culturally specific notions of selfhood that they represent. Women and men freely expressed their emotions of *wŏn*, or the sense of being wronged, in their legal narratives. The sovereign and authorities, sharing the same culture, comprehended the importance of relieving one's negative emotions that stemmed from injustice.

The primary goal of this study is to explore the concept of *wŏn*, which was the kernel of legal discourse and legal narrative. As shown in Malgŭm's petition, the beginning and ending of her narrative mention grievances or the emotions of *wŏn*. In order to understand how grievances were addressed, it is necessary to first recognize the meaning of *wŏn*. In 1401, during T'aejong's reign (r. 1400–18), the Chosŏn state installed the "petition drum" (*sinmun'go*) to allow people to directly petition the sovereign by striking the drum installed in front of the State Tribunal (Ŭigŭmbu). The petition drum provided subjects with an opportunity to redress grievances that had not been rectified in lower courts. This petition drum was institutionalized under the influence of a Neo-Confucian vision that the monarch's mandate relied on listening to his people.[10] Although subjects had been authorized to petition the government during the Koryŏ dynasty (918–1392), the legal channel to voice concerns directly to the sovereign was not instituted until the Chosŏn dynasty was established.[11] This new type of appeals system was referred to as *sowŏn* in Korean, with *sowŏn* meaning "to appeal *wŏn*."

The term *wŏn* is often translated as "injustice," "grievance," or "wrong" in English. However, these English translations do not fully capture the way in which the term was used in Korea and particularly its emotional aspects. *Wŏn* was aroused specifically when subjects were legally violated or wronged. Negative emotions such as vengeance, hatred, anger, grief, remorse, and pain were merged into a single emotion known as *wŏn*. The more petitioners embodied *wŏn*, the stronger their justification became for demanding the state to redress their grievances. The very term used for the appeals system in the Chosŏn shows how the emotions of *wŏn* provided sufficient grounds for subjects to appeal to the state. What this implies is that law and emotions were not always mutually exclusive but in fact closely interrelated when it came to seeking legal justice.[12]

Dispensing justice in the Confucian setting depended on whether the emotions of *wŏn* were relieved. The sense of justice was not only about royal compassion and sympathy but it was also cultivated from negative emotions such as vengeance, hatred, anger, grief, remorse, and pain.[13] It is my contention that the emotions of *wŏn*, which encompassed these negative emotions, played the most critical role in the performance of justice during the Chosŏn. The cases examined in this book deal with these negative emotions under the umbrella of *wŏn*. Furthermore, I argue that relieving the emotions of *wŏn* was the mechanism by which to achieve justice and the primary motive that led ordinary people to turn to courts.

The Chinese character 義 (K: *ŭi* Ch.: *yi*) is translated as "justice" or "righteousness." However, *ŭi* is not the term we often find in legal documents. We do find officials using *ŭi* or *gongŭi* (righteousness/public justice) but more often when discussing political affairs than legal matters. Relieving *wŏn* was the language employed in petition sources to express justice in the legal context of the Chosŏn. While placing the emotions at the center of analysis, this study concerns itself with the way legal culture and different subjectivities within it were constructed. From early to later in the dynasty, the legal culture of the Chosŏn was shaped through linguistic practices, the appropriation of legal channels, and the utilization of different strategies and modes of petitioning. We will see how the display of the varied emotions of *wŏn* by multiple subjects using diverse narratives shaped and molded a distinctive legal culture of Korea.

By tracing a discourse of emotions and linguistic practices in the juridical field of the Chosŏn, this study articulates a new way of conceptualizing justice by pushing the theoretical, methodological, and empirical boundaries of our understanding of justice in the context of Confucian Chosŏn society. Every legal system, Western and non-Western, has sui generis features and simultaneously shares some aspects that provide useful insights across cultural boundaries. This examination of the intersection of law, emotions, gender, and status, furthers the interdisciplinary dialogue and expands the historical scholarship on the topic of justice.

## TOWARD A NEW HISTORIOGRAPHICAL PARADIGM

Only a few scholars within or outside of Korea have explored the field of Korean legal history. Within Korea, the existing historiography on this topic echoes that of the anticolonialist historians, who have placed Chosŏn history on a trajectory such that Korea would autonomously have modernized had Japanese imperialism not intervened. This group of historians, writing against the Japanese colonial portrayal of Chosŏn history as stagnant and backward, has sought to identify internal change in the Chosŏn structure prior to the Japanese occupation. However, this view of internal development theory (*naejaejŏk palchŏn non*) has been challenged by another group of scholars outside of Korea, who contend that the economic development of the Chosŏn was very limited and that the agents of change identified by anticolonial historians were insufficient to have led to modernity.

Korean legal historians similarly follow the logic of anticolonial historians. Some scholars have argued that indigenous Korean customs were suppressed and distorted by the Japanese authorities as part of their colonial policy. In order to give prominence to Korea's indigenous legal tradition, eminent Korean legal historians such as Pak Pyŏng-ho and others have argued that legal precedents and customary laws governed Chosŏn Korea.[14] However, Marie S. Kim has challenged this view by claiming that it is necessary to distinguish customs and custom in order to discuss customary law in Chosŏn to argue that Korean traditional society maintained a legal order based on private law.[15] She shares the view of Jérôme Bourgon, who has argued that the notion of customary law was absent in China, and suggests that there are methodological flaws in approaching Korean legal tradition by applying Western concepts.[16]

Kim's critique of Korean legal historians has a point in that the application of Western terminology is especially problematic when little attention has been paid to how the concept should be applied in the Chosŏn context. She makes a compelling argument that customary law was "nonexistent in traditional East Asia within the imperial Chinese legal sphere."[17] According to her, the notion of customary and civil laws was introduced to East Asia only when Japan first imported European civil law during the Meiji Restoration and then introduced it to Korea in order to enforce Japanese legal order on colonial subjects.[18]

I concur that scholarship showing the existence of Western customary or civil law in the context of premodern Korea misrepresents Chosŏn law and its legal system. I also agree that the Chosŏn legal system primarily consisted of penal and administrative law and that civil law was subsumed under the framework of punishments. However, I disagree with the claims that "the Chosŏn law served no interest in resolving disputes between individuals" and that "the notion of royal justice was absent because the state was responsible for maintaining social order but not for dispensing justice in private relations."[19] In discussing the Chosŏn law, claims based on official representation and not actual legal practice are of limited value.[20] The examples provided in this book show how the authorities as well as the king were concerned to "resolve legal disputes between private individuals." In fact, in order to administer justice, the ruling authorities had to execute proper judgment and timely adjudications of both criminal and civil lawsuits.[21]

Previous scholarship on legal history in Korea primarily has focused on whether the Chosŏn judicial system was up to par with legal criteria set by the West.[22] The present study avoids engaging in such a hollow debate. Western legal concepts cannot adequately guide one's approach to investigating non-Western legal systems. This account of petitioning practice incorporates indigenous meanings as much as possible and compares this practice with that of other cultures when necessary to gain a broader understanding.

Not only did the Chosŏn legal system function differently but also the Chosŏn perception of emotions was dissimilar from that of the West. In Europe, the Cartesian mind-body dualism associated emotion and the body with women, and the mind and rationality with men. It was also the case that with the rise of modernity, emotions have been treated as antithetical to law in the West. Modeled on Immanuel Kant's view of separating reason from the inclinations, law was considered a product of reason and thus the opposite of emotion. By the early twentieth century in the West, emotions came to be treated as having no prominent role in civilized society as they were recognized as "primitive."[23]

In the context of Chosŏn Korea, the dichotomy between emotion and reason seems to have been not always so clear.[24] The term *chŏng* (Ch. *qing*) can be translated as "emotion," "feeling," and "sentiment."[25] The meaning of *chŏng* has a different semantic level from its Western usage in that it is closely tied to an array of other Korean philosophical concepts such as human nature (*insŏng*), mind of the Way (*tosim*), mind of man (*insim*), mind of Heaven (*ch'ŏnsim*), Four Beginnings (*sadan*), principle (*li*), and material force (*ki*). In Confucian cultures, it is not possible to discuss emotions without deep understanding of human nature, and the human mind in particular.[26]

In *The Book of Rites* (Yesŏ) there is a conventional list of the Seven Emotions (*Ch'iljŏng*): desire, hate, love, fear, grief, anger, and joy. The concept of Seven Emotions developed metaphysically with the Four Beginnings that was based on the classical Chinese philosopher Mencius's essential view that human nature is good.[27] In the sixteenth century, two representative Confucian thinkers of Korea, T'oegye (Yi Hwang, 1501–70) and Yulgok (Yi I, 1536–84), conducted an intellectual and philosophical conversation, known as the Four-Seven Debate, which addressed concerns about how the Four Beginnings and the Seven Emotions should be understood in the context of the principle and material-force dualism.[28] This debate is recognized as a famous controversy that influenced subsequent generations of thinkers and shaped Korean Neo-Confucian philosophy.

Although it is beyond the scope of this study to elaborate on the details of the Four-Seven Debate, what is worth mentioning here is that the central theme of the debate involved various kinds of positive and negative emotions and the way they originate based on principle and material force. More specifically, Korean scholars debated whether abstract principles or the materiality of objects and the human mind controlled human behavior. Although the debate created a polarity between principle and material force, the prevalent view was they were never separated but were closely intertwined.[29]

According to Neo-Confucians, the universe was perceived as "a single organic whole where humans and all other creatures lived in a harmonious unity."[30] This perception of maintaining equilibrium and harmony in the continuum of all living things extended to legal cosmology in the practice of justice. The emotions of *wŏn* were treated as negative energy that damaged harmony and eventually causing natural disaster by breaking the equilibrium. Therefore, it was crucial to relieve people's *wŏn* as every individual had the potential of generating this negative energy. The idea of harmony between man and nature is very well reflected in the legal discourse examined in chapter 1.[31]

In the study of emotions, recent scientific research in various fields including psychology, anthropology, and philosophy has shown that emotions and reason cannot be opposed. There has been a paradigm shift in the study of emotions, which is called "the cognitive turn." Scholars who study emotions are influenced by the cognitivism that allows them to think of emotions and reason together. Influenced by "the cognitive theories" of emotions, philosopher Robert C. Solomon argues that emotions are a kind of evaluative judgment and are central to our sense of justice.[32] Philosopher Martha Nussbaum similarly claims that emotions are involved in making moral decisions and judgments.[33] Neuroscientist Antonio Damasio has found that emotions are critical to making intelligent and rational decisions and suggests that they connect the mind and body.[34]

Historians have been also influenced by cognitive theories and have applied them in studying the history of emotions. Several historians have offered analytical tools to examine emotions.[35] Among them, William Reddy has produced work most helpful for this study. In his book *Navigation of Feeling*, Reddy coined the term "emotive" by appropriating the model of John Austin's term "performative" in linguistics. He regards statements about emotions as performative in the sense that they do change things; they change the state of the speaker or of the world around the speaker. These are the emotions that, when expressed and acted upon, transform reality. When this idea is applied to historical processes, it offers a way for us to perceive emotions, which themselves do change, as a powerful device of social change.[36] Reddy's notion of emotives can be fruitfully employed to examine the emotions of *wŏn*, or the sense of being wronged, at a particular time in Korean history in order to understand the performance of justice. In studying emotions, it is crucial to understand the cultural importance and meaning of these notions that may differ according to time and space.

## THE EMOTIONS OF *WŎN*: GENDER, STATUS, AND LAW

With the advent of the petition drum, which authorized subjects to strike the drum and address their grievances by expressing *wŏn* in public, the state allowed each person's voice to reach the apex of the power structure. In a highly stratified and gender-segregated society such as the Chosŏn, the puzzling question is how it was possible for the state to recognize every subject regardless of gender or status as an independent legal subject.[37] More specifically, what was the source of conferring legal capacity to women of all social statuses, including female slaves?

From a comparative perspective, this question is particularly significant when taking into consideration the fact that other contemporary patriarchal societies such as China or England subordinated women's legal status to men. Furthermore, as Daniel Smail has shown in his study of medieval Europe, in Marseille, France, members of the unfree and marginalized groups—such as domestic servants, serfs, Muslims, and Jews—were not allowed to "publicize" their anger in the law courts because it was thought to be too dangerous to the state.[38] In this regard, the Chosŏn judicial system is worthy of study because it provides useful insights into how emotions played a role in a legal institution to sustain social harmony by recognizing *wŏn* horizontally as well as vertically. William Shaw's study on legal norms of the late Chosŏn shows how the judicial system discriminated against subjects on the one hand but simultaneously minimized such discrimination on the other hand. Although he eloquently demonstrates that "legal rationality" existed in the late Chosŏn through an examination of crime and punishment, Shaw does not explore the implications of a legal system that operated in a somewhat contradictory fashion.[39]

During the Chosŏn, relieving the emotions of *wŏn* was the primary motive that led ordinary people to turn to courts. And by providing emotional satisfaction to people who addressed grievances to the sovereign, the state could not only create power but also reinforce the essence of social order. The emotions of *wŏn*, which functioned as a key element in legal narratives, were perceived as natural emotions that could not be repressed, unlike other emotions such as personal desire (*sayok*) or sexual desire (*ŭmyok*). Although these latter desires were also considered to be natural feelings, they had to be controlled and suppressed in order to maintain social order. The state, in contrast, thought that repressing the *wŏn* of anyone, regardless of gender and social status, was dangerous and would cause social disorder. Unlike the Marseille government, the Chosŏn state perceived that it was necessary to relieve negative emotions in order to prevent rebellion against the government. *Wŏn* was treated as an egalitarian sentiment that served as a channel for every legal subject to seek rectification.

During the Chosŏn, the hereditary status system and the official representation of Confucian gender norms treated nonelites and women as subordinate subjects. The concept of gender and status was a crucial element in organizing the Chosŏn society. Laws that represented inequality were evident in places such as punishments, procedures, sumptuary rules, and the commutation of certain penalties to monetary fines for officials or elite aristocrats.[40] Despite these salient unequal aspects of the law, recognizing every subject as holding some legal power and allowing each to express the sentiment of *wŏn* neutralized gender and status hierarchies to a certain extent in the judicial domain and minimized discrimination in the outcome of criminal trials and civil lawsuits. The legal space was one of the few places, if not the only place, where the nonelite could publicly challenge the elite, in this case by exercising their legal capacity to petition. The practice of such recognition generated a distinctive feature of the Confucian judicial system where legal subjects interacted in the realm of law without gender or status distinctions.

Examination of interactions among a variety of subjects demonstrates how each social status group enjoyed a certain amount of freedom within its status boundary. Even slaves such as Malgŭm, who were recognized as both property and human beings, had the legal capacity to not only file a petition but also make legal transactions such as buying or selling, lending or borrowing, entering into contracts, and making bequests. Although there was the limitation that slaves could not file suit against their own masters, they could bring complaints against elites or commoners if they had been legally violated.

In the Chosŏn, the Confucian judicial system protected subjects within their status boundaries while concurrently preventing them from defying the social order. Conversely, while petitioning activity functioned as a safety valve, it reinforced the state's legitimacy by regulating subjects to prevent them from transgressing social norms. The state authorized subjects to voice their grievances but also rigorously sanctioned them when they crossed a status boundary to challenge their ascribed role. Insofar as people within each status group performed their roles within the hereditary status system, all subjects could equally seek legitimate recourse through the law to rectify injustice done to them. This obviously does not mean that the modern notion of "equality" existed, because clearly the hereditary status system served to produce social inequality and hierarchical relations. But subjects who were deprived of privileges that they were able to enjoy *within* the boundary of their status were at least given the equal opportunity to file complaints with the state.[41]

The distinction between elite and nonelite was relatively clear even when there was instability in the status system toward the late Chosŏn. Until the Japanese-sponsored Kabo reform took place in 1894, there was no sign at the state level of interest in abolishing the hereditary status system. In the case of China, the state's goal prior to the Qing dynasty (1644–1911) was preserving status hierarchy, which was distinguished by varying norms of sexual propriety. However, during the Qing, the state's goal under the Manchus was to enforce new norms of gender order based on common moral standards that applied to both elites and nonelites. Matthew Sommer has demonstrated that the shift from status to gender performance was intended to protect familial roles especially in peasant families during the Qing.[42]

Conditions during the Chosŏn were not ripe for implementing a gender order based on common moral standards that uniformly applied to women of all social statuses. Although the two wars that took place in the Chosŏn, the Imjin War (1592–98) and the Manchu invasion (1627 and 1636–37), brought significant changes to Korea in the latter half of the dynasty, the situation was not grave enough to alter the basis of gender and status order, as happened in China. For instance, during the late Chosŏn, the state regulated elite women's sexual conduct even more rigorously than it did earlier in the dynasty, by executing elite women who committed adultery. However, there was no such legal regulation on nonelite women in the Chosŏn legal codes.[43]

As is saliently reflected in the indigenous legal codes, the distinctive element of the appeals system in the Chosŏn was an outcome of the Neo-Confucian polity that was intricately interwoven with the hereditary status system. In a society where social order was framed by status distinction, the ruling class, without a doubt, possessed far more privileges than the lower class. Although the state adopted a Confucian civil service examination system that was to a degree meritocratic in nature, it was the hereditary male aristocrats at the center of political affairs who dominated the bureaucratic realm.[44]

However, subordinate subjects such as women and the lowborn embodied much greater *wŏn* than privileged aristocrat men, which generated solid grounds for them to redress grievances. Thus, it is possible to claim that no group in the Chosŏn society was entirely excluded from performing a political role, as every subject was empowered to petition and thereby exerted some influence in shaping the legislation of the state. For instance, two laws that regulated social injustice in the late Chosŏn, which are examined in chapter 5, precisely stemmed from grievances that had been addressed by petitioners from the early period of the dynasty, and women were active agents who reported such injustice. These two laws, which were related to regulating "the mistreatment of commoners as slaves" and "magistrates' abuse of punishment," represent how the judicial realm was used as a site to negotiate the meaning of grievance between the state and society.

## IN THE LEGAL ARCHIVE: GENRE, NARRATIVE, AND PETITION

The term "petition" is generally used to mean a request, demand, or complaint that is made by a private individual to the government. Legal historians have distinguished petitions that were filed for favors from those for justice. Petitions for favors refer to requests made to higher persons for an act of mercy or aid. Petitions for justice are usually directed against an opponent and focus on a formalized legal remedy in an ordinary court process or a legal means of redress as the right of appeal.[45] The petition documents examined here include both grievances that were filed to request mercy or aid and those that sought legal redress and demanded justice, the majority being the latter. Petitions signed by a large number of people and collective petitions that deal with communal grievances are beyond the scope of this study as they are more relevant in studying social movements.[46]

What, then, is the legal type of petition? What is its significance, and how should historians read such petitions? The petition sources used in this study are (1) judicial writing to persuade the authorities and the king for redress; (2) stories that narrate emotions of *wŏn* to seek justice; and (3) personal or family accounts of negative encounters with relatives or the community. The characteristics of petitioners' performance of writing and speaking of their grievances must be considered in the context of their audiences, who were the authorities and the king.

In *Fiction in the Archives*, Natalie Z. Davis provides an insightful method of reading letters of remission in sixteenth-century France. By using a "fictional" lens in observing the documents, she emphasizes the role of "crafting" in shaping the narratives. By "fictional" she does not refer to "feigned elements" but how people "formed, shaped, and molded" their stories as they constructed their narratives.[47] Although grasping fictional elements is useful and I am inspired by her approach in reading petition documents, the method is not sufficient to understand the complexity of orality and textuality that the Korean petition sources entail.[48] The "crafting of narrative" elements exist in both written and oral petitions, but the way in which they were addressed cannot be comprehended by merely exploring fictional components in petitioners' narratives. In this study, I adopt a similar approach of reading "fictional" elements, but also look more seriously into performative aspects of linguistic practices.

Performative aspects of petitioning are apparent not only in petitioners' physical display of *wŏn* in public but also in the orality and textuality that were closely associated with the two modes of petitioning in the Chosŏn: oral and written. Through these two methods petitioners narrated their events on the theatrical stage of petitioning, and it was authorities who observed and evaluated the performance of petitioners through their communication skills. The narrative that was used to express the *wŏn* defined hierarchies of relationships and shaped the legal identities of the actors involved. For example, petitioners in general used humble words in narrating their grievances to the state. The authorities, by contrast, responded with their authoritative voice in their written judgments. In the context of early Ireland, Robin Stacey shows how verbal art was intimately related to exercising one's legal power.[49] Similarly, the performance of law through speech and writing in the Chosŏn was inevitably tied to the linguistic practice of culture and the exercise of power.

When addressing grievances to the state, subjects were able to present either written or oral petitions. When submitting written petitions, petitioners narrated their grievances through classical Chinese, which was the official written language for legal petitions. Some elite women, however, submitted their petitions in vernacular Korean, the written language they were educated with, thereby challenging official literary space. It is most likely that the majority of the illiterate population such as women and nonelite men relied on scriveners when submitting written petitions in classical Chinese. It is not far-fetched to assume that Malgŭm's petition, introduced earlier, was drafted by a scrivener.[50] Despite the fact that scriveners were involved in drafting written petitions, this does not mean that the voices of original petitioners are absent from the petitions we can find in the legal archives. The purpose of employing scriveners was not for them to create stories from scratch but that they would articulate the existing grievance of petitioners so that they could effectively persuade the authorities and win favor. The grievances of petitioners were first conveyed through speech in a *pre-textual* mode, and that spoken language was *textualized* to produce written petitions.[51] The narrative of *wŏn* constructed in written petitions during the Chosŏn was thus generated by multiple actors.

In oral petitions, we see a similar process, but it was authorities from the Board of Punishments (Hyŏngjo) who textualized the grievances of petitioners to report to the king. Unlike the case with written petitions, in which the aim was to heighten the petitioners' grievances in order to convey their emotions to the authorities or the king, oral petitioners were able to display their grievances directly to the authorities. Despite the benefit that those petitioners were able to perform their *wŏn* right in front of the authorities, the original voices of petitioners were inevitably lost in reaching the ultimate point of justice. This is because the authorities recorded the gist of a grievance and advised the king whether it was a serious or petty grievance. After reading the report, the king had the final decision-making power to determine whether the grievance had merit. Through verbal performance, the grievances of oral petitions were conducted in a pre-textual mode, but the government authorities were given the task of textualizing petitioners' grievances by describing, interpreting, and making sense of their experiences.[52] Petitioners' verbal performance, despite its orality, could be seen as inherently textual in the sense that it generated a text through which to convey the grievance to the king. In the legal culture of the Chosŏn, the production of both written and oral petitions we find in the legal archives was a "collaborative, dialogic, and jointly orchestrated affair"[53] in that it entailed multiple processes. In both written and oral petitions, orality and textuality crisscrossed the two modes of petitioning.[54] It is thus possible to define the petition as a mixed genre of discourse that orality and textuality developed jointly in constructing the narrative of *wŏn* through scripted performance.[55]

But why examine the petition rather than another type of legal document? Why is it such an invaluable source in studying emotions and justice? Previous studies of Korean legal history have used criminal records such as *Records of Stating and Hearing* (Simnirok) and inquest records (*kŏman*).[56] These are useful sources along with petitions in that they offer a window to examine the lives of nonelites, who remain mostly invisible in historical archives. When studying the history of emotions, however, these other sources lack the emotional tone that is rich in petitions. The testimonies given by the accused and witnesses were pulled together into a single narrative by authorities when writing interrogation records. In order to maintain "objectivity" or an "unbiased" view, the authorities purposefully maintained an impersonal tone in their records. As a result, the structure of court transcripts is an "emotionless architectonic" form, and it is very difficult to recover emotions in those documents.[57] Although it is possible to infer what emotions were involved in homicide cases through testimonies, the records' emotional neutrality in shaping the "narrative" of document makes it a precarious endeavor.[58] In contrast, petitions were constructed precisely to amplify petitioners' emotions, especially their *wŏn*, and they document physical and emotional reactions expressed by gesture and tone of speech. Furthermore, unlike the interrogation or criminal records that sustain a single and monotone narrative, petitions provide multifaceted narratives of storytelling according to the petitioner's gender, age, and social status, and it is possible to discern different narrative strategies of petitioners.

In order to effectively utilize petition sources that are rich in anecdotes, this book focuses on various issues women complained about and the kinds of narrative strategies they employed in structuring their arguments.[59] Although women's petitions are primarily represented here, their lives are not explored in isolation. Women are the key actors in this study, but it is a gender history in that it includes male-female relations on individual as well as institutional levels.[60] Most of the petitions women addressed were filed against males, who were relatives, neighbors, or county magistrates. Through petitions it is possible to compare the social conflicts of various groups, such as ruined literati versus nouveaux riches, affluent versus destitute commoners, and former masters versus ex-slaves. In addition, because it was imperative to identify one's status in addition to one's gender when petitioning, these two are crucial constructing themes.

There are nearly six hundred records of women's petitions from the Chosŏn, including at both local and capital levels, and most petitions are from the eighteenth and nineteenth centuries. Approximately 25 percent of the six hundred petitions are from county and provincial levels; these petitions exist in original form and are extremely rich in anecdotes. Such petitions can be located in the *Komunsŏ* (Old documents) compiled by the Kyujanggak Archives of Seoul National University and the Changsŏgak Archives of Academy of Korean Studies. Unlike petitions submitted at local courts, most of the petitions presented to the king are recorded in official documents such as the *Veritable Records of the Kings of the Chosŏn Dynasty* (Chosŏn wangjo sillok), Records of Daily Reflections (Ilsŏngnok), *Records of the Royal Secretariat* (Sŭngjŏngwŏn ilgi), *Records of the Border Defense Command* (Pibyŏnsa tŭngnok), and *Records of Stating and Hearings* (Simnirok).[61]

There were various terms used in Korean to refer to the "petition." First, the term *soji* referred to general petitions that were presented at county and provincial courts. This includes petitions filed as complaints to seek legal remedy as well as requests for tax relief, endorsement, material help, permits, dispensation, and so on. *Wŏnjŏng* and *tanja* are different terms for petitions. *Wŏnjŏng* was used to refer to petitions submitted to county courts, but *tanja* was used specifically to indicate petitions submitted by ruling aristocrats, the *yangban*. A petition submitted at the provincial office, which functioned as a higher court, was called a *ŭisong*. People appealed to the provincial office when their grievances were not redressed at the county level. Finally, petitions presented to the king, as a final resort, were divided into written and oral petitions; the written were referred to as *sangŏn* and the oral as *kyŏkchaeng*. For the sake of this study, I do not make distinctions in terminology among these different types and use "petition" broadly to denote grievances addressed to local authorities as well as to the sovereign, and I explain a petition's specific characteristics as I illustrate each case.

The existence of these various Korean terms for petitions reflects the fact that subjects had to go through different levels of court, which demanded an incredible amount of effort, before they could actually appeal to the king. Thus, it was never an easy matter for petitioners to approach the sovereign. The state strictly punished subjects who bypassed intermediate courts and did not abide by the legal procedures. It is worth noting that women had to go through long and difficult journeys to voice their grievances.

Although memorials (*sangso*) presented to the king by officials and Confucian literati on political affairs are also referred to as "petitions," they are not included in this study,[62] which focuses on petitions presented by ordinary subjects to make a request or seek legal remedy. When officials with especially high-ranking positions had grievances to address to the king, they often chose to appeal via written memorials. Memorial-type petitions were not submitted through the appeals system because it was believed that voicing grievances through the appeals system was intended for the general populace rather than for officials with privileged status.

Groups of people of both genders submitted collective grievances with multiple signatories through the appeals system. For example, women submitted collective grievances around the turn of the twentieth century to demand their right to public education. However, this type of collective petition is not the object of this study, which focuses on women's personal and family grievances, which are as significant as collective grievances in the sense that they had an equal power to force the government to listen to their complaints. From the state's point of view, relieving the emotions of *wŏn* that stemmed from either personal or collective grievances was critical in administering justice and maintaining social harmony.

Chapters in this book are divided thematically, and the book begins by examining the discourse on the emotions of *wŏn* and its connection to the justice system. In 1401, the Chosŏn state institutionalized the petition drum as a way for petitioners to present their joys and woes based on the rationale that the people are the root of the state. With the advent of the petition system, marginalized subjects such as women and slaves were empowered to directly petition the king in a highly stratified and gender-segregated society. The establishment of a legal channel to display emotions of *wŏn* directly to the sovereign was critical in reinforcing the legitimacy of the sovereign through his performance of royal justice. It played an essential role in constructing the image of a benevolent ruler and the making of a Confucian sage king.

The next chapter examines how the linguistic practice was manifested in petitions and demonstrates the significance of orality and textuality in petitions presented at local and capital levels. The performance of women's writing enabled vernacular Korean, which was treated as a vulgar script, to be visible in the public literary space previously dominated by classical Chinese. As women submitted petitions in both classical Chinese and vernacular Korean, they became the medium for connecting the two written languages, enabling the culture of diglossia to be reflected in public writing.

Continuing to focus on the linguistic practice, chapter 3 examines narrative strategies used when articulating various personal grievances appealed at county and provincial levels. Although women and men regardless of status sought to relieve their *wŏn*, I argue that the *wŏn* narrated in petitions was gendered in that a narrative trope established in petitions conformed to cultural conventions of gender norms. Gender played a far more important role than status in constructing the narrative of *wŏn*. When presenting their cases, women emphasized the pain they embodied as weaker and subordinate subjects by utilizing a narrative of pity. Such a narrative allowed women to represent greater *wŏn* than male petitioners and strengthened their rationale for entering the courts of law.

In addition to addressing personal grievance, petitioning on behalf of family members was one of the distinctive characteristics of legal practice, especially in the late Chosŏn. By examining how the practice of petitioning came to include family grievances and not just personal ones, chapter 4 focuses on women's petitions on behalf of family members. When the petition drum was first institutionalized in the early fifteenth century, the state limited petitioners to bringing forth matters confined only to themselves. However, as the society Confucianized, people began to actively appeal on behalf of their family members. By the early eighteenth century, the state came to legally allow sons, wives, younger brothers, and slaves to represent the *wŏn* on behalf of fathers, husbands, elder brothers, and masters, respectively. By examining the practice of petitioning about family grievances at the capital level, with particular focus on wives petitioning for husbands, this chapter demonstrates how the emotions of *wŏn* were shared by family members and how domestic values such as filial piety and fidelity were carried into legal roles.

Finally, in chapter 5, I focus on the petitions that were made in the case of family members' unjust deaths. By investigating two major injustices of the late Chosŏn— "oppressing commoners as slaves" and "making accusations against unjust county magistrates"—this chapter shows how petitioning was negotiated between the state and society in defining what grievances could be addressed in courts. Throughout the Chosŏn, the modes of petitioning and the meaning of grievance were molded and shaped by the multifarious issues people addressed to the state. The two laws specifically discussed in this chapter represent the changes that took place in the early eighteenth century as a result of petitions from the previous period. When examining the narratives of *wŏn* regarding the two kinds of injustices, we can see that the petitioners emphasized the sentiment of pain they shared with their family members who had been murdered. In order to enhance the merit of the appeals, petitioners described their own vicarious suffering in addition to the pain that was personified in the wronged. They spoke on behalf of their dead family members, becoming "inventors of language," and communicated the reality of family members' suffering to government authorities. The display of pain and grief in court transformed those emotions into a condition that could be quantified as the basis for rectification.

*Chapter One*

# THE CONFUCIAN STATE, LAW, AND EMOTIONS

No man is devoid of a heart sensitive to the suffering of others. . . .
Whoever is devoid of the heart of right and wrong is not human.

*—Mencius 2A6*

The condition before joy, anger, grief, or pleasure is aroused is called equilibrium; after they are aroused and each attains proper measure, it is called harmony. Equilibrium is the great foundation of the universe; harmony is its universal path.

*—The Doctrine of the Mean Ch. 1. 4*

As STATED IN *THE DOCTRINE OF THE MEAN*, THE CHOSŎN STATE, which was founded on Neo- Confucian ideology, envisioned an ideal society lacking in legal disputes and maintaining social equilibrium. Chosŏn legal archives, however, show that people not only engaged in criminal suits but also filed a flood of civil suits and appeals concerning land, slaves, debt, inheritance, gravesites, and adoption. Examining these civil cases, some scholars have claimed that the widespread civil litigations and appeals testify to the growth of people's legal consciousness during the Chosŏn period.[1] Others, however, caution that it is wrong to equate the common practices of suing and appealing with the development of legal consciousness.[2] Legal consciousness, however, is insufficiently defined in the context of premodern Korea and is simply used in search of a modern concept of "rights" embedded in the Chosŏn law. When legal consciousness is defined in a modern sense of asserting the private rights of individuals, it is clear that such did not exist in Korea until the late nineteenth century.

When studying Korean legal history, we need to move beyond comparison with the West. Also, we should avoid the methodological flaw of directly applying modern Western concepts to the Chosŏn. If our goal is to find a Western notion of civil law or private law that can be associated with "rights" in the Chosŏn, we will misunderstand judicial practice in Neo-Confucian Chosŏn society. When studying Chosŏn law, we should not be setting Western law as our criterion, as this generates only pointless debate. Instead, it is more fruitful to investigate the underlying logic of indigenous legal practice.

What was the driving force behind litigators of different statuses turning to courts within a rigid hierarchical society that valued status distinction? More specifically, what motivated subjects of low status to challenge elites by filing complaints against them, and what was the mechanism that enabled such interaction between different statuses in the legal realm? Given that the increase in the use of litigation and petitioning was perceived as a sign of serious moral decline in the populace, why did people continuously go to court to file complaints against relatives, neighbors, and magistrates? Why did the practice persist and even thrive throughout the dynasty?

In a hierarchical society such as the Chosŏn, relying on legal measures was the last recourse for nonelites to seek their interests and protection. Petitioning the state was not based on "rights" consciousness but on the petitioner's sense of injustice.[3] Under what circumstances did users of the court feel injustice and when did they resort to the justice system? In China, the practice of resolving disputes through informal mediation prior to seeking formal court adjudication seems to have been active in a "third realm of justice."[4] In Korea, although the community compact (*hyangyak*) at the village level headed by elite aristocrats had a similar function, it failed to play a significant role as an informal justice system to mediate disputes between individuals.[5] In addition, when it came to petitioning on a bona fide grievance, this was excluded from the rules of the community compact, and petitioners were expected to turn to the formal justice system.[6] From the establishment of the petition drum in 1401, people often bypassed the intermediate court and even went directly to the king as he was perceived to be the final arbiter of justice.

When examining Korean customary law, there is the view that customary law as it was practiced in the West did not exist in the Chosŏn. Also, the lack of private law that regulated disputes between individuals implied a lack of interest by the state in resolving litigation cases. If the state showed interest, it was only when it dealt with cases that went against social morality. In Korea, as in China, law existed not as a means of resolving disputes between individuals but as an instrument of administrative power and public order. The lack of private law indicates that the Chosŏn legal system did not operate to resolve disputes between private individuals. The function of the Board of Punishments (Hyŏngjo) was to administer not justice but order. Although the legal system in East Asia was concerned with ensuring "fairness," it operated merely to execute social harmony and order, and the concept of royal justice was largely absent.[7]

However, does the lack of Western civil or private law mean that the Chosŏn state did not address disputes between individuals and was not concerned with dispensing justice in private relations? There is no doubt that the critical aspect of state law (*kukpŏp*) was to maintain social harmony and public order. But these were maintained only when the state intervened and settled disputes that occurred between individuals. Many examples show that the state was concerned with resolving private disputes because the fundamental duty of the state was to relieve *wŏn* that stemmed from civil and criminal suits. The lack of Western "private law" cannot be understood to mean that the mechanism of the judicial system in the Chosŏn was only executing public order and not justice.

When dealing with property rights in Qing China (1644–1911), for example, there is no Qing law that specifies the meaning of "rights of ownership." This lack of Qing law related to property ownership could imply that the state was concerned only with executing "social order" because the focus of Qing law was punishing those who violated others' property. However, the fact that litigators commonly relied on the justice system to seek protection of their property suggests that "its practical consequence was to protect property rights," regardless of the law's intentions.[8]

Although laws relevant to civil suits existed in the Chosŏn, the state's primary concern, as was the case in China, was on punishment, and the code was not as detailed on civil law as on penal law. Despite the weakness of laws in the Chosŏn's code, the fact that people heavily relied on the justice system to file petitions and suits shows that it had the "practical consequence" of protecting their interests. According to a recent collaborative study on lawsuits of the Chosŏn, there were 666 litigations in 1400 and 12,797 litigations in 1414 alone, as seen in the *Veritable Records of the Kings of the Chosŏn Dynasty* (Chosŏn wangjo sillok). Taking into consideration that the population in the fifteenth and sixteenth centuries was approximately six to seven million, the number of litigations was strikingly high.[9] We need to be able to explain how so many lawsuits were brought despite the fact that the state envisioned an ideal society without legal disputes.

In the Chosŏn, where the judiciary was not independent from the administrative apparatus, the state was concerned with administering not only public and social order but also justice.[10] These two played a mutually constitutive rather than exclusive role. More specifically, the ruling authorities strove to maintain status order while empowering all subjects to petition to relieve their *wŏn*. However, the state struggled to overcome the tension between the two as ordinary people filed complaints against unjust magistrates at the local level, which authorities in central government saw as a challenge to the status quo. Throughout the Chosŏn, the state grappled with the question of whether maintaining status order preceded relieving people's *wŏn* or vice versa.

The establishment of a legal channel to voice grievances directly to the sovereign, which functioned as the highest appellate court, was critical in reinforcing the legitimacy of the sovereign through his performance of royal justice. It played an essential role in constructing the image of a benevolent ruler and the making of a Confucian sage king. The very legitimacy of the Mandate of Heaven relied on listening to the people. The state's vision of "fairness" involved empowering subjects of all social statuses to seek rectification.

In the first admonition to King T'aejo (r. 1392–98) shortly after the Chosŏn dynasty was established in 1392, the Office of the Inspector General (Sahŏnbu) stated in a memorial, "First, establish rules and laws (*kigang*). One who wishes to rule his state well should not be concerned about safety and peril; rather, he should be concerned with whether the rules and laws are properly implemented."[11] In administering justice, the state's utmost concerns were the misjudgment of a criminal or civil lawsuit,[12] delay of adjudication,[13] unresolved lawsuit between a commoner and a lowborn person such as a slave,[14] dispute between an ex-slave and former master,[15] and a magistrate's abuse of punishment.[16] In order to maintain social harmony and order based on status distinctions, it was crucial that the state did not neglect disputes between individuals, especially those of different statuses. By dealing with these disputes, the state was able to reinforce the status system and moral customs by monitoring those who violated them.

Justice in the Chosŏn was certainly not about modern notions of equal rights or equal distribution. It was about corrective justice that dealt with rectifying injustice through executing fair punishment based on social status. More specifically, justice was deeply interrelated with emotions of *wŏn*. In the Chosŏn, justice was performed through expressing people's emotions of *wŏn*, or the sense of being wronged, via filing complaints related to civil or criminal suits and the state relieving their *wŏn* through fair adjudication.

Justice was not only about righting wrong but also seeking emotional satisfaction through relieving *wŏn*.[17] The state's mandate to relieve people's *wŏn* was essential because it was intimately tied to maintaining broader cosmic order.

The Chosŏn state's conferring of legal capacity to subjects regardless of gender or status is often explained in terms of Confucian politics that emphasized "people as the basis of the state" (*minbon*).[18] While it is the case that the Chosŏn state more strictly adhered to Neo-Confucian ideology than China, its country of origin, there are questions to be asked, such as why women in the Chosŏn were authorized to enter courts without male representation while women in China had to employ a male proxy. The Confucian political philosophy of *minbon* was certainly the guiding principle of ruling the people. However, in order to better understand the judiciary practice of the Chosŏn, it is essential to recognize the state's role and logic behind empowering subjects regardless of gender or status. The performance of petitioning the state and the state's endeavor to relieve *wŏn* were fundamental aspects of legal practice, but they also functioned to reinforce the image of the Confucian sage king as a benevolent ruler.

## ROYAL JUSTICE AND THE POLITICIZATION OF WŎN

Prior to the transplantation of a modern Western legal system into East Asia, the judicial systems in China, Japan, and Korea shared a structure in which there was no separation of power between the administration, legislature, and judiciary. The judicial domain was an integral part of the administrative apparatus where administrators had to function also as judges. The two most salient differences from the Western legal system were a lack of legal professionals such as lawyers and notaries, and no clear distinction between civil and criminal suits. Although there were terms in Chosŏn that distinguished between the two types of suits, civil suits (*sasong*) and criminal suits (*oksong*), civil procedure was merged with criminal in that it entailed punishments, and the application of law was not different from that of penal cases. The term "civil suit" as it was used in the Chosŏn denotes lawsuits litigated through documents. For civil matters, it was extremely important to preserve one's documents that proved ownership of land or slave and submit them as evidence. Without documents as evidence, it was very unlikely that one could win the case.[19]

During the Chosŏn, the central organs that dealt with legal disputes of civil and criminal matters were divided into four main judicial institutions:

the Office of the Inspector General was one of three major censor organs but also had jurisdiction over litigation cases; the State Tribunal (Ŭigŭmbu) was a special organ that functioned only when there were royal orders for the ad hoc consideration of political cases such as treason or lèse-majesté relating to the official class; the Capital Magistracy (Hansŏngbu) had jurisdiction over a diverse range of affairs in Seoul and was responsible for cases such as land disputes and gravesite litigation;[20] and the Board of Punishments had jurisdiction over both civil and criminal matters and managed all death penalty cases.[21] The founding edict of King T'aejo states that "the Ministry of Punishments (Hyŏngjo) will be in charge of criminal code, litigation, and criminal investigations and punishments. The constabulary (P'odoch'ŏng), on the other hand, will be in charge of patrolling, catching thieves, and maintaining order."[22]

The king-appointed governors of the eight provinces had initial jurisdiction over legal cases in their provinces and made the final adjudications of crimes punishable by banishment or less. The central government assigned a magistrate to each county, which was the lowest level of administration, and the county magistrates exercised jurisdiction over all government affairs in their areas.[23] When it came to appointing magistrates to counties, the central government was keen to select those who were "just, fair, upright, and capable."[24] After serving thirty months of their term, they were promoted if their performance was outstanding but blamed if they failed to fulfill expectations.[25]

Although it is unclear when the appeals system or the practice of appealing to a higher court first appeared in Korean history, extant sources show that it was practiced in the Koryŏ dynasty.[26] The ideas and practices of justice, however, underwent a significant change in the following Chosŏn dynasty as every subject was authorized to appeal to the sovereign when a grievance had not been redressed at lower courts. Subjects headed to the capital to voice concerns on every imaginable issue, ranging from property to seeking the restoration of honor. In the Neo-Confucian Chosŏn society, if the ruler failed to relieve his people's grievances or resentment, this neglect was thought to ultimately bring disorder to the society. Thus, the ruler paid heed to petitioners' voices, and this concurrently led to a strengthening of his authority to preserve peace and social harmony by regulating those who transgressed the laws or social norms.

Although Korea was influenced by Chinese law prior to the Chosŏn dynasty, it was during the Chosŏn that the state adopted the *Great Ming Code* (K. Taemyŏngnyul, Ch. Da ming lü) and applied its penal law throughout the

MAP 1. Map of Kore[a,]
eighteenth century
(Tonggukdaejido).
Courtesy of Nationa[l]
Museum of Korea.

FIGURE 1.1. A Chosŏn county court. From *Paintings on the Evolution of the Legal System* (Shihō seido enkaku zufu). Call no. 5100–18. Courtesy of the Central Library of Seoul National University

dynasty. The first comprehensive volume of Chosŏn legal codes, the *Great Code of Administration* (Kyŏngguk taejŏn), explicitly states that the *Great Ming Code* should be applied to criminal matters. However, the Chosŏn legal codes continuously underwent revision process and numerous substatutes were added to the volume. These changes reached their zenith during the eighteenth century and were eventually incorporated into the *Continuation of the Great Code* (Sok taejŏn) in 1744 during Yŏngjo's reign (r. 1724–76) as a supplement to the previous one.[27] In this second compiled volume, it states that the two *Great Codes* of the Chosŏn precedes the *Great Ming Code*. In order to improve its quality even further, King Chŏngjo (r. 1776–1800) in 1785 promulgated new comprehensive dynastic codes, the *Comprehensive Great Code* (Taejŏn t'ongp'yŏn), which combined all the major provisions of earlier codes into a single volume. Despite the heavy influence of Chinese law and legal system, the Chosŏn government envisioned justice based on the idea of a just and fair society that complied with Korean custom and the status system.

Influenced by the Chinese practice of the petition system, the Chosŏn state installed the "petition drum" (*sinmun'go*) in 1401 during T'aejong's reign based on a Confucian vision that the monarch's mandate rested on listening to his people.[28] Although subjects had been authorized to appeal and petition the government during the Koryŏ dynasty, the legal channel to voice concerns directly to the sovereign was not instituted until nine years after the Chosŏn dynasty was established. The drum was installed in front of the State Tribunal to provide subjects with an opportunity to redress grievances that had not been rectified in county, provincial, and capital courts. The advent of the petition drum system allowed each person's voice to reach the apex of the power structure.

Prior to installing the drum, T'aejong had consulted Ha Yun (1347–1416) and other officials about institutionalizing the petition drum system. Ha suggested that implementing a legal channel to appeal to the sovereign would force magistrates in lower courts to execute fair adjudications and administer justice in order to avoid causing people to file complaints with the sovereign. Taking Ha's suggestion into account, the king commanded the installation of the petition drum and promulgated its related law in 1401.[29] The king then issued an edict in the first month of 1402 concerning the petition drum and pronounced its three primary objectives: the first was to allow people to freely express their opinions on politics and for the monarch to embrace their voices if they had merit; the second was to redress the grievances of those who had been wronged; and the third was to encourage people to report to the state on clandestine schemes of treason or rebellion. The edict stated:

> Because I succeeded the throne without virtue, I feared [for my position]
> night and day and worked unceasingly to maintain peace. However, my ears
> and eyes were unable to reach every corner of this country, and I am afraid
> this will obscure wise ruling. I therefore install the petition drum. Those
> who wish to address the gain and loss of politics and people's joys and woes
> shall beat the drum. If the words addressed have merit, then they shall be
> adopted immediately. Even if not, they shall be forgiven. Those who wish
> to redress grievances shall initially appeal to the government office in their
> region. Those in the capital shall appeal to the Seoul magistrate and others to
> county magistrates and provincial governors. If grievances are not redressed
> properly, then they shall appeal to the Office of the Inspector General. If they
> still have not been properly redressed, then they shall beat the drum. The
> grievances of subjects should be clearly redressed. If those in office do not

adjudicate the cases fairly, they will be punished according to law. Those who bypass the lower courts will also be punished according to law. If someone is covertly preparing for treason or rebellion and is putting the country in peril, then subjects are allowed to beat the drum collectively.[30]

This edict was later codified in the first comprehensive volume of legal codes, the *Great Code of Administration*, under the statute of "Appealing grievances" (Sowŏn).[31]

In a study of the petition drum, Han U-gŭn concludes that early on it failed to be adopted by the general populace; aristocratic families residing in the metropolitan area appropriated the system to address state affairs and their own economic issues.[32] There is no doubt that the petition drum was limited in its usage in this initial stage compared to the latter part of the dynasty. However, there are records from the early period showing that non-elites were not entirely excluded from using the petition drum. For example, in 1409, Oh Kŭmnok petitioned the Office of the Inspector General to restore the commoner status of his family; they had been demoted to slave status during the last few years of the Koryŏ dynasty.[33] When Yu Pak and Kim Ikchŏng at the Office of the Inspector General rejected his petition, Kŭmnok beat the petition drum to appeal his grievance to the king. When Kŭmnok's petition was reported to T'aejong, the king exiled Yu and relieved Kim from his official post for denying the petition.[34]

In 1428, a female slave, Chajae, struck the great bell at Kwanghwa-mun to appeal her grievance. When an official from the Royal Secretariat (Sŭngjŏngwŏn) asked Chajae why she had struck the bell instead of the drum, she replied saying that "officials from the State Tribunal prohibited me from beating the petition drum." When her statement was verified to the king, Sejong relieved the officials Kim Chungsŏng and Yu Mi from their posts. Sejong commented: "The petition drum was instituted so that people could beat the drum whenever they wished to redress grievances. By listening to their words, it is possible to allow people's voices to reach the upper apparatus of the government. Why did they prohibit her? . . . There must be several petitioners who were prevented from beating the drum. Tell the Board of Punishments to interrogate the officials who prohibited Chajae from beating the drum."[35]

About five decades after the petition drum was installed, King Sejo (r. 1455–68) issued an order to the Board of Punishments, stating: "Recently, there have been many ignorant people (*umin*) who dared to appeal in front of the royal carriage outside the palace. Let them abide by the existing rules and beat the petition drum placed in front of the State Tribunal. Prohibit petitioners from making appeals elsewhere. From now on, do not receive petitions presented in front of the royal carriage."[36] The order given by Sejo implies that nonelites attempted to beat the petition drum during the royal procession as early as the middle of the fifteenth century.

The legal channel to approach the king was quickly adopted as a public stage by subjects of a broad population. By appealing grievances, petitioners could seek royal justice and display their emotions of *wŏn*. Even as the legal system served the interests of royal or communal authority, it also provided subjects with a way to publicize their grievances to seek rectification. Through the appeals system, there was constant interaction between the authorities and the petitioners; the petitioners engaged in dialogue, either textually or verbally, with the authorities by filing complaints to seek justice, and the authorities responded to the petitioners' appeals through endorsement and writing comments. These groups were able to interact not only at the local but also at the central government level, and various political, social, and economic interests were involved and negotiated. The dialogue between the state and the petitioners generated an important social site that produced multilayered meanings for the parties involved.

If subjects continuously internalized the feelings of *wŏn*, this would cause moral and ritual impropriety that would disrupt the social, legal, and cosmic harmony, ultimately destroying equilibrium. Legal justice was conceived of as fluid, an entity that traversed the moral and cosmic universes. In Sino-Korean legal tradition, law was not just for maintaining social and legal order but also an integral part of broader cosmic order. As in the making of the *Great Ming Code* in early Ming China (1368–1644), there were two pillars, heavenly principle (*ch'ŏlli*) and human feeling (*injŏng*), that were central to understanding Chinese legal cosmology.[37] As in China, in the Chosŏn the concepts of heavenly principle and human feeling were deeply implanted in the law. These two concepts were complexly intertwined with the Confucian classical thinking of "the harmony of man and nature."[38]

The legal discourse of the Chosŏn stemmed from the Confucian ideology that Heaven responds to the people's minds and that the sovereign should rule according to the people's will. In other words, if the sovereign does not relieve the *wŏn* or grievances of his people, this will create negative energy and thereby destroy the yin-yang harmony of man and nature. If the sovereign rules by virtue and gains the support of people's minds, this will bring positive energy and will prevent natural disaster. Only if the sovereign governs according to Heaven's will can he receive the Mandate of Heaven and legitimately rule his people. During the Chosŏn, the most critical issue in political affairs was thought to be relieving the *wŏn* of people. In 1570, during the reign of Sŏnjo, one official stated:

> There is nothing more urgent than redressing grievances in political affairs.
> There is nothing more serious than the *wŏn* that accumulated for a long
> period of time. Since the negative energy already got depleted under the sun,
> the long accumulated emotions must be relieved on a bright clear day. In the
> end, how could we deceive people's minds and Heavenly principle?[39]

The official's statement implies that it was crucial to relieve *wŏn* in a timely manner because it was impossible to fool the people and Heaven. If cases were misruled and delayed, then natural disasters would ultimately result. Such discourse based on Confucian ideology, law, and emotions persisted throughout the Chosŏn period.

This relationship of law and cosmic order is very well reflected in the *Veritable Records of the Kings of the Chosŏn Dynasty*.[40] For example, in the fifth month of 1407, during the reign of T'aejong, the king sought advice from officials from various ministries, including the Board of Punishments, about the prolonged drought in the country. The king asked whether the reason for the drought was his lack of virtue, impropriety of the royal family's relatives, or officials' misgovernment.

Chŏng Ch'o (d. 1434) was one of the first officials to reply, and he stated that "Heaven and man are one principle and Heaven reacts to human affairs."[41] He claimed that the reason for the drought was the suffering of the poor that stemmed from the newly enacted tax law, which forced them to borrow grains from the rich to pay their taxes. T'aejong responded that the law should be revised if people complained, although it had been codified after he had conducted serious discussions with officials. The king then asked officials to speak of all the people's sufferings of which they were aware.

An Nosaeng, an official from the Board of Punishments, spoke about people's *wŏn* that stemmed from civil lawsuits. He began by stating that the king institutionalized the petition drum so that the people's voices could reach the sovereign and thereby he could relieve their *wŏn* if it had not been redressed at the lower courts. However, land and slave disputes among family members continuously increased, and he was concerned that this caused discord among family members. He claimed, "Brothers engaging in litigation because they did not receive equal distribution goes against Heavenly principle and human feeling."[42]

Delay of adjudication and misjudgment of civil lawsuits were the critical reasons that people felt *wŏn*. When there was a drought in the seventh month of 1402, T'aejong asked his officials about the complaints of people at the time. Ha Yun responded that people's *wŏn* increased when in the eighth month of 1401 the state prohibited people from appealing to an appellate court even if the case was misjudged at a lower court. In addition, people claimed that civil lawsuits would only increase if cases were left unresolved. He then suggested repealing what was enforced in 1401 and allowing people to seek rectification of misruled lawsuits.[43] Similarly, when there was another drought in the following year, the king asked whether it was because civil lawsuits were judged unfairly and people's *wŏn* could not be relieved.[44] In 1416, Ha again reported to the king, stating that the role of magistrates was to adjudicate lawsuits but they were incapable of resolving disputes. Due to their delaying, litigators' *wŏn* increased day by day.[45]

The discussion of how the misjudgment and delay of civil lawsuits escalated the *wŏn* of people and thereby caused natural disasters such as drought extended beyond T'aejong's reign. In 1424, during Sejong's reign (r. 1418–50), due to the increase in *wŏn* that stemmed from the misjudgment and delay of civil lawsuits, Sejong commanded that an endorsement document (*iban*) be drafted within ten days of the adjudication of a case.[46] In 1427, U Sŭngbŏm memorialized to the throne about the inefficiency of the legal procedure. He stated that the judgment of civil lawsuits could not be delayed because it concerned relieving the *wŏn* of the people. When the higher court, the Board of Punishments or Capital Magistracy, sent the civil case back to county courts, the case was delayed because it could not be reinvestigated until a new magistrate was assigned. In between, the litigators had nowhere to turn but only wait and worry. In order to overcome its inefficiency, U advised the king to order a different county office to immediately resolve the dispute and thereby bring peace to the people.[47]

There is no doubt that the Chosŏn state envisioned an ideal society without litigation as they even used the term *tansong* (stop suits), in the sixteenth-century handbook *Classification of Legal Proceedings* (Sasong yuch'wi). It is evident that the Confucian state preferred maintaining social harmony to engaging in legal disputes. Also, rule by virtue was considered more desirable than rule by law. However, it was only in theory that the meaning of *tansong* had its significance and we should be careful not to take the term too literally.[48] Although the state envisioned an ideal society without legal wrangling, in reality, the state's goal was to end litigation by resolving each individual case without procrastination. The state's intention was not necessarily to eliminate suits from society but efficiently adjudicate legal cases in timely manner.

When the state recognized the *wŏn* of subjects, it was critical for authorities to relieve their *wŏn* by judging cases fairly and promptly in order to maintain equilibrium and harmony. The state, however, strictly punished litigators when they filed lawsuits for petty grievances or complaints without legitimate reasons. These litigators were called "those who love to initiate improper lawsuits" (*piri hosong*), and they were regarded as the source of social disorder. Although engaging in lawsuits was not encouraged, at the same time it was not discouraged if there were genuine grievances to appeal. Carefully reading the sources in which the term *tansong* appears, we can see that the goal was to resolve disputes without delaying their adjudication so that every lawsuit could end in timely manner. For example, during the reign of Sŏngjong (r. 1469–94), the king specified, "In the *Great Codes* (Taejŏn), it is stated that civil suits must be ceased and it should not be heard and investigated. Although the *Great Codes* are the universal norms, *tansong* is also just a temporary policy. There are about four hundred people spending their days waiting for their unresolved civil suits to be heard at the Board of Slaves (Changyewŏn). It is impossible not to settle those cases."[49] As can be seen in Sŏngjong's statement, *tansong* was used as a temporary measure in this case to minimize the number of civil lawsuits by efficiently adjudicating cases so that the negative emotions of *wŏn* would not disrupt the equilibrium.[50]

As much as the state was concerned with resolving civil lawsuits between private individuals, executing the right punishment in criminal cases was just as important. Throughout the dynasty, balancing crime and punishment was a critical issue, and it was also closely intertwined with maintaining cosmic order.[51] The state's concern with civil lawsuits that were prolonged without proper judgment was similarly pertinent to criminal suits.[52] The Confucian notions of penal benevolence and judicial prudence (*humhyul*) were deeply embedded in the practice of criminal law.[53] For example, on the seventeenth day of the sixth month in 1425, Sejong proclaimed a new law to relieve the suffering of the people due to a severe drought. In his proclamation, Sejong ordered that descendants of criminals be allowed to take the civil service examination if the law stated that they were exempted from being implicated in the original crimes. In addition, he ordered that prolonged criminal cases be effectively cleared, as prisoners had been imprisoned for longer than necessary, which thereby intensified their *wŏn*.[54] On the twenty-third day of the sixth month, Sejong declared an ordinance of amnesty. In this ordinance, he expressed his concern for the escalation of people's emotions of *wŏn* that could be due to improper punishment. He thus ordered those whose sentence was less than capital punishment be pardoned.[55]

In maintaining the social, legal, and cosmic harmony, it was imperative for the state to dispense justice, and its vision of "fairness" rested on empowering subjects across all social statuses to seek rectification. The state perceived that one's capacity to appeal could not be tied to one's social status.[56] When examining a criminal case, Sejong stated, "The sovereign's duty is to rule all creation on behalf of Heaven. . . . The sovereign should clearly rule all creation consistently. How could there be a difference between the common people and the lowborn (*yangch'ŏn*)?"[57]

The emotions of *wŏn* were understood as an egalitarian sentiment in the sense that it was located in every human being regardless of gender or status. When the king referred to his people, the "people" here were the Heaven's people (*ch'ŏnmin*) that the sovereign had to treat equally, especially when listening to their grievances. In Confucian thinking, there is a difference between "natural equality" and "evaluative inequality." While the Confucians recognized men's equality at birth, the idea of equality was mixed with social hierarchies creating the notion of aristocracy in merit.[58] When the state refers to Heaven's people in legal discourse, it designates all groups of people, including elite aristocrats, commoners, and the lowborn, as being born equal but being unequal in the evaluative sense. When it came to relieving *wŏn*, the notion of "fairness" in the application of law applied *equally* in that the state treated subjects of different statuses and genders as Heaven's people. However, when Heaven's people were perceived as objects of punishment, they were treated differently and the law was applied *unequally* according to merit, discriminating against those who were recognized as having less merit.


TENSION BETWEEN INSTITUTIONAL ORDER AND RELIEVING WŎN

Throughout the Chosŏn dynasty, establishing institutional order was a major concern of the state. When the Office of the Inspector General wrote one of its earliest memorials to the Chosŏn founder, T'aejo, the very first thing they admonished the king to do was to establish institutional order by putting laws and ordinances into effect.[59] However, this institutional order often conflicted with the practice of allowing people to air grievances to the king based on the Confucian political philosophy that the people are the root of the state.[60]

In order to balance the strengthening of the institutional order and listening to subjects' voices, the state limited grievances to those that stemmed from a private-private relationship. This limitation prohibited subjects from making accusations against county magistrates, which ultimately protected the power of public officials. The rationale behind this prohibition was that county magistrates represented king at the local level.[61] The symbolic relationship between county magistrate and local subject was treated equally with that of ruler-official, father-son, and master-slave. Since hierarchy between superior and inferior constituted the basis of social order, it was crucial for the state to enforce laws that protected the vertical relationship such that the inferior could not challenge the superior. In a Confucian state, accusing one's ruler, father, or master was regarded as an absolute crime, and this similarly applied to local subjects' accusing county magistrates.[62]

During Sejong's reign, a serious debate took place on whether protecting magistrates' authority despite their misdeeds preceded the importance of relieving people's *wŏn*. Sejong and Hŏ Cho in particular had conflicting ideas about allowing subjects to make accusations against magistrates. In a discussion with Hŏ Cho in the first month of 1431, Sejong stated that if an inferior was prohibited from filing a complaint against a superior, people would not be able to relieve their *wŏn*. He then suggested that authorities should listen to people's grievances on urgent matters but disregard others. He stated, "If people's *wŏn* cannot be relieved, how could that be the way of executing politics? If a magistrate misjudged someone's land case and that person appealed to seek rectification, how could we consider that to be accusing the magistrate?"[63]

Sejong took a firm stance on the issue throughout the discussion with his officials and claimed it was necessary to allow people to file complaints against magistrates if grievances stemmed from their misjudgment or unjust ruling. While he agreed with Hŏ that accusing magistrates was breaking the status distinction and damaging the power of authority, he pointed out that the ruler's legitimacy would be in jeopardy if the legal channel to address people's grievances was obstructed.

Unlike Sejong, Hŏ defended the magistrates' position despite their misjudgment or unjust behavior. He steadfastly argued that allowing people to accuse magistrates would bring disorder to the social hierarchy and eventually destroy indigenous customs. He claimed that the Koryŏ had lasted for five hundred years precisely because the state banned disrespecting one's superior. Furthermore, he claimed that the practice of sending special emissaries to listen to people's grievances about magistrates harmed the status distinction by misleading people into thinking that they could easily challenge their superior.

Sejong acknowledged that it was contradictory to prohibit people from filing complaints against magistrates with the king but allow them to report their mistakes to special emissaries. Sejong, however, remained adamant in claiming that it was unreasonable to entirely forbid people from accusing unjust magistrates. An Sungsŏn, one of the officials who participated in the debate, commented that the legitimacy of the sovereign would be weakened if people's grievances could not reach the king.[64]

In the early years of the dynasty, special emissaries were used only for administrative and economic issues. As magistrates' abuse of the justice system continuously increased, the central government expanded the role of special emissaries to include monitoring magistrates.[65] Civil and criminal suits began to soar as early as the fifteenth century and continued into the eighteenth century. Yŏngjo (r. 1724–76) and Chŏngjo (r. 1776–1800) actively appropriated the use of special emissaries to scrutinize provincial administration and check whether justice was properly administered.[66]

In 1432, officials even proposed including the issue of making accusations against unjust magistrates or superiors as a question to be asked in the civil service examination.[67] As they were unable to agree or compromise on the matter, Sejong and Hŏ continued their discussion in 1432. The capital court was already overflowing with petitions that addressed misjudgment of legal cases in the early fifteenth century. According to Hŏ, people petitioned because magistrates were not penalized for their mistakes but simultaneously claimed that these people were recklessly petitioning because they failed to achieve their interests. Sejong was well aware of people petitioning petty grievances. He decided that it was not possible to punish every petitioner who addressed frivolous grievances, but he or she should be punished if petitioning again on the same matter. Sejong's greater concern was how he should deal with so many officials who had misjudged cases and triggered people's *wŏn*. Sejong expressed his concern by referring to the emperor of Ming China's (1368–1644) statement that Yuan China (1271–1368) had lost the mandate to rule because the emperor had shifted the burden of executing political affairs to his officials. In this, Sejong implied that it was the king's duty to execute officials who misruled cases and the job could not be put in the hands of other officials.[68]

Hŏ Cho replied to the king by emphasizing that the Chosŏn system was more efficient than the Ming system in terms of conducting discussions with many officials through a variety of channels. He stated that the emperor in Ming China makes the decision without consulting with his officials when executing punishments and it was likely that some people were unjustly sentenced to death. Therefore, the Chosŏn should not follow China's way of executing punishments. The message Hŏ attempted to convey to the king was that he should continue to consult with officials because it was dangerous if the king solely seized the decision-making power.[69]

In 1433, Sejong reiterated his position that if the state rejected complaints filed against unjust magistrates and paid no attention to relieving people's *wŏn*, it would bring undesirable consequences to the society. Therefore, he concluded that the state should allow people to accuse magistrates but at the same time exempt magistrates from being punished for their misdeeds.[70] Sejong in the end took a balanced approach by protecting magistrates' authority and also relieving the wŏn of people.

Despite Sejong's efforts, the tension between the two did not come to an end until law was finally codified in the *Continuation of the Great Code* during Yŏngjo's reign in the early eighteenth century. A balance was difficult to achieve, and the issue continued to haunt the Chosŏn government for another two centuries. The law that prohibited accusing magistrates was initially codified in the *Great Code of Administration*, but this law was finally revised in the eighteenth century, empowering subjects to file complaints against magistrates when their family members had died from excessive torture.[71]


CONCLUSION

The legal channel to address grievances in the Chosŏn was integrated into the appellate system that had the dual function of taking higher appeals and receiving petitions to redress grievances. The limitation of the premodern legal system was precisely in that it did not separate the two functions. The lack of separation restricted the development of civil procedure because people often went directly to the sovereign to settle legal disputes.[72] In principle, it was against the law to bypass intermediate courts. However, in practice, we find that the state accepted those petitions if it recognized that the grievances were valid.

In the Neo-Confucian Chosŏn society, authorities tended to equate the increase in number of lawsuits with the moral decline of the people. The state thus naturally discouraged people from initiating litigation and strictly punished those who instigated filing lawsuits or simply entered into litigation for frivolous reasons. While maintaining such a view, the state left the legal channel open to those whose grievances derived from unfair adjudication or unjust treatment by magistrates or powerful elites. Because the legitimacy of the sovereign depended on listening to the will of people, it was imperative for the state to permit people's voices to reach the apex of the power structure.

The lack of private law, or the difference in legal procedure from the Western legal system, did not necessarily mean that the state was unconcerned with resolving disputes between individuals. People turned to local courts and appealed to the sovereign to resolve disputes not because they had legal knowledge or legal consciousness. What motivated subjects to go to different levels of courts, from county to capital and ultimately to the king, was their sense of injustice or what Mencius discussed of human's natural feeling of right and wrong. This sense of injustice was aroused when they were legally violated of what they were entitled to, such as life and property. If an elite aristocrat arbitrarily deprived a slave of property or life, that aroused the *wŏn* of the slave or the dead slave's family members and he or she had a legitimate reason to demand that the state right wrong.

The Chosŏn government's primary aim of listening to people's grievances was to reinforce the sovereign's legitimacy by relieving the *wŏn* of the people. Royal justice was performed through relieving the *wŏn* of those who suffered from misjudgment or the unjust ruling of lawsuits at the local level. The legal channel that allowed subjects of low status to seek protection by filing complaints against people of higher status may have empowered them to a certain extent. This does not, however, mean that the state approved lower status people to challenge their superior without legitimate reason. It was actually the opposite; the state's primary concern was to maintain the status system by ensuring that people not cross their status boundary. In order to reinforce the rigid status system, the state listened to nonelites' grievances, which led them to monitor whether they challenged the status order. The state's ultimate goal was to secure both order and justice.

The increased number of litigations or appeals signified how people actively took advantage of the legal system. However, this does not necessarily mean that the legal system functioned efficiently or that justice was achieved in every case. Seeking justice was one thing, and achieving justice another.

People actively petitioned the state based on their personal sense of injustice; however, the fact that numerous complaints were filed throughout the dynasty also suggests that people turned to the court because of the inefficiency of the legal structure and the incapability of magistrates at the local level. This was why people often bypassed middle courts and went directly to the king to settle disputes. Nevertheless, evidence that many subjects filed lawsuits and appeals suggests that it did have certain "practical consequences" for those engaged in various disputes, as it was never an easy journey to go all the way to the capital to petition the sovereign.

*Chapter Two*

# GENDER, WRITING, AND LEGAL PERFORMANCE

Appeals from the provincial judges to the Board of Punishments and from it to the sovereign are allowed. In petitioning the king two methods are employed: In one, the petitioner, bearing his prayer, written on a large roll of the finest paper and bound round with red strips, goes to the palace gate, spreads his mat, and there takes his seat, the petition resting upright against the wall. In this position he remains until someone is sent out from the palace to take his petition and present it to the king. Another mode of petitioning is for a person to take an empty brass rice bowl and strike it as the king passes along in one of his progresses. Should the king choose to receive the petition the procession stops and it is presented to him then and there.

—W. Woodville Rockhill, "Notes on Some of the<br>Laws, Customs, and Superstitions of Korea"

W. WOODVILLE ROCKHILL, THE UNITED STATES CHARGÉ d'affaires in Korea from 1886 to 1887, described two petitioning methods of Korea in an article in *American Anthropologist*.[1] Of the two methods he mentioned, the first refers to the written petition (*sangŏn*) and the second to the oral petition (*kyŏkchaeng*).[2] These two modes, which were used to petition the king, had evolved from the original practice of beating the petition drum that was first institutionalized in 1401.[3] The practice of beating the petition drum was inspired by China, but the petitioning practice unfolded and manifested differently in Korea. As the petitioning process evolved, beating the petition drum was replaced by striking a gong, and then other major changes occurred in the content and context of the grievances addressed to the government.

Although the Chosŏn judicial system was heavily influenced by China, Korean Neo-Confucian bureaucrats incorporated and adjusted the system according to indigenous culture. By the eighteenth century, the Chosŏn state officially allowed every subject to directly petition the sovereign during his royal procession. Compared to China or Japan, the legal channel of the Chosŏn was relatively more open in that people were allowed to directly approach the king to petition. In Qing China (1644–1911), petitioners attempted to appeal to the emperor along his imperial procession, but this remained illegal and they were harshly punished regardless of the basis of their petitions.[4] Similarly, in Japan, it was strictly prohibited to appeal directly to the shogun during the Tokugawa period (1603–1868).[5]

Petitioning in the Chosŏn was used to create a theatrical space to not only display one's emotions but also gendered identity. The interplay between legal procedure and the performative force of petitioning provides a view of legal events through the lens of procedure. When investigating petitioning activities, it is not difficult to detect theatrical productions within them. The power of the performance was in its ability to create a distinct legal culture of actors performing the law.

Women's written petitions, especially those drafted in vernacular Korean, show how women's gendered identity was exhibited through vernacular writing. The practice of petitioning was performed in a culturally restricted setting that was regulated by legal codes and was bound within preexisting norms. Nevertheless, women actively appropriated the modes of petitioning and challenged the official literary space by using vernacular Korean. It was only through women's performance of petitioning that the two written languages used during the Chosŏn became visible in the space of legal writing that was dominated by classical Chinese.


THE THEATRICAL SPACE OF PETITIONING

It is not clear when the appeals system first appeared in Korea, but extant sources show that the practice of appealing to higher courts existed from the Koryŏ dynasty (918–1392).[6] The ideas and practices of justice, however, underwent a significant change in the following Chosŏn dynasty as every subject was authorized to appeal to the sovereign when a grievance had not been redressed at lower courts. Subjects headed to the capital to voice concerns on every imaginable issue, ranging from ownership of property to restoration of honor. In the Neo-Confucian Chosŏn society, if the ruler failed to relieve his people's grievances or resentment, this neglect was thought to ultimately bring disorder to the society. Thus, the ruler paid heed to the petitioners' voices, and this concurrently led to the strengthening of his authority to preserve peace and social harmony by regulating those who transgressed the laws or social norms.

The legal channel to approach the king was quickly adopted as a public stage by a broad population. By appealing grievances, petitioners could seek royal justice and perform petitioning through a display of emotions via speech and writings. Even as the legal system served the interests of royal or communal authority, it also provided subjects with a way to publicize their grievances to seek rectification. Through the appeals system, there was constant interaction between the authorities and the petitioners; the petitioners engaged in dialogue, either textually or verbally, with the authorities by filing complaints to seek justice, and the authorities responded to the petitioners' appeals through endorsement and written judgments. These groups were able to interact not only at the local but also at the central government levels, and various political, social, and economic interests were negotiated through petitioning. The interactive dialogue between the state and the petitioners generated an important social site that produced multilayered meanings for the parties involved.


*From Beating the Petition Drum to Striking the Gong*

As noted previously, the Chosŏn state installed the "petition drum" (*sinmun'go*) in 1401 based on the Neo-Confucian vision that the monarch's mandate relied on listening to his people. The drum was installed in front of the State Tribunal (Ŭigŭmbu) to provide subjects with an opportunity to strike the drum to appeal grievances that had not been rectified in lower courts.[7] Female petitioners, like their male counterparts, engaged in this early stage of petitioning by beating the petition drum. The earliest extant petition by a woman is from the second month of 1409, during T'aejong's reign. In this earliest case, the wife of the high official Ch'oi Kŭmgang beat the petition drum to appeal a grievance on behalf of her imprisoned husband.[8] The next earliest petition was appealed during Sejong's reign; twenty-nine blind women collectively struck the petition drum in 1422 and asked the sovereign whether it was possible for them to pay back their state loan of grain (*hwanja*) in paper money (*chŏhwa*).[9] In 1428, a female slave, Chajae, struck the great bell at Kwanghwamun to appeal her grievance.[10]

As early as 1492, during Sŏngjong's reign (r. 1470–94), the wife of Ch'ŏng Yŏnsu struck a gong and appealed on the day of the civil service examination, when the king was present in the examination hall. She struck the gong to attract the king's attention by climbing up somewhere higher than the hall, thereby making herself visible to the king.[11] Also in that same year, a wife of the royal clan petitioned on the street during the king's royal tour outside the palace concerning her ownership of slaves.

Because of these two petitions, Hŏ Chip, an official of the Office of the Inspector General, told the king that women were petitioning in the streets without going through the proper channels. He proposed punishing the head of household of the wife of the royal clan because her petitioning disturbed public morals.[12] Although both women petitioned inappropriately, Hŏ criticized only the wife of the royal clan. The social status of Ch'ŏng Yŏnsu's wife is unknown, but Hŏ did not reproach her for appealing during the civil service examination. During the early part of the Chosŏn, the state began to strictly regulate the moral conduct of women of the royal families, which gradually spread to *yangban* women in the seventeenth and eighteenth centuries.[13]

The petitions examined here indicate that the gong was already in use in the late fifteenth century, in addition to the petition drum, and that petitioners attempted to appeal not only in front of the royal carriage but also in other locations. Although we do not know how these petitioners were informed of the king's itinerary, we can see that petitioners were well prepared to appeal to the king during his outside tours and that they devised their own performing strategies of petitioning. As people increasingly found ringing a gong to be more convenient to use in a variety of places, the practice of beating the petition drum gradually vanished sometime in the sixteenth century.


## *The Two Modes of Petitioning: Written and Oral Petitions*

In the sixteenth century, the theatrical construction of petitioning was complicated as the government further systematized the appeals system and specified two ways to address grievances to the king: written and oral.[14] Within the two petitioning modes, the performance of petitioning during the royal procession was conducted in a variety of ways. When petitioning the king, people usually waited for the royal procession to come by and then struck the gong to attract the authorities' attention. Some petitioners even stood in front of the palace gate every day waiting for the king's procession.[15] In order to stand out from other petitioners, some climbed up somewhere high above the ground.[16] Others used their voices and shouted loudly, making strange noises as the king approached.[17] The petitioners also cried agonizingly to express their *wŏn*, and this occasionally attracted the king's attention during his procession. When the king heard the tragic sound, he immediately ordered officials to find out the grievance of the petitioner at the site.[18]

Another common petitioning strategy was creating a visual effect by writing the petition with blood from a cut finger.[19] This type of writing was known as *hyŏlsŏ*.[20] Not only did petitioners write in blood but some also held banners written in blood that conveyed the message of their grievance.[21] Although it was illegal to submit petitions written in blood, some petitioners chose self-infliction as a way to demonstrate their extreme emotions of *wŏn* and the sincerity of their suffering. The performance of blood writing in petitioning activity was not merely a "symbolic behavior" but aimed for practical effect to achieve petitioners' interest.[22]

The state directed the two modes of petitioning differently. When petitioners submitted written petitions to the king, they either sat in front of the palace gate or struck the gong during the royal procession and waited for the authorities to take their petitions. The Royal Secretariat (Sŭngjŏngwŏn) was responsible for reviewing written petitions and filtering out frivolous or extraneous ones before reporting to the king. Once a petition was officially registered, the petitioner had to show his or her identification tag to authenticate the petition within three days.

The official language for written petitions was classical Chinese. However, as women were educated in the vernacular Korean (*ŏnmun*) that was treated as "vulgar" script, as opposed to classical Chinese "true" script, and as women, especially elite *yangban* women, began to present written petitions in their accustomed language, the practice challenged the state's official norm. Although vernacular Korean petitions were officially recognized at county and provincial levels in the late Chosŏn, the state continued to take issue with the language when the petitions were presented to the king. When a petition was not perceived as relating to a true grievance, the state questioned whether it was drafted in proper written language.[23] Unlike written petitions submitted at county and provincial levels, Korean-script petitions were deemed inappropriate to present to the sovereign.[24] Even when Korean-script petitions were tolerated in some cases, they were transcribed into classical Chinese in official documents in the guise of male language; this transcription diminished women's power. Therefore, Korean-script petitions subverted the norm but only in a limited sense, because they were later transcribed into classical

Chinese and thereby became invisible in official records.[25] Despite these limits, women's capacity to petition enabled them to challenge the official literary space, dominated by classical Chinese, by inscribing their identity and raison d'être through Korean script.

The recognition of vernacular petitions in public space is vital because it reflects how women, as legal agents, actively capitalized on their capacity to petition the state. The absence of men's Korean-script petitions until the late nineteenth century further substantiates how it was women who successfully introduced vernacular Korean to the petitioning process.[26] It was possible, at least at the county and provincial levels, to reflect diglossic culture in literary space through the very performance of women's legal writing.

Although it is likely that elite women wrote vernacular petitions by themselves, most female petitioners had to rely on professional scriveners or men in their family or community to draft their petitions either in classical Chinese or vernacular Korean. Some scholars thus consider that women's voices and roles were limited in the petitioning process as many of them relied on men in composing their petitions.[27] When viewed this way, it is not only female petitioners whose roles were limited, as the same could be said of illiterate, nonelite men. Even if those who wrote the petitions were not the petitioners themselves, it cannot be denied that both illiterate female and male petitioners shaped their own narratives. Whoever wrote the petitions could not have put pen to paper without the stories told by the petitioners. However, scriveners may have employed narrative skills to better articulate grievances when producing written petitions.[28] Unfortunately, we have no access to the original stories told by female petitioners to scriveners. It is difficult to assess to what extent the stories presented in petitions followed the petitioners' original stories. However, it is clear that the role of the drafters was not to invent new stories but to effectively package the grievances of petitioners to win favor.[29]

When taking into consideration that even men relied on professional male scriveners, there is not much point in discussing whether it was women's voices in their written petitions. From a gender perspective, what is more noteworthy in the context of Confucian society is the multilayered process of storytelling in petitioning and how the process eventually generated gendered legal narrative. In other words, instead of focusing on whether women ipso facto wrote their petitions, it is more fruitful to discuss the gendered narrative that was produced as a result of multiple actors involved in the storytelling. If petitioners told their grievances, then it was the scriveners' task to "craft" those stories to amplify the emotions of *wŏn*.[30] The process of producing written petitions entailed multiple layers of storytelling, which ultimately generated a bifurcated, gendered legal narrative that conformed to the conventional norms.

When petitioning orally, petitioners were taken to the Board of Punishments and given the opportunity to present their grievances. Unlike literate people who mostly chose to submit written petitions when seeking redress, illiterate people were attracted to oral petitions due to their vernacular component. The lower social strata expressed their emotions of *wŏn* far more frequently via oral petitions than written petitions when petitioning the king.[31] However, literate petitioners occasionally preferred the oral mode because, unlike written petitions that could be submitted only twice, oral petitions could be presented unlimited times. Nevertheless, oral petitions were not without disadvantages. Petitioners presenting orally were initially treated as criminals and transferred to the Board of Punishments to be interrogated, the justification being that they disturbed the king by striking the gong and bringing the royal carriage to a halt. The purpose of the interrogation was to hinder people from pleading false grievances.

Unlike the Royal Secretariat, the Board of Punishments had to report every oral petition to the king, even those with frivolous or extraneous contents. Thus, oral petitions had greater possibility than written ones of being heard by the sovereign. And unlike written petitions, which sometimes involved male scriveners in the process of constructing the narrative, oral petitions were presented solely by petitioners. Thus in the case of oral petitions, it entirely depended on petitioners to convey the narrative of *wŏn* through their own voice. It was through their verbal performance that the Board of Punishments determined whether their display of *wŏn* was legitimate. If the petitioners seemed to be faking grievances during the interrogation procedure, then there was a possibility that they would be tortured as a form of punishment. Instead of male scriveners, officials from the Board of Punishments drafted written reports, which they based on the interrogation they conducted. The officials' role was not to amplify *wŏn* in their reports but to "objectively" convey what the petitioners' grievances were, regardless of whether they were serious or frivolous. It was the king who ultimately decided whether the grievances were grave matters. As with written petitions, oral petitions were also associated with scripted performance because petitioners' voices of both genders were written down in classical Chinese.

If writing was the primary element that constituted performing *wŏn* through written petitions, oral petitions were more organized around the bodies of petitioners, their physical and emotional reactions expressed by gesture, tone of speech, and facial expression.[32] However, this does not mean that the element of body was absent in written petitions, as petitioners similarly had to perform with their body on the theatrical stage in presenting their petitions. In either the written or oral mode of presenting grievances, body and language functioned as mediums through which to express an individual's emotions in public. Through legal performance, petitioners' emotions were exhibited in front of a great number of audiences—men, women, seniors, and children—especially where people stood along the street to watch the royal procession. According to the *Veritable Records* of *King Chŏngjo*, "those who came out to watch the procession covered mountain and hills."[33] In depicting the scenery of the royal procession in the late nineteenth century, another source similarly states that thousands of people gathered around to see the king, and the procession was considered the event of the year for the people to watch.[34]

## Broadening the Meaning of "Grievance" in the Eighteenth Century

In the sixteenth century, the government expanded the allowable scope of petitions to the king from personal grievances to issues concerning a petitioner's corporal punishment, paternity, familial status as wife or concubine, or social status as commoner or slave. In addition, the state also broadened the meaning of grievance, which had been confined to the individual, to include family grievances. Although this came to be officially legalized only in the latter part of the Chosŏn, appeals were made on behalf of family members as early as the fifteenth century (see chapter 4). In order to adjust to changing practices, King Sukchong (r. 1674–1720) in the late seventeenth century authorized petitioners to address not only personal grievances but also those of their family members. The state legitimized the practice of a son petitioning for his father, a wife for her husband, a younger brother for his elder brother, and a slave for a master.[35] These four new categories were later codified in the *Continuation of Great Code*, which was compiled in 1746, during Yŏngjo's reign.[36]

The introduction of these categories increased the number of petitions as well as the diversity of their content. Previously, petitions were mostly limited to seeking legal justice by redressing grievances, but now they extended to requesting official commendation for an ancestor's or other individual's virtuous conduct.[37] For example, loyal subjects, filial sons, and faithful wives

FIGURE 2.1. King Chŏngjo's procession to Hyŏllŭngwŏn, showing spectators gathered around, sitting and standing. Kim Tŭksin (1754–1822), *Hwasŏng Nŭnghaengdo*, 1795, folding screen, 151.5 × 66.4 cm. Deoksu 1042. Courtesy of National Museum of Korea.

FIGURE 2.2 (*opposite*). People would have petitioned during the king's and official's procession, with spectators standing on both sides of the street, as in this painting. Landscape, hanging scroll, 72.2 × 43.0 cm. Deoksu 4013. Courtesy of National Museum of Korea.

FIGURE 2.3. Two men who appear to be commoners, at the bottom of the picture, kneel down to petition their grievances before the magistrate. The man on his knees closest to the magistrate is a local clerk ready to write down the grievances being addressed. From Kim Hongdo's (1745–?) pictorial records of travel, folding screen, 90.9 × 42.7 cm Deoksu 1313. Courtesy of National Museum of Korea.

were granted official commendations through petitioner appeals. In addition to petitioners' requests for family members, local communities also submitted collective petitions to honor exemplary subjects.

Officials during Chŏngjo's reign initially opposed the acknowledgment of these petitions because they were unrelated to redressing grievances. However, Chŏngjo had a different view. Although not directly related to grievance, filial piety and public righteousness (*kongŭi*), respectively, were what motivated individuals and communities to petition.[38] By expanding the definition of "grievance," or *wŏn*, the petitioning practice in the late eighteenth century was reorganized to administer reward and punishment within the larger framework of the justice system.[39]

The final and most significant reforms of the appeals system were conducted during Chŏngjo's reign. Chŏngjo was the first to legalize the practice of appealing in front of the royal carriage. Previously, petitioners could only strike a gong and present petitions in front of the palace gate. This practice had been established in the sixteenth century, especially during the reigns of Chungjong and Myŏngjong (r. 1545–67). Some petitioners even illegally crossed the boundary of the palace gate to appeal to the king. During Myŏngjong's reign, Kim Yuhyŏn, a slave, disguised himself as a soldier and, carrying a sword, snuck into the palace. He struck a gong and cried out to request the postponement of a county magistrate's term of service. Officials recommended that he be punished according to the law that sentenced capital punishment to those who carried a sword inside the palace. However, after conducting an interrogation, the king reduced the sentence and banished Yuhyŏn instead, because the slave had no intention of harming the king.[40]

There was a similar case in 1692, during Sukchong's reign, when a man recklessly entered the palace carrying an arrow and struck the gong; the king banished him for impropriety.[41] Although some petitioners succeeded in trespassing through the palace gate without permission, the practice of striking the gong in front of the palace yard or during the royal procession was the custom that remained intact in the late Chosŏn. The petitioners' performance of *wŏn* in the theatrical space of petitioning eventually led the state to further systematize the mode of petitioning.

Another reform that Chŏngjo implemented in the late eighteenth century was expanding the petitionable categories to include a wide range of socioeconomic issues. Previously, the kind of grievances that could be addressed to the sovereign were limited to issues that dealt with Confucian cardinal relationships. However, as petitions about socioeconomic grievances, such as unjustly levied taxes, corrupt officials, the abusive usage of corporal punishment, the usurpation of land, and so on, continuously increased, Chŏngjo once again authorized an existing practice. Chŏngjo's reforms tremendously encouraged people to further engage in petitioning activity, and petitions flooded into the capital as a result.[42]

Female petitioners, especially commoner women, emerged as active agents in voicing grievances to the king in the late Chosŏn.[43] The issues of women's petitions varied broadly according to their social status. For example, elite women predominantly petitioned on adoption, which was tied to both the succession of the family line and the issue of inheritance. The choice of a suitable heir was a critical matter for elite families. These women also appealed regarding the restoration of a family member's honor, the distribution of family property, and the ownership of slaves.[44] By contrast, the majority of lower status women's petitions concerned grievances associated with socioeconomic problems such as taxes, land ownership, and the resolution of debts. These women also appealed regarding their social status. Elite families often exploited destitute commoners' labor through coercion, treating them as slaves and extorting money from them. An eighteenth-century law punished those who treated commoners as slaves; this law was codified based on grievances appealed by petitioners.

## DIGLOSSIA IN LEGAL WRITING, AND WOMEN'S CHOICE OF LANGUAGE

The emotional display found in petitioning procedures offers us insights into especially the vernacular culture of the Chosŏn. Through either verbal or textual performance to display *wŏn*, people's petitioning strategies and the language they employed on the public stage defined their gender and status identity. Female petitioners possessed a keen gender consciousness, and they constructed their identity through a particular vocabulary of gender behavior.[45] Women negotiated a position for their identity in relation to established prescriptive norms, and gender identity in the Chosŏn was deeply related to linguistic choices they made in their representations of *wŏn*.

In 1446, King Sejong (r. 1418–50) promulgated the new Korean alphabet of twenty-eight letters, which he called *Hunmin Chŏngŭm* (correct sounds for the instruction of the people). This can be described as the most epochal event in Korean culture in the premodern period. Prior to the invention of the alphabet, literary culture in Korea consisted of writings in classical Chinese, which bore little syntactic relationship to Korean. After the invention, Koreans were able to write their spoken language phonetically, and, as a result, vernacular literary culture emerged. This vernacular Korean, however, did not replace classical Chinese in the literary space until the late nineteenth century. The hegemony of classical Chinese in literary culture remained unchallenged throughout the period. In other words, all official documents, including legal petitions, had to be written in classical Chinese by law.[46] Because classical Chinese was perceived as a man's language and was also difficult to learn, women were educated with vernacular Korean, which was much easier to acquire. Although the two representative volumes of Chosŏn legal codes, the *Great Code of Administration* and the *Continuation of the Great Code*, do not explicitly stipulate the written language of petitioning, it was taken for granted that petitions should be submitted in classical Chinese, as were all other public documents.

Women's participation in the appeals system complicated legal writing as some women submitted legal petitions in vernacular Korean. Although it is difficult to verify whether every woman petitioner actually wrote her own petition, significance lies in the fact that it was only female petitioners who submitted petitions in vernacular Korean. Most men's petitions that are extant in legal archives were written in classical Chinese.[47] The vernacular Korean petitions submitted by women challenge previous notions of diglossia that had been often discussed in terms of simple binaries: classical Chinese was public, male, and universal, whereas vernacular Korean was private, female, and local.[48] These binaries are useful in describing the general contours of the dual literary culture, but they create an impression that the two written cultures were mutually exclusive, each having developed in isolation from or in opposition to the other.

Recent scholarship on the usage of vernacular Korean has shown the break of these binaries in dual literary culture. Although it is true that each culture had its own trajectory, each evolved as the two had continuous interactions with the other, and both were shaped by the same cultural and political forces of each historical moment. It is necessary to think about the question of choice—why some women chose to submit petitions with vernacular Korean. The cultural and political meaning of literary cultures of premodern Korea can be approached through an analysis of literary culture as rhetoric of power.[49] Going beyond simple binaries and complicating the dual literary culture by examining the intersection of language, vernacular, and gender, investigation of women's performance of petitioning shows how legal writing became more complex when classical Chinese and vernacular Korean coex-isted in the realm of law and how they were shaped by the same cultural and political forces of the period.

Although it is likely that most nonelite women's either classical Chinese or vernacular Korean petitions were drafted by scriveners, the significance of vernacular Korean petitions written by *yangban* women lies in its reflection of the diglossia in legal writing. It is well known that elite women largely participated in the production of vernacular literary culture in the late Chosŏn dynasty, and so it is nothing new to discuss their usage of vernacular Korean.[50] However, most studies of elite women's usage of vernacular Korean are limited to their writings in the private realm. The existence of vernacular Korean petitions raises several questions: How did the vernacular Korean petitions complicate legal writing that was dominated by classical Chinese? Why did women choose to enter the public space through vernacular lan-guage when they could have translated their writing into classical Chinese? Why did women risk being punished by submitting their petitions in ver-nacular Korean? What does the lack of men's vernacular Korean petitions imply? If it is the case that the Korean alphabet was created for women and the nonelite strata, why is it difficult to find nonelite men's vernacular writ-ings? Although it is impossible to address all these questions here, my aim is to underline the significance of elite women's usage of vernacular Korean in legal petitions and to demonstrate how they challenged the division and hierarchy between the two literary spaces that are often discussed in terms of binaries. Examination of vernacular Korean petitions shows how entering the theatrical stage of petitioning was a way for female subjects, especially *yangban* women, to perform their gendered identity through narrating their *wŏn* in the vernacular.

The earliest Korean-script petition I found was submitted in 1509, during the reign of Chungjong (r. 1506–44), by a daughter of the royal clan whose name was Ch'ŏlbi. She appealed her punishment of demotion to private slave. Court officials argued that her crime was unpardonable and further criticized her for writing the petition in the Korean script, which digressed from the proper form.[51] Nevertheless, the king granted her immunity from demotion.[52] During the Kwanghae-gun period (r. 1608–23) government officials discussed seriously at court whether Korean-script petitions should be accepted.[53] Although the state made no effort to legalize them, it eventually acknowl-edged such petitions because rejecting them countered the state's intention of redressing grievances.[54]

In my research, I found 155 petitions by women that were submitted at county and provincial courts during the late Chosŏn.[55] Of those 155 petitions, 30 were drafted in vernacular Korean and the rest in classical Chinese. Of the 30 vernacular Korean petitions, 16 were presented by elite *yangban* women and 14 by commoner women (for an example of a vernacular Korean petition submitted by a commoner woman, see fig. 2.4). Although the numbers show that women submitted classical Chinese petitions in greater number than vernacular Korean ones, what is vital about the petitions written in the Korean script is that they were officially recognized by local governments despite the fact that such petitions were illegal.

Although the state continued to take issue with women's Korean-script petitions when they were presented to the king, such petitions submitted at county and provincial levels show that women succeeded in receiving official red seals using the same language that they employed in domestic spaces. Some scholars suggest that female petitioners must have relied on scriveners or male kin even when they drafted the petitions in vernacular Korean.[56] Whether or not women literally wrote the petitions themselves is not the point. What is noteworthy is their participation in the process of drafting the petitions and the fact that it was female subjects rather than their male counterparts who submitted their petitions in the Korean script. If women relied entirely on men's assistance, it would hardly have been likely for vernacular Korean petitions to appear in court. It is thus my contention that it was a woman's choice to draft a petition in the language she knew. This was a way of performing her gender identity and representing femaleness through public writing to narrate her *wŏn*. Through petitioning activity, women extended the usage of vernacular Korean into legal writing, which was previously dominated by classical Chinese.

The manifestation of diglossia in the juridical domain is evident in petitions submitted in both classical Chinese and vernacular Korean. The following petition in classical Chinese submitted by an elite woman is peculiar in the sense that she did not petition to redress existing *wŏn* but to prevent a grievance that might occur in the future. It is not common to find petitions in which petitioners appealed to gain legal knowledge so that they could act accordingly and prevent a dispute from taking place. A petition submitted by Madam Im was such a case; she appealed to seek legal advice from a provincial governor concerning the distribution of property. In the twelfth month of 1652 she submitted a petition in classical Chinese to the governor of Chŏlla. She narrated at length to explicate the details of her family succession and

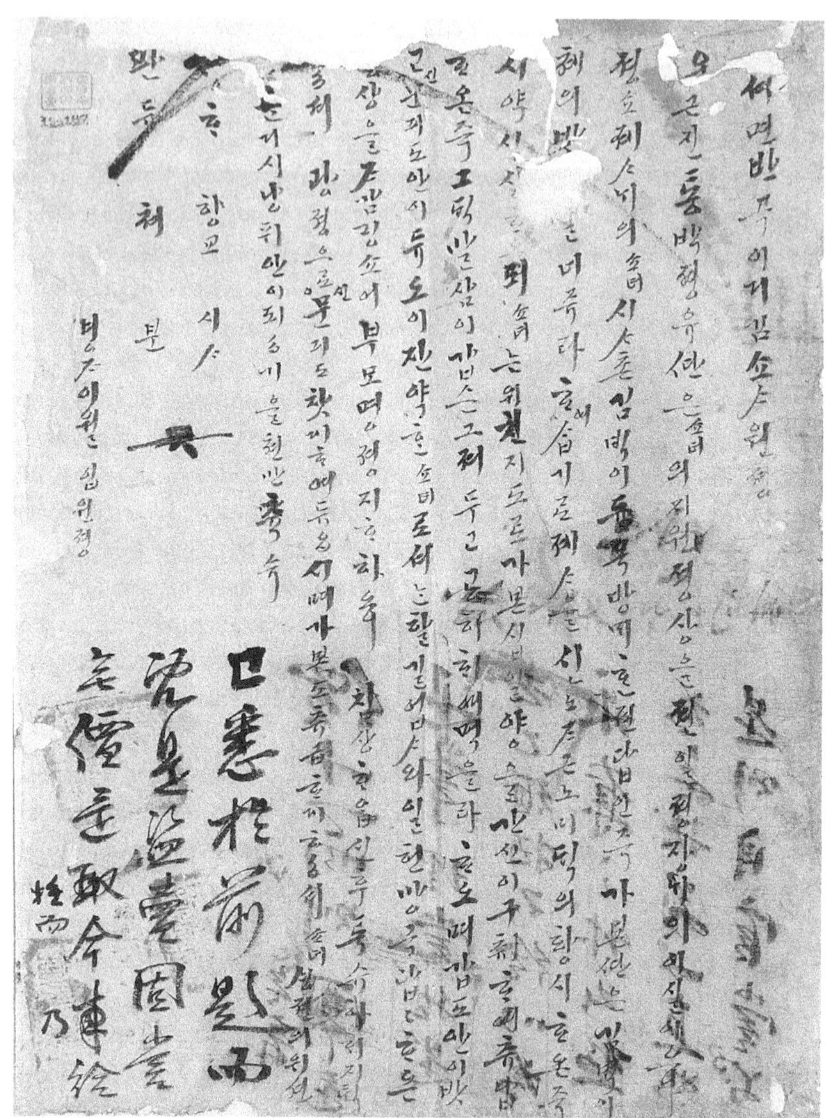

FIGURE 2.4. The vernacular petition (land dispute) of a commoner woman Kim. *Komunsŏ* 194167. Courtesy of Kyujanggak Archives, Seoul National University.

property issue. Madam Im and her husband, O Sinnam (d. 1632), did not have a son but had two daughters from concubines. The couple therefore decided to adopt O Sangji, who was Sinnam's grandnephew, and brought him home before he was three years old. Sinnam, who served as a military and diplomatic envoy, was away from home most of the time after the adoption. During the Manchu invasion of China, he served as a commanding general leading Chosŏn troops to support the Ming dynasty. He was captured as a prisoner of war by the Manchus and was incapable of returning home for more than ten years. Madam Im stated in the petition that whenever her husband sent letters, he was concerned about Sangji because he was the only existing heir who could perform ancestor worship.

When Sinnam returned home, he was delighted to see Sangji, but his joy did not last long because he was once again ordered to go to China as a diplomatic envoy. From that point on, Sinnam kept traveling back and forth between China and Korea, and he died in 1632. Madam Im, in her petition, addressed how Sangji had faithfully performed his duty as lineal heir after her husband's death. She emphasized that he had arranged her husband's funeral and mourned for three whole years. In addition, he took care of ancestor shrines, gravesites, and ritual worship for twenty years, as she had conferred all those duties to him. Madam Im wished to persuade the provincial governor that Sangji had sincerely performed the role of lineal heir.

Madam Im had reasons for asserting this, because there were two major defects in Sangji's legitimacy. First, according to adoption law, a son must be adopted from a collateral agnate of an appropriate generation. Sangji was from a collateral agnate, but from an inappropriate generation. In other words, an adopted son must be selected from one of the adoptee's nephews, but Sangji was Sinnam's grandnephew. Second, adoption and lineal succession were two distinct matters; an adoptee did not automatically become the lineal heir of the family. In order to be established as lineal heir, an adopted son needed official recognition. In Sangji's case, he had not yet been recognized by the Board of Rites due to Sinnam's untimely death. Despite these defects in the case, Madam Im supported her claim by emphasizing that her husband had clearly stated his intention by appointing Sangji as lineal heir in "special gift writ" (*pyŏlgŭp mun'gi*), which was an inheritance document given to an individual on certain occasions such as a birth, wedding, examination success, and so on. She further argued that kin had also recognized Sangji as lineal heir.

Sangji's legitimacy emerged as a critical issue when distributing Sinnam's property. Only once his position had been accredited would he be able to receive the largest share of property. If Sinnam was alive and Sangji was officially recognized as the lineal heir, then his status would have been unquestionable. However, Sinnam's untimely death made things complicated for Madam Im. In order to consolidate Sangji's position, Madam Im gave her land to Sangji after having consulted with her three natal brothers who also acknowledged him as lineal heir.

When Madam Im first decided to distribute her husband's property to his children, she assembled all the family members including the head of kin and other relatives. Yun Inch'ŏl, a son-in-law, claimed that the property should be evenly distributed because it was improper to accept Sangji as lineal heir. If Madam Im wished to guarantee Sangji's share, then it was necessary to request that the government officially recognize him as jural heir. In the petition, Madam Im addressed her motive for petitioning, saying that it was to prevent Yun and the other son-in-law from filing suit against Sangji. In order to avoid such a legal dispute, she felt the need to distribute property according to law. Thus, before drafting an inheritance document for the second time, Madam Im decided to seek legal advice from the provincial governor concerning four specific queries she had. She stated:

> I write this petition because there are many laws of which I am not aware and thus wish to be taught by Your Honorable Governor. First, although it is clear that my husband and I adopted Sangji before he was three years old and it is explicit that we have already recognized him as the ritual heir, I do not know whether I should distribute equal shares to the concubines' children. For instance, should my son-in-law, Yun Inchŏl, receive a share equal to Sangji's? I am sure there must be differences between children of the direct descent line and those of the secondary line. If so, how much of a share do I have to give to the concubines' children? Second, the mother of one of the daughters, who lives in the capital city, used to be a slave. However, after my husband took her as his concubine, he purchased her commoner status but did not register with the Supplementary Department (Poch'ungdae). Moreover, she failed to preserve chastity and left for another man. Do I have to consider her as my husband's concubine of lowborn or of commoner status? Third, when I distribute the property, my relationship with the adopted son seems legally appropriate to be treated as a mother-son relationship. However, when I consider my relationship with the sons-in-law, I feel it should be different because they are the husbands of concubines' daughters. Would it be more appropriate to receive the government's endorsement for the inheritance

document that I will draft? Or would it not be necessary? Fourth, regarding land and slaves for the services dedicated to the direct lineal antecedents, I do not know how I should distribute them, since my husband was an official of the second rank.[57]

After listing the four inquiries, Madam Im concluded her petition by asking the provincial governor to issue a written judgment. She stated, "Not only am I not aware of the related laws but also live in a remote region, which makes it difficult for me to consult with someone on these matters. Thus, I dare write this petition. . . . Please issue your written judgment so that there will not be a dispute among the descendants. Please do not read this petition as you treat any other ordinary petition written by common people; please be kind enough to devise a scheme for the four questions that I have raised according to strict laws."[58]

When comparing her narrative with other women's petitions, Madam Im suppressed her emotions despite the fact that Yun had challenged her authority to distribute the property. She sought to maintain a neutral tone throughout the petition but revealed her desire to protect Sangji in her four questions. The real intention of seeking legal advice was to assure that no more than necessary of her husband's property would go to the concubines' children. This was not uncommon for elite women when tensions arose with concubines' children on the issue of property. Madam Im's double position as widow and senior member of the household empowered her to exercise significant influence within the family. It is striking that she decided to distribute property only after having controlled it for more than two whole decades. This reflects how she maintained her authority by possessing economic power and control over an adult son. The significance of her petition, though, is that she had sought legal advice in order to prevent the *wŏn* that might later arise. Whereas most petitions were submitted after the *wŏn* was evoked, Madam Im's petition was presented beforehand in order to avoid having a dispute with the concubines' children. Engaging in intertextual dialogue with the provincial governor, Madam Im's petition shows how she actively appropriated the system by expanding the practice from addressing the existing grievance to seeking legal advice to prevent a future dispute.

The provincial governor replied to Madam Im by first praising her effort to prevent potential discord among descendants. His written judgment primarily focused on the first question and provided details of how the property should be distributed according to one's status based on the laws stipulated in the *Great Code of Administration.* He pointed out that adoption from an inappropriate generation was illegal but suggested that there was an exception. If the adopted child was from a close relative of the same descent group, then he could be recognized as the lineal heir despite the fact that he was from an inappropriate generation. Based on this exception, he assured Madam Im that Sangji's legitimacy could not be considered problematic. Furthermore, the fact that Sangji's adoption was conducted before he was three years old and that he was referred to as the lineal heir by his adoptive father in the special gift writ confirmed his legitimacy.

The provincial governor then elaborated on the details of the law and concluded that it was improper to evenly distribute the property. He stated that Sangji should receive a larger share than the concubines' children. Per Madam Im's second question, the provincial governor suggested that the concubine's daughter should be treated as a slave and receive her share accordingly. Although the mother had gained commoner status, she was a slave when the daughter was born and therefore the daughter could not be treated the same as the daughter of the concubine who was from commoner status. In response to the third question, he suggested that receiving endorsement depended on the will of the property owner. For the last question, he stated that it was six slaves for those above the rank of *taebu* and four slaves for those under the rank of *sa.*[59]

Although Madam Im's petition was deviant in that instead of seeking redress she inquired for the purpose of gaining legal knowledge to prevent problems that might occur later on, the provincial governor was sincere in answering all of her questions. Furthermore, the petition does not provide any information regarding whether Madam Im drafted the petition herself or relied on a male family member to write it on her behalf. This petition shows how Madam Im conformed to the norms of the written format but actively utilized the appeals system to communicate with authorities by deviating in terms of content. As long as what was addressed in a petition was related to preserving harmony within the family as well as the greater society, it seems that the state widely embraced the petitioner, whether his or her grievance already existed or not.

Although Madam Im's petition was peculiar in that it sought legal knowledge, the written language she used conformed to official language. The following vernacular petitions had content the state had officially acknowledged but they deviated from the proper form of writing. When petitioning, it was not uncommon for women to strategically use both languages and submit several petitions. For example, Madam Cho, who was involved in a property dispute, submitted four petitions in total; the first petition, submitted in the ninth month of 1816, was written in classical Chinese, but the other three petitions submitted in the following month were all drafted in vernacular Korean.[60] When petitions written in classical Chinese and vernacular Korean are compared, there is not much difference in the content, which makes it difficult to find out the petitioner's reason for choosing the language used. The petitions do not provide even a hint concerning the language issue. However, it is not far-fetched to assume that it was the female subjects themselves who made the language choice.

For instance, Madam Yi's petition states that she actually drafted the petition herself. In the will she left for her children, she emphasized that she was writing in vernacular Korean with her own handwriting to show that she was the drafter.[61] Similarly, in the petition she filed against Sŏgu, who was the concubine's son of her stepson, she used vernacular Korean. She appealed to punish him for attempting to usurp the lineal heir's position, along with other crimes he had committed.

Madam Yi was the second wife of Hwang Yŏil (1556–?), who was a high-ranking scholar-official during the reign of King Sŏnjo (r. 1567–1608). Hwang had a son named Sŭngji with his first wife and then had four sons with Madam Yi: Chungmin, Chunghŏn, Chungsun, and Chungwŏn. Sŭngji, who was the lineal heir, failed to produce a son with his legal wife and thus needed to adopt a son in order to maintain the patriline. Sŭngji's father, before his death, had ordered Sŭngji to adopt one of his half-brothers' sons. Following this wish, Sŭngji decided to adopt Sŏngnae, Chunghŏn's son. However, Sŭngji's untimely death led Sŏgu to covet Sŏngnae's position and conspire to replace him with Chungmin's son. Sŏgu claimed that it was illegitimate to adopt Chunghŏn's son while Chungmin's son, who was the eldest in the line, was alive. Madam Yi regarded Sŏgu's action as a challenge and petitioned the king in order to report his attempt to go against his father's will in selecting the heir of the family.[62]

After reviewing Madam Yi's petition, the state banished Sŏgu to Paengnyŏng Island for three years. Madam Yi, concerned that he would continue to cause trouble, decided to write a will to confirm Sŏngnae's position as lineal heir. On the twentieth day of the third month in 1651, she drafted a will stating that if Sŏgu and Chungmin fabricated the document of family succession and attempted to displace Sŏngnae, then other family members should take her testimony as evidence to report to the government, asking to punish them.

She ended the will stating that she drafted it herself in vernacular Korean to show her determination to maintain family order.[63]

On the eighth day of the first month in 1656, Madam Yi drafted a petition to submit to the magistrate of her county. Unlike other petition documents, this petition lacks an official's written judgment, which implies that it was either never submitted to the county office or was a copy of the version that had been submitted. Whatever the case, Madam Yi wrote the petition in vernacular Korean and intended to have Sŏgu punished for a second time. She addressed how Sŏgu had continued to misbehave even after his release from Paengnyŏng Island. Sŏgu stole Madam Yi's document and bribed powerful officials at the central bureaucracy to gain their support. Moreover, he tore up the letter she sent to him asking him to return the document he stole. She stated in her petition:

I am extremely afraid to report to Your Honor, who is in such a high position. I am old and sick but I write this petition without any shame or fear because my rage has soared up to the sky. . . . When he [Sŏgu] read the note, he tore it into pieces and humiliated me in every possible way and never showed up. How on earth can he be so insolent and vicious! He cannot behave this way to the legitimate grandmother when his secondary status is taken into consideration. Not to mention our relationship as master and slave. I first pitied him because he was, in one way or another, one of my family members. Because I pitied him, I am humiliated by him today. I do not know what his next move will be if I left him without taking any further actions. Thus, I no longer wish to consider him as my family member and wish to take legal action against him. Please consider the following six crimes he has committed and punish him strictly based on the laws: the crime of humiliating the legitimate grandmother of the family, the crime of betraying the master-slave relationship, the crime of attempting to succeed to his father's lineage by following the father's bloodline instead of his mother's, the crime of stealing the family document and selling it, the crime of not participating in the ancestral rituals for his father, and the crime of abandoning his mother. Please consider each of these six points by applying all the existing laws to make him realize the importance of state law. By doing so, please protect this aged and weak woman. I will end here as I am afraid to write any further.[64]

Although Madam Yi's grievance stemmed from Sŏgu's attempt to deprive Sŏngnae of his rightful position, the tone of her petition resonates more of her rage provoked by humiliation or frustration. Madam Yi was determined to punish Sŏgu for disrespecting the senior member of the household and challenging her authority. It was possible for Madam Yi to make a complaint against Sŏgu because their relationship was not tied by blood.

She also noted her relationship with Sŏgu as master-slave: Sŏgu's mother was previously Madam Yi's slave. Madam Yi had allowed Sŭngji to take her slave as a concubine when he had asked for permission. According to the matrifilial succession law (*chongmo pŏp*), the status of offspring was defined by the mother's status. If Sŏgu's mother bore him without having gained commoner status, then in principle his status would have been slave. Because his master was the grandmother and senior member of the family, it was possible for him to live a life that distinguished him from ordinary slaves.

Madam Yi wrote the petition herself using vernacular Korean. She decided to submit the petition to the county office in the language she was accustomed to based on her own discretion. As early as 1509, women similarly utilized vernacular Korean to communicate with authorities at the capital level. However, Korean script petitions, although not entirely rejected, continued to be criticized when presented to the king. Nevertheless, elite women were not discouraged from using the written language they were versed in when submitting petitions to the king. Not only did they write in vernacular Korean when petitioning, they also actively appropriated the petition system to engage in dialogue with the sovereign. In addition to addressing grievances, female subjects also used petitioning as communicative space to seek legal advice or express gratitude.

Despite also being written in vernacular Korean, the following petitions by Madam Kim are different from Madam Yi's in that her vernacular Korean petitions were submitted directly to the sovereign. Her petitioning was performed in a theatrical space to express her gratitude toward the king by kneeling in front of the royal palace until she received a response from the king. By engaging in interactive dialogue with the sovereign, Madam Kim's two petitions submitted to Yŏngjo (r. 1724–76) show how a woman of a high-ranking official family actively utilized the petition system to pursue her interest.

Madam Kim's (1655–1736) husband's kin underwent a downfall during the late seventeenth and early eighteenth centuries when the factional strife within the Chosŏn court was at its zenith. Madam Kim, a widow and senior member of the household, risked her life by recounting the details of key political affairs via petitioning in order to save her grandson, who was the only lineal heir of the family. She had two objectives in appealing to the king: one was to protect her grandson from being punished and the other was to prove her brother-in-law's innocence. Madam Kim not only narrated the most public male power rivalry in the Chosŏn court but also had the courage to imperil her own life by criticizing her family's opponents.

Madam Kim presented her two written petitions during the first three years after Yŏngjo ascended the throne in 1724. Although the purpose of both petitions was to protect her husband's patriline, the tone of language in the second petition diverged from the first one. While the first petition, submitted in 1725, was written to express gratitude for the king's leniency,[65] the second petition, presented two years later, was drafted to defend her grandson and brother-in-law, and it carried a desperate tone.[66] Madam Kim was a daughter of Kim Manjung (1637–92), a high-ranking Confucian scholar-official and prominent member of the Noron faction. He was also the author of two famous novels, the *Nine-Cloud Dream* (Kuun mong) and *Madam Sa's Conquest of the South* (Sassi Namjŏng ki). Coming from a prestigious family, Madam Kim was well educated in Confucian norms and versed in the vernacular Korean script. Her husband, Yi Imyŏng (1658–1722), was one of the four leading figures of the Noron faction, which also included Kim Ch'angjip (1648–1722), Yi Kŏnmyŏng (1663–1722), and Cho T'aech'ae (1660–1722). The members of Noron were involved in bitter factional strife with the Soron faction, which led to the literati purge of 1721–22 called the *Sinim Sahwa*. All four Noron ministers along with many others were executed for treason or for signing a memorial supporting Yŏngjo's regency during King Kyŏngjong's reign (r. 1720–24).

The factional strife between Noron and Soron that endangered Madam Kim's household began in the Sukchong period and continued throughout the two subsequent reigns. A colorful love triangle at the Yi court during the reign of Sukchong was a foreboding of the purge of the Noron faction. In 1681, Sukchong married Queen Inhyŏn, who has often been portrayed as an ideal of Confucian womanhood of the Chosŏn dynasty. When Inhyŏn could not bear an heir after eight years of marriage, the king took as a concubine Lady Chang, who was from a low status. When Chang gave birth to a son, who later became Kyŏngjong (1688–1724), Sukchong dethroned Inhyŏn, demoting her to commoner status, and enthroned Chang in 1689. After abandoning Inhyŏn for five years, Sukchong regretted his action and restored her queenship in 1694, demoting Chang to secondary consort. Inhyŏn died of illness, believed to have been caused by black magic practiced by Chang, in 1701. The romances of Sukchong ended when he sentenced Chang to death.

Factionalism in the Chosŏn dynasty rested on two principal sources. While factions were formed according to familial, regional, and scholastic tendencies, the political and social issues of each period were also determining factors.[67] The cleavage between Noron and Soron became deeper when Lady Chang gave birth to a son. While Soron members advocated that Kyŏngjong become the regent, Noron members supported another son, Yŏngjo, the child of a lowborn secondary consort, Lady Ch'oe. One of the reasons Noron members supported Yŏngjo's regency was because they were the ones who strove to restore Inhyŏn's queenship and called for the punishment of Chang. Thus, it was inappropriate for them to support Kyŏngjong's regency. The purge of 1721–22 took place when the Noron urged that Yŏngjo be appointed heir apparent as Kyŏngjong ascended the throne.

Madam Kim's family, both natal and in-law, were affiliated with the Noron faction. Her father was exiled for supporting Inhyŏn when Sukchong first decided to dethrone her.[68] Three of the four Noron ministers, Yi Imyŏng, Yi Kŏnmyŏng, and Kim Ch'angjip, had a familial relationship with Madam Kim. Yi Kŏnmyŏng was a cousin of Yi Imyŏng, and Kim Ch'angjip was the father of Yi Imyŏng's daughter-in-law. Although Madam Kim was from one of the most prestigious families of the time, her kin paid the price by becoming the victims of factional strife. Her husband was executed; her son, Yi Kiji, was tortured to death; her grandson, Yi Pongsang, was to be enslaved; her brother-in-law, Yi Ingmyŏng, was exiled; and the three women in the family—Madam Kim, her daughter-in-law, and her granddaughter-in-law—were exiled to Puan, Chŏlla province. All the family members mentioned were punished accordingly, except Pongsang.[69]

When the state decided to enslave Pongsang, Madam Kim was worried because her husband's family line would then be severed. As the senior member of the household, Madam Kim devised a plan to save her grandson. When she first heard that the state was going to enslave him, in the middle of the night, she desperately discussed the matter with his wet nurse. The wet nurse had a son who was about Pongsang's age, and the two boys fortunately or unfortunately had similar countenances. In order to save her grandson, Madam Kim asked the wet nurse's son if he could sacrifice his life for his master so that Pongsang could flee. The wet nurse's son willingly agreed and thereupon threw himself into a river and died. When government authorities arrived to execute the state's order, they were told that Pongsang was already dead, and the corpse was shown as evidence. Thereafter, Pongsang's case was closed and no longer discussed at the court.[70]

To save her grandson, Madam Kim committed two crimes. One was inducing the slave boy to commit suicide, and the other was going against the state's command by helping her grandson to escape. Madam Kim was cognizant of her crimes and decided to confess. However, she refrained from making a confession during the reign of Kyŏngjong; she strategically waited for the right time, which was when the political climate shifted favorably toward her family as Yŏngjo ascended the throne.[71] When Yŏngjo seized power, he restored the posthumous official titles of the four Noron ministers.[72] He further commanded that the ancestral tablets of these four ministers be enshrined in private academies.[73] Whereas Madam Kim remained silent during the reign of Kyŏngjong, she finally showed the courage to speak of her crimes after the untimely death of Kyŏngjong.[74]

When Yi Imyŏng's honor was restored during the first year of Yŏngjo's reign, his brother, Yi Ingmyŏng, implored the king to pardon Pongsang. The memorial concerning Pongsang was sent to the king shortly after Yi Ingmyŏng himself was released from exile. He stated in the memorial that the grandson, whom he thought was dead, turned out to be alive and would soon appear before the king to confess his crime.[75] After reading the memorial, Yŏngjo withdrew the charge against the fugitive Pongsang.[76] Shortly thereafter, Pongsang showed up at the royal court and was granted an official rank.[77]

When Madam Kim heard that her grandson's charge had been dropped and that he had even been offered an official post, she considered that it was now her turn to confess and to convey gratitude to the king for his benevolence. Although Yi Ingmyŏng had already mentioned the grandson's situation to the king, Madam Kim felt obliged to readdress the issue because of her subject position as his grandmother as well as senior member of the household. It was her role to petition the king on behalf of the family. Less than a month after Yi Ingmyŏng's memorial was sent to the throne, Madam Kim drafted her first petition and took the long journey to the capital from Puyŏ, Ch'ungch'ŏng province.[78]

Madam Kim began the petition by expressing her appreciation to Yŏngjo. She then proceeded to confess in detail the crimes she had committed:

A few years ago, my grandson, Pongsang, fled in order to save his life. I recently heard from my husband's brother, Yi Ingmyŏng, that Your Majesty not only pardoned Pongsang, but also granted him an official rank. Your Majesty has saved my grandson's life. Even the vast ocean cannot encompass Your Majesty's heavenly benevolence. But how can I dare ask to be forgiven for the crime

I have committed? Therefore, I ask to be punished after I convey these words. My deceased husband had a single son, Yi Kiji. Yi Kiji had two sons but one of them was blind, so Pongsang, the only other son, had to continue the family line. Pongsang reached the age of sixteen several years ago, whilst the state was in disarray. I was suddenly informed that the state had commanded that Yi Kiji be executed, his family property confiscated, and his wife and children be degraded to slave status.[79] How could I have been afraid of the punishment I would receive by disobeying the state's order under these circumstances? Thus, I said to my daughter-in-law, "Since Yi Kiji is already out of town, this is a good opportunity to save his life. How could this not be heaven's intention? But how should we take care of Pongsang?" Fortunately, there was a slave boy in the house who was about the same age as Pongsang, and who even resembled him in appearance. I told him that Pongsang was in dire straits and that I hoped he could save the family by sacrificing his life. The boy was enraged after hearing about the situation and threw himself into the river without hesitation and died. Pongsang was able to escape through this boy's sacrifice. The government authorities took the boy's corpse after it was put into a coffin to conduct an autopsy, and we buried it and had a tablet made when it was returned. We did not hear a word from Pongsang after that—there was no way to find out whether he was alive or dead. I finally heard that he was safe in the second month of this year, and I immediately started searching for him so that I could tell him what we had done, but I then heard from my husband's brother that Pongsang had already been granted an official rank. Had it not been for Your Majesty's magnanimity it would have been impossible to save our grandson, the heir to our family line, and restore our family's reputation. Thus, I dare to report the truth of my actions and kneel down awaiting punishment.[80]

After reading this petition, Yŏngjo responded by saying, "I am saddened by Madam Kim's appeal. A slave boy sacrificing his life for [his] master is truly rare. Send someone to convey my words to Madam Kim to not await the punishment. Also, reward the family of the slave boy who sacrificed his life for Pongsang." He then had a meeting with Pongsang and told him about his grandfather's loyalty and how he had thought the family line of Yi Imyŏng had been severed due to the purge of 1721–22. He also expressed his joy about being able to restore Yi's family line. Pongsang then told the story of his days as a fugitive to the king.[81]

Unlike usual petitions that asked that a grievance be redressed, this petition is distinctive in that its aim was to make a confession and to convey gratitude to the king. Madam Kim used the legal channel as an available mode of communication. She personally engaged in interactive dialogue with the king through the medium of petitioning and by actively performing her legal capacity to petition.

Although Madam Kim had violated the state's command by helping her grandson to flee, the consequences of her actions seem to have turned out favorably. According to the autobiography of Pongsang's son, Yi Yŏn'gyu, the idea to conceal Pongsang was initially suggested by Madam Kim's son-in-law, Kim Siryŏm.[82] Whether or not the idea was Madam Kim's, she carried out the plan. Because her domestic role to serve the family was far more critical than obeying the state's order, it was her gender that made it much easier for her rather than a male family member to help Pongsang flee. If Yi Imyŏng had been in control of the household, it would have been difficult for him to disobey the state's order due to his required loyalty to the state. However, Madam Kim's loyalty did not extend to the public realm, the state, but remained within the family as her foremost duty was confined to the domestic space. Furthermore, she would have faced less severe consequences than any male family member by disobeying the state's command. During the Chosŏn dynasty, it was the patriarch of the household that often suffered the consequence of a wife's wrongful deed. However, Madam Kim's husband had already died during the purge, so that would not have been a consideration for her.

When Yŏngjo first ascended the throne, it seemed as though the political climate was shifting favorably toward Madam Kim. However, Yŏngjo's implementation of the magnificent harmony (*t'angp'yŏng*) policy soon changed the situation, and members of the Soron faction gradually began to raise their voice in the bureaucracy. In 1727, members of the Soron once again attacked the members of Noron, including Madam Kim's family. The Office of the Inspector General argued that Pongsang should be punished for having disobeyed the state's order because others would emulate him if he were easily pardoned. The officials claimed that Yi Ingmyŏng should be exiled for plotting Pongsang's flight and concealing the truth.[83]

In order to defend Pongsang and Yi Ingmyŏng, Madam Kim wrote her second petition to the king. It is clear that Madam Kim was well informed of what was discussed at the court because it was less than a month before she submitted her second petition that the two men's names had been raised. She sensed a menace looming toward her family and headed to the capital once again. As in the first petition, she narrated the details of what had happened on the night of Pongsang's flight. However, in her second petition, she emphasized that she was the only one who was responsible for the flight. Madam Kim had three objectives in writing the second petition: the first was to plead for the king to disregard the claim made by Soron; the second was to beg for the king's leniency once again; the third was to vindicate Yi Ingmyŏng. While gratitude was the tone of the first petition, in the second petition it was desperation. After having enjoyed two short years of the king's protection, Madam Kim was in another dire extremity in which she had to raise her voice to defend the family.

In the second petition, which was written in vernacular Korean, she stated that she thought of committing suicide when she first became aware of the Office of the Inspector General's claim.[84] However, she had second thoughts and changed her mind because she would be disloyal to the king by disregarding his benevolence if she killed herself. Not only was her grandson granted an official rank, but also Madam Kim had been provided with a monthly provision.[85] She then mentioned her husband's loyalty to Yŏngjo and evoked his memory by relying on her detailed knowledge of the discussion the king once had with her husband. She stated the following:

> It is not because of this poor old widow that Your Majesty showed mercy; the real reason lies in my husband's loyalty. He devoted his whole life to bringing peace to the state. Your Majesty described my husband as a patriot who worried about the state day and night, neglecting his own household for more than ten years. You also referred to his loyalty and the extent to which it impressed the heavens. Your Majesty disliked the thought of my husband not having a grandson and lineal heir who would worship his grief-stricken soul. My husband's enemy is now attempting to sever my husband's lineage by executing Pongsang, and I am afraid that Your Majesty's will to live in harmony might be misrepresented by taking their request into consideration.[86]

In the *Veritable Records of King Yŏngjo*, there is a record that shows how Yŏngjo was moved by Yi Imyŏng's loyalty when he was alive. Yi had once expressed his loyalty to Yŏngjo by writing, "Worry about the state, and forget about your family (*uguk mangga*)."[87] Madam Kim precisely quoted her husband's words in her petition. As wife, she was well aware of even the most intimate conversations between her husband and the king.

After explaining her motive for writing the petition, she shifted the topic to defend her brother-in-law. She emphasized that it was impossible for him to have plotted Pongsang's flight because he was exiled to a region that was far distant from their home. Furthermore, she stated that he was suffering from such severe dysentery then that he was incapable of recognizing people, and there was even a witness who could testify to his health condition at the time. She concluded the petition by expressing her grievance and pleaded to the king saying that it was unfair of Soron to attempt to eliminate her patriline by executing both her grandson and brother-in-law. She wrote: "The crime was committed solely by me; he [Yi Ingmyŏng] is truly innocent. The enemy is trying to eliminate him without any reasonable grounds because merely hurting this powerless woman would mean nothing to them. How could I not be grieved? I would not refuse to die ten thousand times for the crime I have committed. I even ask to be punished with the execution tools. I ask Your Majesty to abandon this woman [instead of Pongsang] and resolve my family's grievance by sparing Pongsang's life so that he will be able to succeed the family lineage, and I beseech Your Majesty to show mercy to Yi Ingmyŏng."[88] In this petition, Madam Kim attempted to persuade Yŏngjo to show leniency by emphasizing her husband's loyalty and criticizing Soron. Despite her desperate appeal, Pongsang was exiled the year after the second petition was submitted. Madam Kim passed away without ever seeing her grandson again. Regarding Madam Kim's petitions, Im Hyŏng-t'aek suggests that her effort was in vain because Pongsang was ultimately exiled in 1729.[89] However, since Madam Kim's primary aim was to continue the family line, it would be more appropriate to recognize that her effort was worthwhile. After eleven years of exile, Pongsang was released in 1740 and was granted various official ranks. However, he declined all offers and chose to live a secluded life. Although Pongsang underwent several crises during his lifetime, Madam Kim accomplished her aim because he lived long enough to produce a son and heir.


CONCLUSION

The performance of petitioning evolved throughout the Chosŏn as people actively appropriated the appeals system. By displaying their *wŏn* on the theatrical stage of petitioning, women sought to acquire legal knowledge, filed complaints against secondary sons who challenged their authority, and communicated gratitude to the sovereign. Exercising the legal capacity to petition enabled female subjects not only to seek judicial protection but also to negotiate their interests with state authorities. Women further sought to engage in dialogue with authorities, which allowed them to assert their personhood embedded in female virtue. Through their articulation of grievance via written and oral petitions, women struggled to defend their own sense of morality by performing their petitioning activity outside their domestic boundary.

Through visualizing legal events and actors, it is possible to detect how the power of performance generated the distinct legal culture of the late Chosŏn. Through verbal or textual performance, people's petitioning strategies and the language they employed on the public stage defined their gender and status identity. Through the written language of petitions, women performed their gender identity through linguistic practice, especially using vernacular Korean. For example, Madam Kim found it to be her duty to save her grandson. It is possible that she strategically used vernacular Korean to emphasize her femaleness and to avoid factionalism while addressing the sensitive political affairs in her petitions.[90] Although it is difficult to know the exact intentions behind the use of vernacular Korean in women's petitions, what is certain is that it challenged the official literary space dominated by classical Chinese. It was through these efforts that the Korean script came to be particularly visible in the legal writing of the late Chosŏn period. Through their practice of writing in the vernacular, women petitioners elevated that which was seen as vulgar script by the literary culture of the Chosŏn to an officially recognized option for legal documents.[91] And because women instead of men submitted petitions in both languages, they became the medium for connecting the two languages and reflecting the practice of diglossia in legal writing.

# Chapter Three

# WOMEN'S GRIEVANCES AND THEIR GENDERED NARRATIVE OF *WŎN*

I address my extreme *wŏn* and painful situation to Your Honor. . . .. If he is left to behave imprudently, then where is law and how could [we] trust the county office's command?...Please investigate his crime for causing disorder in the district and right wrong according to law. I beg to protect my emaciated body so that this widow, who has nothing on which to depend, will be able to preserve the land.

—Commoner woman Hwang, *Komunsŏ* vol. 25

THE LAW COURTS OF THE CHOSŎN WERE A MAJOR PUBLIC VENUE in which women expressed *wŏn* and publicly attacked their neighbors. Women's ability to express hostile emotions in public is of significance in any premodern society because it indicates that they are recognized as free and honorable individuals.[1] Servants, slaves, and Jews in medieval Europe must have held similarly hostile emotions, but they were not permitted to express them in public; in this, the Chosŏn case is significant.[2] In medieval Europe, status and ethnicity seems to have had greater influence than gender when it came to whether it was acceptable to publicly express hostile emotions. In contrast to medieval Europe, during the Chosŏn dynasty one's gender or status did not affect one's ability to display hostile emotions in courts precisely because such negative emotions were thought to damage not only legal but also social and cosmic harmony.

When local- and capital-level petitions are compared, women more often expressed personal and family grievances to county magistrates, whereas they predominantly aired grievances on behalf of family members when appealing to the king.[3] What kinds of grievances did women bring before the local court? What narrative strategies did women use when pleading their interests? How can we understand the grievances women addressed in public courts when their primary role was confined to the domestic space? How can we draw a boundary between personal and family grievances? When widows petitioned on issues such as property, taxes, or debt, it is quite evident that they were pleading their own personal grievances to the court. However, the meaning of personal becomes more ambiguous when we look at cases of married women independently entering the courtroom to address grievances that were related to larger family matters, such as those regarding ancestor's gravesites, rituals, or lineage issues. Such cases blur the boundary between individual and family and further complicate our understanding of female subjectivity in a Confucian society where women were believed to have been silent in the public domain.

According to Suad Joseph, interpersonal relationship is relatively fluid, and one's identity is intimately tied to the other to complete the sense of personhood. In other words, subjects require interaction with others in order to shape their emotions, desires, attitudes, and identities.[4] When married women, whose husbands were unable to appear in court, petitioned on family-related issues, their subjectivities were constructed collaboratively through specific familial relations that affected the individual subjects who held multiple positions within the household. Petitions filed to address the grievances of familial matters cannot be regarded simply as instances of women filing petitions to seek redress on behalf of their family members. The petitions that are discussed in this chapter are thus clearly different from those of female petitioners appealing on behalf of imprisoned or dead family members, which will be discussed in the next two chapters. When speaking on behalf of family members, petitioners constructed their narratives with a focus on relieving the *wŏn* of the family members they represented. In contrast, when a woman entered the court to voice a grievance related to family issues, she built her narrative around relieving her own emotions of *wŏn*. This type of petition, which traverses the realms of personal and family, cannot be perceived as a matter entirely belonging to personal or family. These petitions should be understood as those of women representing their families in a way ultimately tied to their *own* sense of self.

The issues women petitioned on at county and provincial levels described here, including both personal and family grievances, show how the *wŏn* expressed in their petitions relied on a narrative of pity.[5] The petitions show that the *wŏn* expressed in petitions was not necessarily gendered because both women and men of different social statuses displayed such emotions. However, the story used to construct the *wŏn* was gendered in that a narrative trope established in petitions conformed to cultural conventions of gender norms. Gender was emphasized much more than status in constructing the narratives of *wŏn* in women's petitions. While it is difficult to find status differences in the usage of *wŏn*, there are salient distinctions between women and men in the way they articulated their emotion: women's *wŏn* was more frequently associated with pain (*t'ong*), whereas men's was related to anger (*pun*). This is not to suggest that pain was socially recognized as a woman's emotion or anger as a man's. We find both women and men expressing these two emotions in their petitions. However, the emotions of *wŏn* were gendered in the sense that the emotional language reflected in women's petitions was far more frequently associated with pain than anger due to the petitioners' different experiences and the narrative strategies they employed.

When explaining unjust cases, women emphasized the pain they embodied as weaker and subordinate subjects by utilizing a narrative of pity. Such a narrative style allowed women to represent greater *wŏn* than male petitioners and reinforced their rationale for entering the courts of law. During the Chosŏn period, women occupied a subordinate position based on the Confucian patriarchal system. However, with their legal capacity, women regardless of status actively petitioned the state and interacted with men as equally recognized legal agents. Nevertheless, most of the women who appealed grievances were widows or women with incapable husbands.[6] These women shared the fact that they could not receive help from either their husbands. Women of this category were not only sexually vulnerable but also susceptible to becoming victims in their everyday life.[7] Thus, these women became even stronger metaphors for pain and suffering publicly expressed in the Chosŏn legal space. By using a narrative of pity, women conveyed the message that it was difficult to live as women and that the state needed to protect them by redressing their grievances and thereby relieving their *wŏn*.

In men's petitions, we find men often relying on their emotions of anger when constructing their narrative. For example, men expressed their anger in terms of two Chinese characters used together: *punt'ong* (anger/pain), *punwang* (anger/grievance),[8] and *wŏnpun* (grievance/anger). Looking at 155 women's petitions submitted to county and provincial courts, I came across fewer than ten petitions in which a woman used "anger."[9] It was not socially prohibited for women to express anger, but female petitioners predominantly *chose* to rely on the two characters *wŏnt'ong* to emphasize their pain in their narratives. Unlike women, who personified femininity through displaying their weakness and vulnerability, men characterized their masculinity through their stronger and superior position within the society. Instead of relying on narratives of pity and elaborations on why and how they came to be in such miserable situations, men's petitions were more direct about the facts of the case and how their anger was aroused due to the injustice done to them. Men's narrative techniques differed from women's in two ways: they refrained from using a narrative of pity, at least when addressing personal grievances, and they did not make familial connections when representing their male identity.

When women addressed their personal grievances, they usually explicated what had happened to their husbands, how they had been making a living, and the kinds of hardships they went through within their community. Although they entered the legal realm as independently recognized legal subjects, they were also identified as someone's wife in addition to their surname in petitions. Their narrative strategies show that gender hierarchy was emphasized through women's gendered narratives and thereby they appeared to conform to social and community expectations about gender roles. In other words, by carrying gender norms to the legal space, women appropriated the Confucian rhetoric of female virtue in seeking their interests. While limiting their concerns to private matters, women as legal agents were regendering legal identity by constructing a sense of personhood via their narrative strategies. Furthermore, when taking into consideration that there are salient distinctions in the narrative strategies employed by women and men, and that it is difficult to find status differences within them, it could be argued that gender preceded status when identifying women's position in the judicial realm.

Despite the complex process of drafting written petitions, and despite the fact that male scribes wrote the petitions for most of the women and the illiterate men petitioners, petitioners' voices were always contained in the petitions submitted to the state as they were the original narrators of the grievances. Male scribes could not have written the petitions without first hearing the original stories as narrated by the petitioners. The process of constructing the narrative of *wŏn* entailed multiple layers of storytelling and ultimately produced a bifurcated gendered narrative. By minding the conventional norms of womanhood in Confucian society, the role of a scribe involved in drafting a petition was not to invent a new story but to effectively "craft" the grievance to win a magistrate's favor.[10]

While the scriveners helped shape the narrative in written petitions, women also participated in "crafting" the narrative. As will be shown in the chapter 4, commoner and slave women used the Confucian rhetoric of fidelity and filial piety when petitioning orally for their husband. This suggests that women were knowledgeable about what kind of language to use when addressing grievances even without the aid of scriveners. It is thus likely that scriveners did not solely conduct the "crafting" of narrative. Women not only provided the stories of their grievances but also participated in shaping the narratives together with scriveners in such a way as to win the magistrates' favor. In terms of linguistic practice, female petitioners, regardless of status, adopted the Confucian rhetoric of gender norms. This not only enhanced the power of the authority but also empowered female subjects as they demanded that the state listen and redress the grievances of its weaker subjects in order to exercise the benevolence of its Confucian governance.

### THE GENDERING OF LEGAL NARRATIVE

At both local and capital levels, women of commoner status and men of elite status were the most active petitioners.[11] This is well reflected in the guidance text to writing legal documents known as the *Essential Knowledge for Scholar-Officials and Clerks* (Yusŏp'ilji). The author of the text is unknown today, but scholars consider it to have been written sometime in the late eighteenth or early nineteenth century.[12] In this guidance text, the format of writing women's petitions is tailored to commoner women, manifesting their frequent participation in petitioning. The female petitioner was told to first write her county and province of residence followed by her surname and the term that represented her social status. The text states: "When women file petitions, they should first write Resident of . . . and . . . *sosa*'s petition. For example, if a woman's surname is Kim, then it should be stated as Kim *sosa*; if a woman's surname is Yi, then Yi *sosa*.[13] The term must be written after each surname. The opening and closing sentences should be written in this way. Also, when the petitioner is designating herself, she should write 'woman' (*ŭinyŏ*)."[14]

The above quotation is the only mention of female petitioners in the text. The rest of the text deals with the format of men's petitions, mostly elite men's writing. Unlike female petitioners, who had to specify their gender, male petitioners did not: elite men simply referred to themselves as "people" (*min*) and nonelite men used "I" (*ŭisin*).[15] The term *min* in general means "people," but elite men had the privilege of using the term to represent their status in petitions. Elite men also used the term *ŭisin* to refer to themselves, but nonelite men were prohibited from using the word *min*.[16]

When petitioners regardless of gender or status narrated their grievances, they began their first sentence by stating: "I am petitioning for the following reason. I appeal to Your Honor about my *wŏn* (and anger)." In men's petitions, men then explained their complaints and provided details of the circumstances. In women's petitions, women first explained why they came to be involved in a dispute and emphasized their vulnerable status. Women then explained the details of the dispute or the complaints that they had and appealed to the magistrate to sympathize with their suffering. Toward the end of petitions, most women stated "I hope Your Honor will take this into serious consideration and relieve my painful *wŏn*," whereas men often stated "I hope Your Honor will take this into serious consideration as I have failed to overcome my anger and *wŏn*."

When examining various grievances addressed to the state, it is not difficult to find men expressing their anger, which is also well represented in the guidance text of writing legal documents mentioned earlier. For instance, in the case of a gravesite dispute involving elite men, the text reads: "Without knowing the rules of the legal codes, that ignorant man secretly in the evening buried the body where it was prohibited. I could not overcome my anger. Thus, I dare appeal to Your Honor."[17] Similarly, for nonelite men in debt-related cases, the text suggests using the following: "Despite the fact that his financial situation has improved, he delayed paying me back and provided such and such excuses and saying he would pay me back today or tomorrow. However, he still has not paid. How can he not be compared to a robber? I could not overcome my *wŏn* and anger. Thus, I dare appeal."[18]

The emotions of *wŏn* and anger are similarly reflected in the example of a petition submitted in the third month of 1794 to the county magistrate of Namwŏn by an elite man, Yi Ch'igwan. This petition was jointly submitted by Yi Ch'igwan and his three cousins, Yi Chŏngjŏn, Yi Kongjŏn, and Yi Tŭkjŏn, regarding a gravesite dispute they were involved in with a commoner man named Yi Myŏngnin.[19] Gravesites were an issue that petitioners of different genders and statuses commonly petitioned about, along with issues of land and slaves. A gravesite dispute, known as *sansong*, was about the usage of a mountainside or gravesite. Along with suits involving land and slaves, this was one of the three major lawsuits in the late Chosŏn period. Unlike land and slave litigations, the gravesite dispute was rarely witnessed in the earlier years of the dynasty. However, it gradually increased as the society Confucianized toward the later Chosŏn and became the most frequently filed lawsuit, especially in the eighteenth and nineteenth centuries.

Conflicts over gravesites were based on three major aspects: geomancy (K: *p'ungsu*; C: *fengshui*), economic interests, and the spread of Neo-Confucian ideology. Scholars who began to explore the topic in 1980s focused on the issue of geomancy and claimed that geomantic belief coupled with filial piety was the primary cause of dispute.[20] In the 1990s, scholars of this kind of conflict moved beyond the discussion of geomancy and focused on how gravesite disputes were focused on the usage of resources surrounding tombs, such as firewood and lumber, thus were conflicts over forestland ownership.[21] One of the reasons people increasingly engaged in this type of dispute was that the state lacked the ability to devise an appropriate policy regarding the usage of mountains. Although mountains were treated as public property, subjects appropriated various means to possess them. For instance, people demarcated the boundary surrounding an ancestor's gravesite and prevented woodsmen or others from trespassing to gather firewood or cut trees. As the gravesite zone passed down three or four generations, it gradually came to be possessed by private individuals. By the end of the Chosŏn, contracts show that different mountain zones were bought and sold like any other private property. Because the state neither punished nor officially approved the possession of mountain areas by private individuals, the number of gravesite disputes increased and became a major social phenomenon in the late Chosŏn.[22]

Other scholars have emphasized the consolidation of patrilineal society and the spread of Neo-Confucian ideology in the late Chosŏn. Although gravesite disputes were initially considered to be a conflict found only among elite aristocrats, similar conflicts gradually spread to even the lowborn by the late eighteenth century.[23] As can be seen in Yi Ch'igwan's case, the other party involved in this dispute was from commoner status. Yi Ch'igwan wrote in his petition that Yi Myŏngnin had illegally buried a body within his ancestor's gravesite zone. He stated that his family had protected their ancestor's gravesite, which was in Poksang village, for many years but Yi Myŏngnin buried his family member's body there anyway. Yi Ch'igwan claimed that the county office was aware of the boundary of the gravesite, and the magistrate had endorsed his family's usage of the zone. He criticized Yi Myŏngnin for his ignorance of the law, stating that it was illegal to bury a body in someone else's gravesite zone, and accused him of not abiding by the law. He stated, "I could not overcome my anger and *wŏn* (*punwŏn*)."[24]

Examining the narrative structure of the petition, we can see that the petitioner opened his argument by directly pointing to the dispute he was involved in with the commoner man. He then explicated the details of the dispute and conveyed his anger and *wŏn*. He ended his petition by claiming that Yi Myŏngnin should be punished for breaking the law and asking that he be coerced to remove the body from the gravesite zone. In men's petitions, this kind of narrative structure was very common. Male subjects did appeal to emotions, but their narratives tended to be less emotional than those of female petitioners.

How different, then, was a woman's narrative concerning a similar situation? The following case is of commoner woman, Chŏng, who petitioned to protect her father-in-law's gravesite. In the third month of the year *sinhae*, Chŏng, wife of Kim Manbok and resident of Kongju county of Ch'ungch'ŏng province, submitted a petition written in literary Chinese to the magistrate of Kŭmsan county of Chŏlla province.[25] Prior to this petition, she had appealed to the predecessor of the current magistrate in a complaint against Yi Sunbong, who had stealthily dug up the front segment of her father-in-law's gravesite and buried his own relative's body there. The first magistrate issued an order for Yi Sunbong to exhume the body and bury it elsewhere. However, Yi deliberately delayed carrying out the order by providing endless excuses. Chŏng's husband was aggrieved by the situation and ultimately became ill. Chŏng narrated her grievance, stating, "Under such circumstances, how could I sustain my life to tragically live alone? I would plan to grab a hoe and go to Yi Sunbong's gravesite to dig up the body and kill myself afterward. My husband could then recover from this and my mother-in-law would also be able to preserve her life. This is my wish. I bow and implore Your Honor to sympathize with my particular *wŏn*. I beg a thousand and ten thousand times and hope Your Honor will settle this case."[26]

The magistrate gave an order to investigate Yi's crime and to bring a drawing of the two gravesites. The magistrate ruled that if Yi's trespassing of the burial site was explicit, he should be arrested. Although the petition does not provide further information, it seems Yi was directed to exhume the body according to Chŏng's ensuing petition. In the eleventh month of that same year, Chŏng appealed again because Yi had failed to follow the order. She traveled to Kŭmsan and sojourned there for about twenty days waiting to directly petition the magistrate, who was out of town. When he returned, she pleaded to him once again about her situation. After reviewing the petition, the magistrate commanded that Yi be punished with beating, and this time he specifically stipulated a date by which the body had to be exhumed.[27]

Despite the magistrate's command, Yi continued to shrink from the exhumation. Chǒng had no choice but to visit Kǔmsan for a third time in the eighth month of the year *ǔlmyo*.[28] However, the magistrate was suddenly reassigned to a post in Taegu and was replaced by a new one. Chǒng reiterated to the new magistrate what had been previously addressed and entreated him to redress her grievance. She stated, "I feel that even if I use my ten fingers to dig the ground, this [conflict] will end only when the body has been moved. I bow and plead to Your Honor to examine the documents of this case in detail and sympathize with my *wǒn*. Please urge [Yi] to exhume [the body] by a stipulated date so that my husband and I, whose lives are about to cease, can sustain our lives. I beg a thousand and ten thousand times with my tears of blood and hope that Your Honor will settle this case."[29]

The magistrate ordered that Yi be arrested and interrogated as to why he was not exhuming the body even though he had lost the litigation. He commanded Yi to exhume it by the tenth day of the tenth month.[30] As Yi failed to execute this new order, Chǒng desperately petitioned the magistrate again in the same month. She stated that when her husband heard of the magistrate's command, there was hope for him to recover. However, his joy lasted only momentarily, as Yi again neglected the order. The magistrate, like his predecessors, commanded that Yi be vigorously pressed and arrested.[31]

In Chǒng's case, Yi had continuously put off digging up the body by appropriating a loophole in the law. In principle, only the person who had buried the body was permitted to exhume it, and those who arbitrarily dug without authorization were exiled. Even the county office was not allowed to order compulsory exhumation unless the case was considered particularly extreme. Thus, if the defender risked being punished to protect the gravesite zone, it was difficult to arbitrate the case.[32] Yi was aware of this and he continued to delay exhuming the body. The outcome of Chǒng's case remains unknown, other than the fact that Yi was ordered to move the body. Nevertheless, the significance of Chǒng's petitions lies in her effort to appeal several times to the county office, which was far away from her residence, in order to reclaim the gravesite of her father-in-law, even though her husband was alive and technically should have taken on the role of petitioner.

Unlike men, women used a narrative of pity and evoked their female gender when petitioning to convey that the degree of grievance or the sense of being wronged was particularly difficult for widows, wives, and mothers. However, this does not necessarily mean that such a narrative implied only female weakness. For instance, Chǒng stressed her pain as a wife by elaborat-

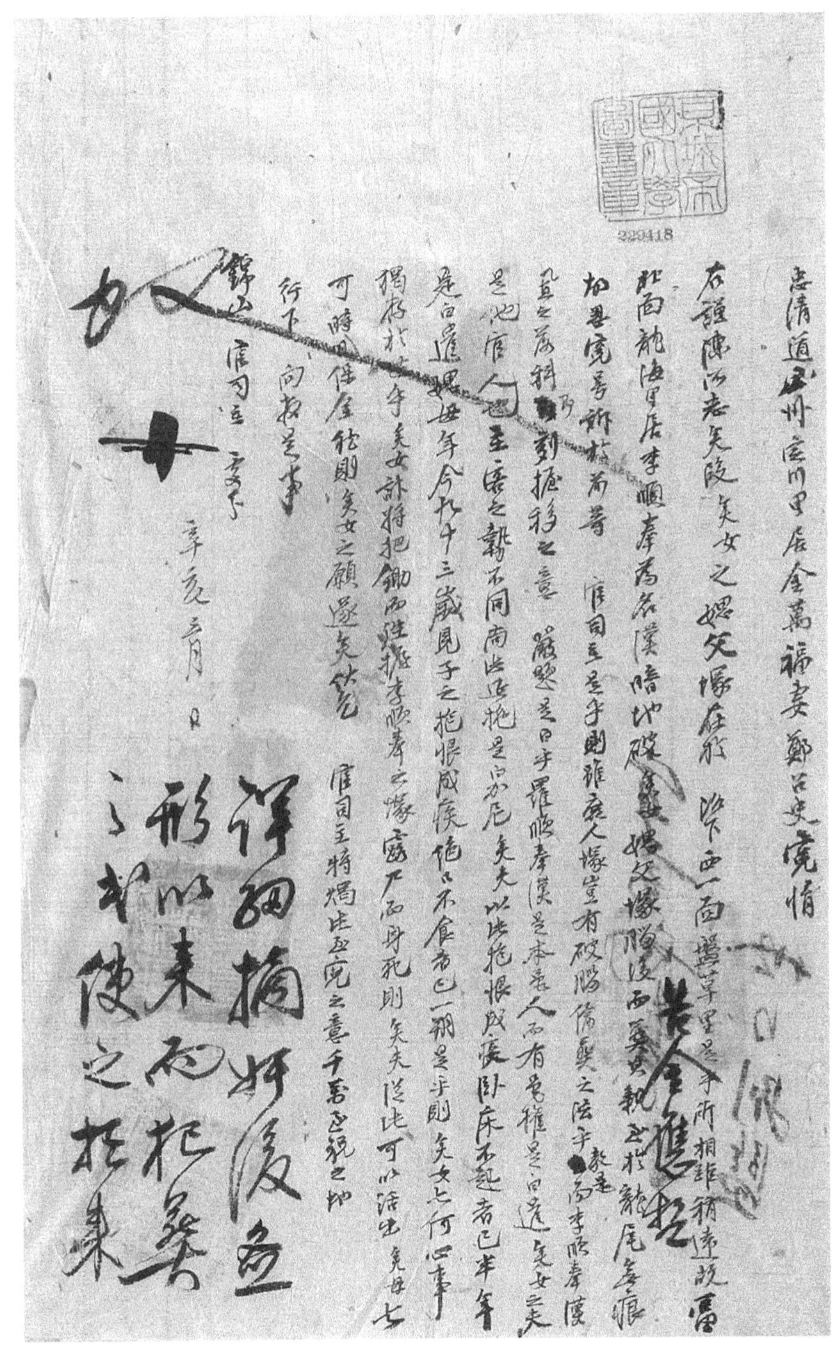

FIGURE 3.1. The first petition (gravesite dispute) of a commoner woman Chŏng. *Komunsŏ* 229418. Courtesy of Kyujanggak Archives, Seoul National University.

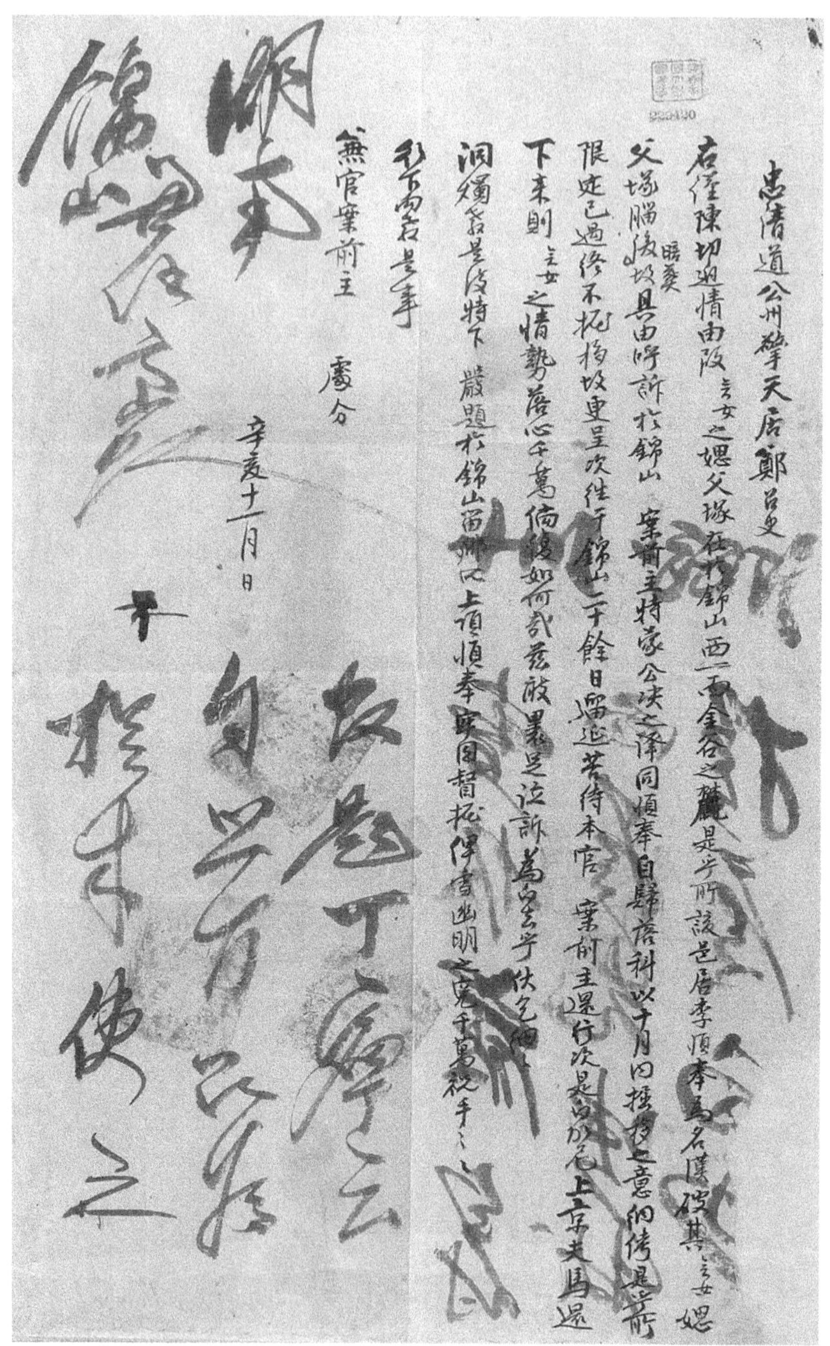

FIGURE 3.2. Commoner woman Chŏng's second petition. *Komunsŏ* 229420. Courtesy of Kyujanggak Archives, Seoul National University.

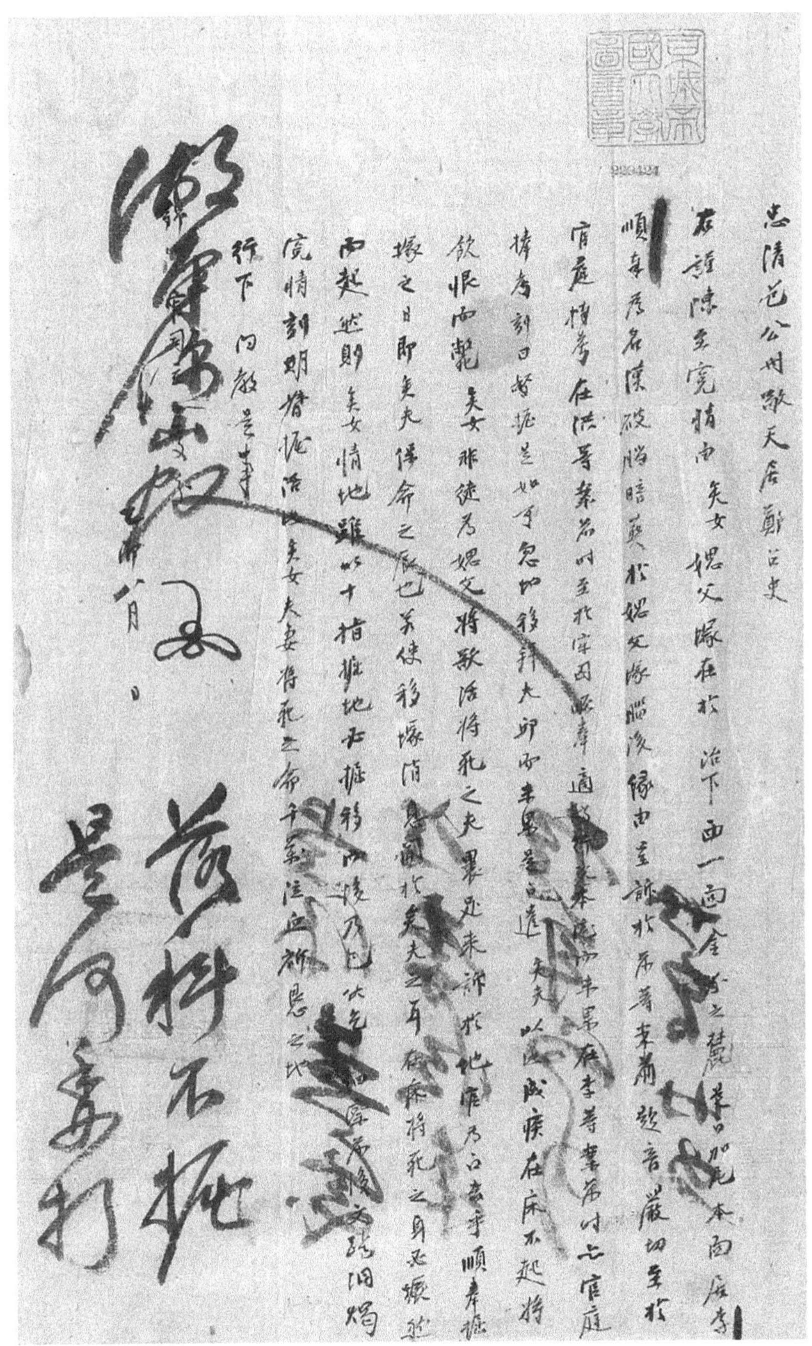

FIGURE 3.3. Commoner woman Chŏng's third petition. *Komunsŏ* 229423. Courtesy of Kyujanggak Archives, Seoul National University.

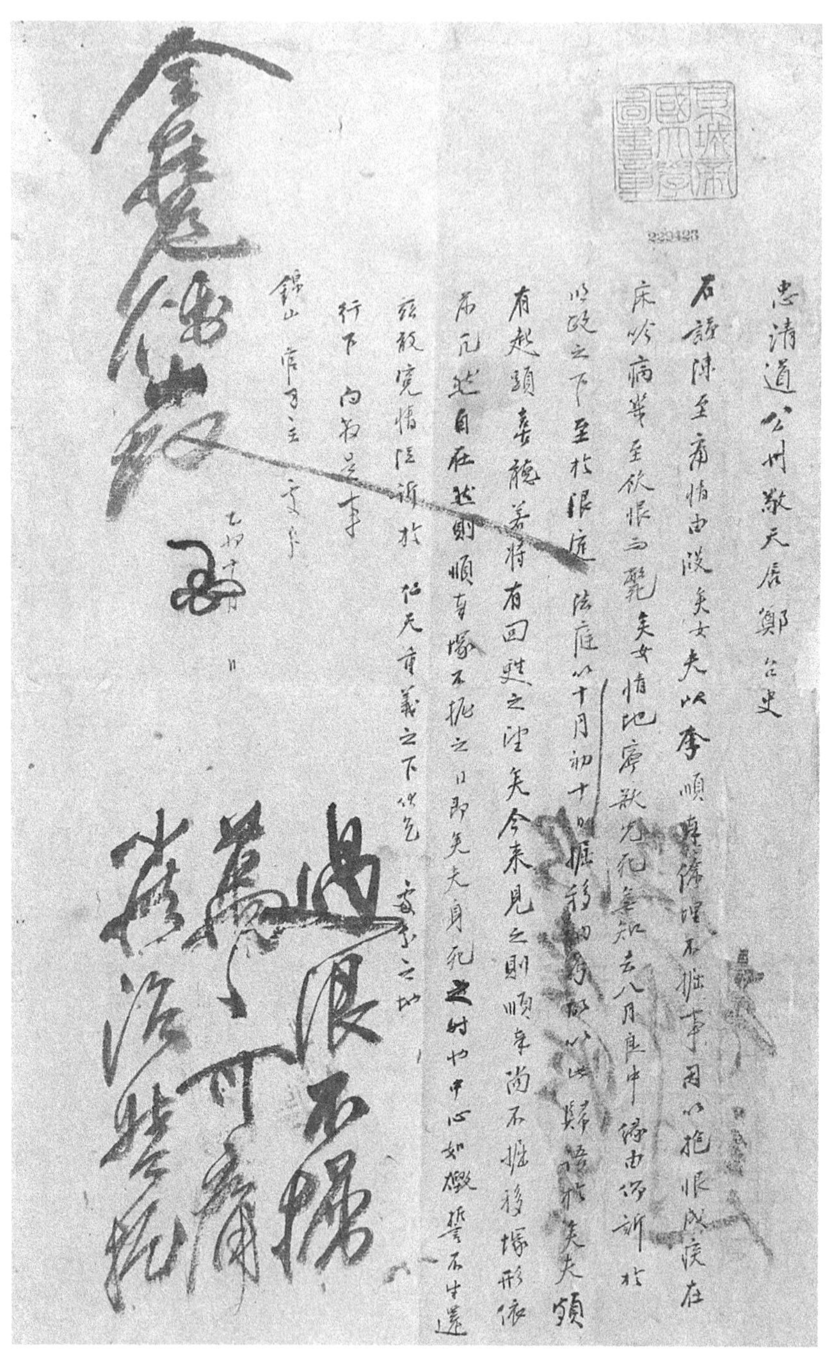

FIGURE 3.4. Commoner woman Chŏng's fourth petition. *Komunsŏ* 229424. Courtesy of Kyujanggak Archives, Seoul National University.

ing on the hardships she endured due to her husband's illness and noted that it was beyond her capacity as a woman to legally resolve the conflict. However, she concurrently characterized herself as a strong agent who was ready to assume a patriarchal role for the sake of the family. She conveyed her firm determination to find some kind of resolution by suggesting that she would go so far as to grab a hoe and exhume the body then kill herself afterward. Because her husband failed to overcome his grief, Chŏng undertook responsibility on the part of the entire family and confronted Yi herself. Whereas her husband became incapable when faced with the dispute, she traveled at least five times to Kŭmsan to reclaim the gravesite of her father-in-law, which reflects the relatively weakness of the husband's authority. It is also possible that this was a narrative strategy: a wife assuming her husband's role could show how desperate the family was and might successfully arouse pity and win the magistrate's favor. Whatever the case, Chŏng was gendering herself but simultaneously reconstructing gender by using a narrative that intricately entwined femininity and masculinity. She was redefining norms of womanhood by representing both femininity and masculinity through executing the legal role of the domestic patriarch.

Because marriage did not affect women's legal capacity, wives assumed their husbands' role when the husbands themselves were incapable of appearing at court. When women did appear to petition on family concerns as wives, their narratives were constructed to show that they appealed for the sake of their husbands and for the benefit of their entire families. Such a narrative allowed women to represent themselves as embodying female virtues and complying with gender norms without defying patriarchal authority. In contrast, when men petitioned as domestic patriarchs, they constructed their narrative without necessarily articulating familial connections, as they themselves were the heads of households. While conforming to the sociocultural convention of women's subordinate position, female petitioners simultaneously represented the family grievance and used a language that ultimately appealed for relief of their own personal *wŏn* rather than focusing on their family members' emotional satisfaction. Such a narrative strategy represented women's self-identity and their emotions in the legal space of the Chosŏn.




Women used the Confucian rhetoric of female virtue that was generally expected by the state when entering the courts, but they constructed their narratives in a way that best suited their interests depending on their position within the household. Although women's lived experiences varied according to their different social statuses, linguistic practices were unified across status boundaries through the Confucian narrative of female virtue. Being able to use such language did not necessarily mean that every female subject lived according to its prescriptive norms. However, through conventional speech, women actively pursued their interests by appealing to the state.

How did women's narratives become Confucianized and why did women regardless of status rely on the Confucian rhetoric of female virtue? When the Chosŏn dynasty was established in 1392 and adopted Neo-Confucianism as its sole ideology, the society underwent drastic changes as the state envisioned a normative Confucian society that implemented the Confucian model of patriarchy and patrilineality. This Confucianization of society was a process of change accomplished through a dynamic interaction between Confucian norms and Korean indigenous practices.[33] Although certain elements of Confucianism were in place before the Chosŏn, it was with the advent of this dynasty that Neo-Confucianism was adopted as official ideology and was accompanied by a reorganization of the indigenous family structure. For example, during the Koryŏ dynasty, sons and daughters were treated as equal members of the family, whether married or unmarried, and received equal share of inheritance. Marriage practice was uxorilocal, and women remained active in their natal homes. Remarriage was not a problem, and women divorced when necessary. The society was bilateral, which allowed daughters' children to succeed the family line.

In the Chosŏn, these practices shifted according to the Confucian patriarchal and patrilineal systems. As ancestral rites were introduced, the ritual duties were given to sons only;[34] daughters were no longer treated as equal members of the family and thus received a smaller share of inheritance;[35] the marriage practice shifted to virilocal, and women left their natal homes to serve their husbands' families; remarriage became socially stigmatized, and restrictions on remarriage were imposed on elite women; clear demarcations were drawn between a legal wife and a concubine, creating hierarchy and tension between them; and the society shifted from bilateral to patrilineal, such that only through sons could the family line be succeeded.

Conventional wisdom on the Confucianization of Korea suggests that these changes actually occurred through a gradual process and only became evident by the mid-seventeenth century.[36] The changes brought adverse effects on women, especially the elite, as they were deprived of ritual, economic, and social privileges. Although we cannot deny the negative effects Confucianization had on women, it must be emphasized that they were not deprived of legal capacity even as they lost other privileges toward the late Chosŏn.

Recent studies on women of the Chosŏn has explored the lives of nonelite women and has demonstrated how many of these women led much more diverse lives than elite women. Their lives show a much more complex picture according to their socioeconomic situations and they were less bound by official representations of gender norms.[37] These recent studies are significant in that they use a variety of sources to examine the lives of nonelite women, who have been mostly invisible throughout Korean history. The results of these recent studies raise critical questions about the late Chosŏn society: To what extent were the lower strata Confucianized? If sexual and marriage practices of nonelites were not greatly influenced by the Confucianization process, then what aspects of Confucianization were reflected in the lives of nonelites, who were the majority of the population? In order to answer these questions, it is necessary to break down the Confucianization process into various components and explore its multilayered representation in the context of a gendered and stratified society.

As far as women's linguistic practices in petitions are concerned, they were Confucianized in the sense that female subjects relied on the rhetoric of Confucian virtue despite their differences in social reality. For example, as women's concerns revolved around domestic affairs, it is very common to find women's narratives emphasizing their marital fidelity and filial piety. Although nonelite women had different lives in many ways from elites, they also utilized the Confucian language when engaging in dialogue with Neo-Confucian bureaucrats.

Now let us turn to various personal grievances that women presented to the state in their petitions. At county and provincial levels, women submitted grievances on issues of land, debt, gravesites, taxes, slaves, marriage, lineage, social status, and battery. Elite women's visibility in petitioning is particularly significant when considering that their other activities were mostly confined to their inner quarters, especially in the late Chosŏn. Compared to petitions of nonelite women, however, their concerns were rather limited to issues of lineage, property, and gravesite disputes. Nonelite women's grievances were much more diverse in content and dealt with practical concerns of their daily life. As seen in commoner woman Chŏng's case, appealing for pity was the common narrative strategy women of all social statuses employed when petitioning on different types of personal grievances. Nonelite women reference their oppressed status in addition to their female gender, which provided them with greater justification to appear at court to relieve their *wŏn*.

To explore the ways that women used the narrative of pity to negotiate their positions as the society Confucianized, we will first examine a petition that aired grievance concerning ancestral rites as elite women lost their privileges. Madam Chŏng's petition was written in vernacular Korean and submitted to the Board of Rites in the seventh month of 1689, during King Sukchong's reign (r. 1674–1720).[38] Madam Chŏng, wife of the deceased private scholar Cho Chiwŏn, was from a highly renowned and privileged kin group in the Seoul district.[39] Her great-great-grandfather, Chŏng Yŏp, was one of the most honorable officials during Sŏnjo's reign. Because Madam Chŏng's father lacked a son, Chŏng Iljang was adopted as the jural heir; his adoption was directly approved by Hyŏnjong (r. 1659–74). The king normally intervened in the adoption process when it concerned agnatic adoption of prestigious kin. However, the family's choice of Iljang as the jural heir turned out to be unfortunate. Iljang was extremely irresponsible and failed to perform his duties as successor. He led a dissipated life and exhausted all the property he had inherited. Moreover, he took a loan from a man named Yŏ P'ilju, and when it was in default the house he inherited was taken by the loan holder. When Yŏ moved into the house, Iljang recklessly disappeared, abandoning the ancestor tablet that remained inside the house. As the only daughter of the family, Madam Chŏng was unable to overlook her natal family's predicament. Thus, she petitioned the Board of Rites to request the state's permission to allow her to take care of the ancestor tablet until Iljang returned home.

From the state's point of view, Madam Chŏng's request was inadmissible because it defied the agnatic principle of the state's ideology. It was not possible to allow a daughter to look after an ancestor tablet when there was a jural heir in the family. The Board of Rites, however, could not simply disregard Madam Chŏng's request, because she was the descendent of a high-ranking official. Also, the king's approval of the jural heir made it even more difficult for the board to handle her case. The Board of Rites sympathized with Madam Chŏng's feeling of chagrin and even praised her effort in trying to sustain the family rituals with her own property. Nevertheless, they were skeptical of the idea of allowing a daughter to look after the ancestor tablet.

During the early Chosŏn, it was not impossible for a married daughter to take care of her natal family's ancestral rituals. However, as the patrilineal system gradually permeated the society, daughters were deprived of this ritual right.[40] Madam Chŏng's case elucidates this process of change that began to manifest in practice by sometime in the mid-seventeenth century. The Board of Rites acknowledged Iljang's recklessness but they could not easily approve Madam Chŏng's request as the agnatic principle was increasingly upheld by society. The board's written judgment stated, "her case has to be considered with extreme caution because accepting her request might appear as if constraint was imposed on the lineal grandson."[41] The Board of Rites refrained from explicitly stating whether Madam Chŏng could look after the ancestor tablet. Their initial response was that her case needed to be taken into serious consideration. According to the *Veritable Records of King Sukchong*, the state replaced Chŏng Iljang with Chŏng Kyejang in 1708 when the male relatives of Madam Chŏng petitioned to annul the jural heir position of Iljang.[42]

Although we cannot know for certain whether Madam Chŏng was permitted to temporarily look after the ancestor tablet, her wish was ultimately calibrated by appointing another jural heir. Madam Chŏng was firmly determined to restore her natal family's honor, and this was well conveyed to the authorities, who lauded her filiality. Although she used the narrative of pity by presenting herself as an ignorant, feeble woman, she emphasized that no one in the family could be more filial and sincere than herself. She stated:

> Although I am just a woman, I am the only direct descent line of Lord Mun
> Suk [Chŏng Yŏp]. How can there be difference between daughter and son
> when the shrines of my parents and grandparents are in the house of others
> being cursed by Yŏ brothers every day? Since I do not know when my brother
> will return, I wish to bring my family shrine [to my home] immediately.
> However, it is improper to bring [it] without the permission of the Board of
> Rites. Please take my situation into serious consideration and issue a written
> judgment.[43]

The fact that Madam Chŏng was the only remaining descendant of honorable ancestors assigned her a heavy responsibility. Filial piety in Confucian society was considered a natural debt to one's birth parents. However, filial allegiance was to be transferred to parents-in-law once a woman married. Thus, this natural emotion toward one's parents was emphasized differently according to gender, because men's filial emotion, which was based on natural moral order, was stressed toward their natal parents, while women's emotion toward their husbands' parents was socially constructed.[44]

However, certain texts, such as the *Instructions for the Inner Quarters* (Naehun), treat a woman's filiality to her natal parents and parents-in-law as no different.[45] This text depicts a woman's filial piety owed to natal and in-law parents as the same, with no fundamental difference based on gender.[46] Madam Chŏng's case shows how a daughter's filial emotion toward her natal parents continued to be expressed even after marriage, and how a married woman's grievance might go so far as to relate to the affairs of her natal family in the late Chosŏn.

The issues of lineage and ancestral rites that Madam Chŏng addressed were primarily confined to elite women. However, grievances related to land, debt, and gravesites were concerns that both elite and nonelite women raised in their petitions. In regards to with land disputes, there were two different types of petitions addressed in the late Chosŏn: disputes over ownership of land and requests to endorse lost documents that approved possession of land.[47] In order to prevent being deprived of one's land, it was necessary to seek an endorsement to claim one's rights. For example, in the ninth month of the year *kyech'uk*, a commoner woman Nam, who was a widow and a resident of Konam in T'aean county of Ch'ungch'ŏng province, petitioned a magistrate to notarize a copy of her original land document, which had been stolen.[48] Nam began her narrative stating that she was widowed at an early age and had neither children nor in-law family members to take care of. She was sustaining her life with five strips of paddy passed down from ancestors.[49] However, a burglar broke into her house and stole the document that verified the land to be 48 *ch'ŏk* in width and 60 *ch'ŏk* in length.[50] She entreated, stating, "Please endorse [the stolen document] so that it could be used as evidence when I sell or buy land in the future." The magistrate ordered the inquisition of three of her neighbors who could corroborate the petition. In that same month, she petitioned again to endorse the document since her case had been verified and the three names had been presented. The magistrate issued an order to endorse it on the eleventh of that month.[51] In about a week or so, Nam succeeded in attaining an endorsement from the magistrate.

Whereas Nam's document had been stolen, Madam O's had been burned when her house caught fire. She similarly requested the magistrate of her county to notarize the document, and she succeeded in achieving her aim. Madam O petitioned in the fifth month of the year *chŏngmyo*,[52] and she began her petition by stating, "I am petitioning for the following reason. My life is ill-fated. I lost my husband when I was young and have lived as widow without any children. . . . Unfortunately, I met with a misfortune last month and my house and [fields?] all were burned. . . . Please examine this case in detail. When my land is verified, please issue an endorsement."[53] Madam O opened her narrative in a similar pattern to Nam's, stating that she was widowed early and had no children. She was sustaining her life with a small amount of property but needed an endorsement in order to prove her ownership of land.

A commoner woman with the surname Pak presented a somewhat different narrative in a petition that was submitted in the first lunar month of the year *ŭllyu*.[54] She similarly began by appealing to pity, stating that she was suffering from a bad harvest that year and was even incapable of paying tax, but she did not stress hardships under her subject position as widow, wife, or mother. She stated, "Because I'm just a feeble woman, I will not be able to sell or buy if I do not get endorsement [of my lost document]. I am submitting my annual list of property in addition [to this petition]. Please take it into consideration and endorse."[55] Unlike other women who normally referred to themselves by their position in the household, Pak designated herself as a single woman (*tongnyŏ*) and identified herself independently.

Requesting the endorsement of a land document was not limited to elite or commoner women. Even female slaves appealed for endorsement. A public (state-owned) slave named Ch'ajŏng petitioned a county magistrate to endorse two documents that had been lost during her father's funeral.[56] One of the documents was the record of land that her father had bought when he was alive, and the other was the inheritance document she received from her father. After first stating that she had a grievance to appeal, she narrated how difficult it was to sustain her life as a public slave in a lean year. In such a situation, it was fortunate that she had inherited land from her father but unfortunate in that she had lost the document that verified her ownership. She stated that she needed the government to substantiate her land claim because people had doubts when she tried to sell. She further stated that she wished to keep such a document as supporting evidence in case her siblings or other relatives attempted to deprive her of her land. The magistrate ordered that the document be notarized when the case was verified.[57]

Although not every petition was successful, magistrates seem to have issued endorsements when petitioners provided enough evidence to prove their ownership of land. Women in general began with narratives of pity to emphasize that the degree of *wŏn* they felt were much greater as females because they were the weak and feeble subjects of the society, and they ended by pleading for the magistrates to protect their interests. Unlike elite women, nonelite women utilized a two-tiered representation as weaker subjects. In addition to relying on their female gender, they also underlined their social status as commoner or slave. The more oppressed or underprivileged subjects were, the greater their *wŏn* and thus the greater their grievance.

When it came to issues of credit and debt, commoner women petitioned far more often than women of other statuses, which implies that they were most actively engaged in the legal transactions of borrowing and lending. In credit- and debt-related cases, emotions such as enmity and *wŏn* inevitably emerged between a debtor and a creditor, especially when either the debtor failed to repay or the creditor unfairly sought interest. Petitioners were hardly averse to using the courts to pursue or resist debt claims, and they appropriated the courts to punish individuals with whom they had fallen out.

The following petitions illustrate the use of language of emotions to characterize social bonds as well as social divisions. In the ninth month of the year *sinch'uk*, commoner woman Sŏ, who was living alone as a widow, related her pitiful situation of how she had lent money to her neighbor Hwang Ch'iryong but was unable to redeem the debt.[58] She first explained that she had been widowed at an early age and had no children, which led her to wander around depending on neighbors. As she reached the age of sixty, she became afraid, thinking that no one would bury her body if she remained penniless. Thus, she began to earn money by pounding rice during the day and sewing at night. When her savings reached 70 *nyang*, she initially planned to put the money out at interest,[59] but she later lent the money to Hwang when he asked to use it for his marriage expense. After he was married, he enjoyed prosperous years of farming and lived affluently. Sŏ thus urged him for repayment, but he refused. She expressed her resentment in the petition, stating: "He not only had a wicked plan to neglect my consistent demand for payment, but also showed disrespect by leaving me with nothing to eat. . . . How could I be more indignant? He must rightfully pay back the money. If a poor woman like me cannot be indemnified, then I will not be able to prepare the money to bury my body. I implore with my blood tears as I have no choice in order to plan things after my death. Please have compassion for this woman whose life is nearing the end. I cry and appeal to you to arrest Hwang Ch'iryong and to immediately press him to compensate my loss." The magistrate of Kimpo county, Kyŏnggi province, in his written judgment, stated that Hwang's behavior could not be overlooked and commanded that Hwang be arrested. He further stated that Sŏ's loss must be recouped so that the lonely widow's grievance would be redressed. On the twentieth day of the ninth month, Hwang was detained in custody at the county office.[60] In this case, Sŏ's narrative strategy was based not only on her vulnerable status as widow but also her seniority, which was not uncommon in aged women's petitions.

A woman involved in a dispute with a younger man often emphasized how disrespectful he was, implying that he was breaking the harmonious communal relationship. Such narrative strategy greatly justified seeking redress and relieving *wŏn*. Whereas Sŏ petitioned as a creditor and appealed for compensation, a petition submitted by commoner woman Hwang was addressed as a debtor. In the twelfth month of the year *chŏngmi*, she filed a complaint against a creditor who had unfairly extracted interest.[61] When her husband was alive, he had borrowed 40 *nyang* from Mr. Yu, who was a *yangban* living in Ch'unch'ŏn county, Kangwŏn province. As the amount increased to 100 *nyang* in the following year due to unfairly charged interest, Mr. Yu demanded that her husband document that he would permanently sell his lands and fields if he failed to pay back the debt. Since there was no way to pay back the debt immediately, her husband drafted the document as demanded. However, when he could still not pay due to a bad harvest, his fields were mortgaged and Mr. Yu continued to collect even larger amounts of money. After her husband's death, Hwang complained that there were hardly any lands left for her.

The petitioner complained that Mr. Yu had unfairly increased the debt from 40 to 100 and even mortgaged fields for an uncollected 15 *nyang*. She asserted that nine years were more than enough to have paid back the initial debt. Further, she indicated that all of her neighbors also acknowledged Mr. Yu's unfair calculation and thus pleaded to redress the grievance. She ended her petition by stating: "Please investigate his crime for causing disorder in the district and right this wrong according to law. I beg to protect my emaciated body so that this widow, who has nothing on which to depend, will be able to preserve the land."[62] In the written judgment, the magistrate reprimanded the petitioner for appealing again when she had already filed complaint. It is common to find a female petitioner submitting several petitions with the same content within a short range of time in order to press the magistrate to adjudicate the case rapidly.[63] It seems Hwang had desperately petitioned again when the case was still under review.

In the second month of the following year, *musin*, Hwang once again lodged a complaint against Mr. Yu.[64] This time, in response to the magistrate, she began her petition by stating that she had previously committed a crime by filing a vexatious petition but she had to risk appealing again. She elaborated on what had occurred during the two months' interval between the last and the current petition. Shortly after her previous petition was submitted, the magistrate adjudicated that Mr. Yu should not dispossess Hwang's fields. After winning the case, Hwang attempted to sell the fields as Mr. Yu continuously interfered. When a buyer showed up, Mr. Yu threatened him by saying that he would lose all of his money because Mr. Yu himself would soon reclaim the fields by appealing to the appellate court. As no one showed up to buy the fields because of Mr. Yu, Hwang decided to look for a tenant farmer. However, Mr. Yu similarly intimidated neighbors by saying that he would not leave them alone if they cultivated the fields.

Under these circumstances, the petitioner stated that owning the fields was useless as she could neither sell nor cultivate them. She stated: "I had already reported Mr. Yu's vile action in my previous petition and the county office examined it. However, it is striking that he is acting even worse toward the end of this month. If he is left to behave imprudently, then where is law and how could [we] trust the county office's command? Mr. Yu has frequently insulted Your Honor with insolent speech. My words may seem as though I am disparaging him. But I was moved by the county office's interrogation and I became indignant when his words offended Your Honor. I thus bow and appeal."[65]

On the nineteenth of the second month, the magistrate in his written judgment stated that Hwang should step back for a while because he did not have discretionary power to arrest Mr. Yu, who was the resident of another county.[66] Compared to the previous petition, in her last one Hwang relied less on a narrative of pity and did not evoke her subject position as widow. She instead maintained a deferential tone and paid attention to avoid appearing as though she were filing a vexatious petition. The tone of the narrative even sounded bold and resolute, unlike that of the previous petitions. She may have gained confidence, since she had won a favorable ruling two months previously. While she relied on a narrative of pity to evoke compassion from the magistrate, she simultaneously made audacious statements such as asking how she could trust a magistrate's command when it was not properly executed. Although she dared not challenge a magistrate's authority, she boldly demanded rectification for the wrong, asking that he relieve the *wŏn* of a weak subject.

In the aforementioned land-, credit-, and debt-related cases, it is difficult to find clear differences between elite and nonelite women's petitions. However, the difference becomes explicit when issues of marriage and social status are examined. In the case of marriage, the depiction of nonelite women's lives shows that they were less bound by chastity ideology even at the turn of the twentieth century.[67] The following petition by a commoner woman with the surname Song illustrates how nonelite women's marriages differed from those of elite women.

Although the petition focuses on a grievance that stemmed from the marriage of a commoner woman's daughter, it is really about a property dispute between Song and her son-in-law; the purpose of the petition was to request an endorsement over her property. In the sixth month of the year *kyemyo* (1903), Song petitioned the magistrate of Wŏnsan county of Hamgyŏng province and filed a complaint against her son-in-law, Kim Chinwŏn, who was a medical practitioner. Song's daughter had married Kim when he came to practice medicine in her hometown. After having lived with her for only a few years, Kim suddenly left his wife and returned to his own hometown, Wŏnsan. Song's daughter waited for her husband to return, but she did not hear from him for three whole years. As it was heartbreaking for Song to watch her daughter suffer emotionally, she decided to set off on a journey with her daughter to Wŏnsan in search of Kim. At first, it seemed that the daughter was fortunate because she was able to reunite with her husband. However, the couple's reunion soon broke because Kim neglected his wife once again.

Song had sold her property in order to move and settle down in Wŏnsan. When her daughter reunited with Kim, Song gave her about 1,000 *nyang* hoping that she would be able to manage and sustain the marriage. Kim, however, took most of his wife's money and bought property under his name and also exhausted the remaining money. To make matters worse, his concubine turned Song's daughter out of the house, so she returned to live with her mother again. Meanwhile, the daughter gave birth to a girl, but the baby soon died from a cold. According to Song, Kim was neglectful of his family even when the poor infant died. From this incident, Song judged that there was no hope for the couple's marriage and decided to leave Wŏnsan and take her daughter back to their own hometown. Because she had given away most of her assets, she needed to reclaim some portion. Song thus asked her son-in-law, but he refused. Feeling extreme resentment against him, she appealed to redress her grievance. She stated that it was not possible for the couple to be reunited, and her petitioning the magistrate indicated that the marital relationship with Kim was severed. After conducting an interrogation, the county magistrate ordered in his written judgment that Kim be arrested.[68]

Although Song articulated in the petition how her daughter's marriage had been broken because of Kim, the aim of the petition was to retrieve her property from her son-in-law. Instead of directing the narrative to elaborate on how Kim had seized her property, Song's strategy was to represent Kim as someone who was immoral and responsible for the shattered marriage. In order to avoid giving the impression that she was making the complaint merely to seek economic interest, she emphasized how her daughter under-went dire circumstances because of Kim and how grievous it was for the two women. Like many other women's petitions, Song's began by explaining that she was widowed at an early age and had lived with her only daughter; the two of them relying on each other. After explaining how the property dispute occurred between her and her son-in-law, she expressed enmity toward him and said that her *wŏn* had reached an extreme due to her son-in-law's unfilial behavior. Such a narrative strategy strongly supported the petition to redress grievance and simultaneously seek economic redress.

Song's petition demonstrates various aspects of a commoner woman's life. First, she portrays a seemingly disparate life from that of an elite woman. The primary difference is the hierarchical relationship between wife and con-cubine. Song stated that "the concubine (*ch'ŏp*) drove the wife (*ch'ŏ* ) out of the house," indicating that there was a lack of the clear hierarchy of women of different social statuses found in elite families. This raises the question of whether a concubine of a commoner man could be from the same social sta-tus as his primary wife. Hierarchy among women in aristocratic families was clearly drawn, and a concubine had to come from a lower status than the legit-imate wife. Although Song did not mention the status of the concubine, her case demonstrates that the hierarchy of women omnipresent in elite families could be absent among nonelites. This does not mean to suggest that such a hierarchy did not exist in any commoner families but only that it is necessary to examine each case to determine the relationship between wife and concu-bine in the case of nonelite families.

The second difference evident in the petition relates to the commitment of marriage. Although the marriage was arranged through a matchmaker, Kim did not take the relationship with his wife seriously. The story of this particular marriage shows that a man of low status was able to easily leave his wife and neglect to fulfill his role as husband without grave consequences. A third difference can be found in the implication about the relationship between Song and her son-in-law as regards Confucian society. It is rare to find a dispute case involving either a woman and her parents-in-law or a man and his father-in-law. However, it is not difficult to find one between a man and his mother-in-law. How can we understand the dispute between the male subject and his mother-in-law? In Confucian society, women were expected to be filial and serve parents-in-law even after the husband's death. In practice, however, some married women looked after their own parents instead. For instance, when a widow of commoner status had no place to go, she depended on her married daughter and resided in her house.[69] Although men did not have an obligation to look after the wife's parents, this did not mean that they were exempted from performing filial duty to parents-in-law.[70] As far as filiality is concerned, women and men had to sincerely carry out their duties to both natal and in-law parents.

Finally, a mother's role in filing complaint against her son-in-law is worthy of consideration, especially considering that Confucian law prohibited a wife from accusing her husband. In Song's case, it seems as though the mother was assuming the daughter's role, as the wife lacked the capacity to petition against her husband. Although women were restricted from accusing their husbands, they were empowered to accuse a daughter's husband. Conversely, while gender functioned as the primary component between wife and husband, it was not gender, but age that became foregrounded in the relationship between wife's mother and son-in-law.

Now let us turn to the issue of social status. During the Chosŏn, social mobility was relatively flexible between commoner and slave women in that it was not rare for a commoner woman to be given slave status and vice versa. In terms of social status, commoner women often appealed when they were unfairly treated as slaves or servants in order to protect their right to freedom as commoners. Powerful elites and wealthy commoners often coercively enslaved destitute commoners or previously manumitted slaves to use their labor.

Petitioners appealed to redress their grievances when they had been violated by the privileged group. Their effort to complain about unfair treatment eventually led the state to legislate a new law in order to prevent such exploitation. The law against "oppressing commoners as slaves" (*amnyangwich'ŏn*) was stipulated in the *Continuation of the Great Code* in the early eighteenth century as a consequence of the appeals of related grievances. The problem of oppressing commoners as slaves, one of the main social injustices in the late Chosŏn, prompted commoner women to construct a narrative of pity when petitioning on their status.

In the fourth month of the year *sinsa*, a commoner woman Kim appealed to the provincial governor and addressed how her daughter had been unjustly treated as a servant.[71] Kim opened her petition stating that "I am petitioning about my *wŏn*. There may be various kinds of grievances in this world but there could not be a more distressing grievance than mine. My parents already passed away in the year *kyemyo* and we (my husband and I) have exhausted family property and we have nothing to depend on."[72] She then explained that she and her husband lived in extreme poverty but were fortunate enough to receive support from Mr. Yi who was of the *yangban* class. The couple first ran errands for Mr. Yi but later depended on Mr. Sin, who was Mr. Yi's brother-in-law. However, when Kim's husband died, she became the concubine of Mr. Sin and had three children with him. Kim's grievance came about after Mr. Sin died, because his son attempted to coercively treat Kim's daughter from her first husband as his servant. She claimed that it was clearly against the law for Mr. Sin's son to treat her daughter as his servant when he did not even own her. In order to prove her claim, she provided the document Mr. Yi had drafted that indicated her commoner status.

The kernel of Kim's case was whether Mr. Sin's son could treat her daughter as a servant. The provincial governor adjudicated that it was inappropriate for the son of Mr. Sin to treat the daughter as a servant because their relationship did not legally bind them as owner and slave. According to his rationale, it was improper of the son to treat the daughter as servant when Kim and her daughter had merely depended on his family for a brief period of time. The provincial governor recognized the *wŏn* of the petitioner and perceived the case falling into the category of oppressing commoners as slaves.[73]

Contrary to petitioning to protect one's freedom as commoner, destitute commoners occasionally enslaved themselves by selling their bodies for economic reasons. Although status was defined by birth, it was not impossible for slaves to be manumitted through purchase and commoners to be enslaved according to their will. Social mobility between commoner and slave seems to have been relatively flexible in the late Chosŏn. For example, in the first month of 1750, commoner woman Kim, wife of Chŏng Poksam, petitioned the magistrate of Kyŏngju and requested an endorsement of her enslavement, elaborating the reasons for selling herself into slavery. Although Kim's husband was alive, she was the one economically supporting the family. Her husband was suffering from a chronic disease and was incapable of working. Due to that year's bad harvest, the family was wandering from one town to another. But as Kim's father-in-law had recently died, she needed to prepare his funeral expenses in addition to providing shelter and food for her remaining family. In order to bail herself out of financial trouble, she decided to sell herself and become a slave. She pleaded her grievous situation to the magistrate and stated that she first wished to escape the dire circumstance by committing suicide, but that choice was not easy. She then decided to fulfill the urgent needs of the family by degrading herself to a lower status. She requested that the magistrate endorse that she was selling herself as a slave so that she could avoid potential conflict that might arise with the owner. The magistrate replied in his written judgment that the petitioner should act according to her discretion but denied her request to endorse.[74]

The purpose of Kim's petition was not to redress a grievance but to prevent a dispute that might occur in the future. The magistrate neither blocked the petitioner's choice to enslave herself nor acceded to her request. Whereas authorities intervened between two parties when it came to redressing an immediate grievance, they seem to have remained relatively aloof to potential grievances. This is one of the differences between petitions presented to the sovereign and to local authorities. In order to administer royal justice, the sovereign not only paid attention to existing grievances petitioners addressed but was also keen to eliminate potential grievances when adjudicating cases. Petitioners often bypassed the intermediate court and directly appealed to the king for various reasons, and the fact that the king was more considerate in redressing the grievances of his subjects seems to have been one of those reasons. The king, who was a fatherlike figure, was a reference point of justice who embraced the voice of every subject and represented fairness by relieving the *wŏn* of petitioners regardless of their gender or status.

CONCLUSION

Petitioning to redress a grievance was a righteous act to restore moral order that had been damaged by injustice. In petitioning, women gained a sense of personhood constructed around the Confucian patriarchal system. Appealing to redress grievances at some times reinforced the gender hierarchy but at other times manifested in a powerful form of female agency. Women's efforts to seek rectification by filing complaints against those who had wronged them were acts to protect their interests. For those who were wronged, petitioning was a measure of self-assertion and self-construction. Women's agency was exercised through the performance of petitioning when female subjects were legally violated as moral individuals. By capitalizing on the legal capacity to petition, women actively engaged in dialogue with authorities, which enabled them to voice their sense of injustice. Through articulating their grievances using the narrative strategy of pity, women struggled to defend their own sense of morality.

These petitions addressed to county and provincial courts show how the narratives used to construct the emotions of *wŏn* were gendered in the cases of both personal and family grievances. While female petitioners often emphasized their pain and suffering, male petitioners represented their anger associated with *wŏn*. In order to emphasize their female gender, women represented their *wŏn* through a narrative of pity underlining their weakness, vulnerability, and subordinate position within the society, but at the same time they boldly demanded that the state follow its mandate to relieve their *wŏn*. While appealing to female weakness, women as legal agents were simultaneously regendering legal identity by making strong and bold statements to protect themselves from being legally violated. Although women were not prohibited from expressing anger in the legal realm, their narrative centered on underlining suffering and pain they experienced as feeble women in the society. By capitalizing on the legal capacity to petition, women engaged in dialogue with the authorities, which enabled them to publicize *wŏn*, and employed gendered narrative strategies to win their favor. Although it is likely that multiple actors were involved in devising such narrative strategies that reinforced gender hierarchy, women themselves were knowledgeable of what narrative to use and how to take advantage of the legal system to relieve their *wŏn* as well as seek their interests.

*Chapter Four*

# SEEKING VINDICATION OR BEGGING
# PARDON ON BEHALF OF THE LIVING

When a husband and a wife enter into a relationship through marriage, they
live together for one hundred years. The husband must be considerate of his
wife, and the wife must obey her husband. If there is discord, the husband
should further suppress his anger, and the wife should further obey him. The
household order will then be preserved.

—Kim Chŏngguk, *Kyŏngminp'yŏn*

IN 1782, DURING THE SIXTH YEAR OF CHŎNGJO'S REIGN (R. 1776–
1800), a commoner woman surnamed Yi, resident of Yech'ŏn county,
Kyŏngsang province, traveled all the way to the capital to present an oral
petition to the king during his royal tour outside the palace. When she succeeded in attracting the attention of authorities by striking a gong, she cried
out on behalf of her husband, Chŏng Yakp'il, who had been held in custody
for homicide. He was accused of beating his distant relative, Chŏng Chaebŏm,
to death during his mother's funeral. When Yi's grievance was publicized,
she was sent to the Board of Punishments to speak further. During her interrogation there, she complained that her husband's slave, Indŭk, who was also
implicated in the crime, was unfairly designating Yakp'il as the principal
murderer to evade responsibility. When the interrogation was over, the Board
of Punishments accepted her oral petition and recounted it to the king.

She reported that on the day of the funeral, an intoxicated Chaebŏm
became unruly, broke the ancestor tablet, and assaulted Yakp'il. He then
headed to Chŏng Chaedae's residence and damaged his house by striking its
pillars with an ax. Continuing his violent behavior, he went to Indŭk's house

and battered his father. Yakp'il, Chaedae, and Indŭk all resisted and ultimately beat Chaebŏm to death. Soon after the incident, Chaebŏm's death was reported to the provincial office, and the three men were detained as suspects. At that point, Yi made her appeal to complain that Indŭk was unfairly shifting the blame to her husband. After hearing the report, the king commanded the governor of Kyŏngsang province to initiate an investigation into Chaebŏm's murder. Based on testimonies and other evidence, the provincial governor substantiated to the king that Yakp'il was the principal offender. The murder trial lasted for eight long years, and when the king finally adjudicated the case in 1790, he banished Yakp'il and exonerated Indŭk.[1]

In the late Chosŏn, when appeals were made to the sovereign on behalf of family members who were accused of homicide, the state's primary concern was to verify the facts of the case. When petitioners presented grievances on behalf of imprisoned family members as the female petitioner Yi did, the state initiated investigations to determine whether the cases were truly those of grievances that aroused the *wŏn* of the wrongfully accused. If they were, then the state sought to rectify and relieve the *wŏn* of those who were imprisoned as well as that of the petitioners. If they were not, then the petitions were disregarded and the petitioners were punished for trying to deceive the sovereign.

What motivated petitioners to travel to the capital to appeal for their family members? How did petitioners articulate a narrative of grievance in publicizing *wŏn* on behalf of their family members? How did petitioners represent or empathize with their family members who had been wronged? What was the implication of women petitioners like Yi representing husbands in a public space, which was a transgression of symbolic or discursive power in Confucian culture? How did women adopt a persona that effectively negotiated the tension between normative prescription and social reality?

Petitions for husbands and fathers were among the most common petitions submitted to the sovereign during the late Chosŏn period. In the fifteenth century, when the petition system was still in its infancy, the state limited petitioners to grievances that concerned them personally. However, as the Chosŏn state adopted Neo-Confucianism as its sole ideology and the Confucianization project gradually permeated various spaces of the society including the juridical domain, the state allowed petitioners to present grievances for others on the basis of Confucian familial relationships. In the early eighteenth century, the state reinforced the sacrosanct kinship bonds by legislating a new set of four categories of allowable petitioning: a son could petition for his father, a wife for her husband, a younger brother for his elder brother, and a slave for his or her master. With the new four categories, the state's perception of legal subjects previously based on the recognition of an individual's *wŏn* shifted to include the *wŏn* of family members. Conversely, the recognition of the individual as an agent of emotions shifted to include the relational self, or intersubjectivity, through the very practice of representing the *wŏn* of family members.

Petitions representing the new four categories, especially those of wives petitioning for husbands, demonstrate the connection between "cross-sub-jective self-enactment" and redressing grievance. The concept of cross-sub-jective self-enactment relies on the idea that expressing one's sense of self is intimately linked to the self of the other, and that people require engagement with others in shaping their emotions and identities. It also refers to mul-tiple subjectivities that are connected through familial relations affecting the individual self.[2] The concept of connectivity is useful in characterizing the economy of relational personhood in the context of Chosŏn society. The prac-tice of petitioning is discussed here in terms of this connectivity to describe the relationality between petitioners and the family members they were rep-resenting. Conversely, intersubjectivity in the legal domain was constructed by representing the *wŏn* of family members.

The set of four categories that was codified in the early eighteenth century was a legalization of what had already been practiced in the previous period. As the number of petitions made on behalf of family members continuously increased, the new provisions were legislated in the *Continuation of the Great Code*, reflecting both the established practice and the state's vision of ideal Con-fucian familial relationships. When addressing grievances for family members, women and men most frequently entered the court when they spoke on behalf of husbands and fathers, respectively. Such a phenomenon attests to how women and men internalized the Confucian exemplars of devoted wife and filial son in the latter half of the dynasty. This implies that the legal sphere of the Chosŏn had been Confucianized in the sense that the two pillars of Confucian ethics, filial piety and fidelity, were present in legal practice. As petitioners came to speak on behalf of family members, women established themselves as defenders of their husbands and men as defenders of their fathers. This does not mean that petitioning for family members was always conducted in the hierarchical order as was stipulated in the legal codes. Nevertheless, the role of wife and the role of son were emphasized when seeking royal justice at the capital level.[3]

What is significant about the new four categories is how the Confucianiza-tion of the society, either intended or unintended, redistributed power within households as the junior and subordinate family members were empowered to speak on behalf of their senior family members in court. These relationships were based on the fundamental Confucian kinship bonds—father and son, husband and wife, and elder brother and younger brother. The new provisions also included the relationship between master and slave, as slaves were treated as extended family members. Although the four categories were based on the hierarchical order within familial relationships, juniors representing seniors in court concurrently enabled the inferiors to subvert the power relationship to some extent.

Women's representation of their husbands reinforced their domestic roles and engaged them in a discourse of domesticity. However, the representation of husbands in the juridical domain complicated power dynamics within patriarchal households. When husbands were incapable of petitioning, they became *dependent* on women's legal capacity for seeking rectification or begging pardon. Their invisibility begot their reliance on wives' performances and narrative strategies. When petitioning to represent the *wŏn* of their husbands, women utilized various narrative strategies that differed from those used when presenting personal grievances. When women narrated their own *wŏn*, they often relied on the narrative of pity and emphasized the pain female petitioners embodied as weaker and subordinate subjects of society. However, when women petitioned as wives, their narratives shifted to reflect the values of fidelity and filial piety to show that they were dutifully acting for the sake of their husbands' and families' well-being. In the Chosŏn, redressing grievance on behalf of family members was dependent on a collaborative and reciprocal petitioning.

As female petitioners actively represented their husbands, the state not only officially approved women as legal agents to speak for their husbands but also reinforced the Confucian female virtue of fidelity in the realm of law. In other words, women's domestic role, which emphasized being faithful to patriarchs, was extended to the legal role of representing the *wŏn* of husbands when they were incapable of defending themselves. In the petitioning activity of the late Chosŏn, the ideology of fidelity was reflected in women's petitioning practice and was one of the factors that drove wives to appeal as they sympathized with their husbands.

The representation of a family grievance at the capital level was normally conducted under one of two circumstances. One was when a family member was imprisoned or exiled due to a crime such as homicide, economic offense, abuse of local authority, or infringement of social custom. Among these four crimes, homicide was the subject of the majority of petitions representing the accused.[4] In this case, petitioners appealed on behalf of imprisoned family members to either vindicate or seek pardon for them. The other circumstance, which is the focus of next chapter, was when family members were unjustly murdered by fellow villagers or by local officials. Petitioners in this type of case, pleaded for justice on behalf of the dead in order to appease the aggrieved souls.

## THE SOCIALITY OF PAIN SHARED BY A VICTIM'S FAMILY MEMBERS

As the number of petitioners representing family members dramatically increased in the late Chosŏn, these petitioners mediated between their family members and government officials. The represented family member was an absent figure who was incapable of presenting the petition in person. Although legitimate representation was limited to hierarchical order within the familial relationship, representation in practice was not necessarily manifested in such order. Very often, a person in a senior position in the family petitioned on behalf of a junior, and multiple variations of representations were made within the familial relationship, with one exception, that is, a master petitioning on behalf of his or her slave. Although petitioners often deviated from the limited realm of possibilities, authorities tolerated such deviation and did not impose restrictions.

Representation can be seen as the means by which mediated knowledge makes an absent entity visible by replacing it with an "image" capable of recalling the entity as it is. Through representation, it is possible to envision something that is absent, which distinguishes what is doing the representing and what is being represented.[5] This conceptualization of representation can be adequately applied to the petitioning activity of the Chosŏn in that a petitioner substituted for the absent figure, who lacked a presence, and mediated between the absent and the authorities by attempting to invoke commiseration. While petitioners represented the grievances of the absent, they also emphasized the emotional pain they themselves were feeling due to injustice exercised on the absent. Thus, the function of the representation here is twofold: to make an absence present and to exhibit the petitioner's own presence as a wronged subject.[6]

The victim of injustice and his or her family members internalized *wŏn* that was intricately bound with power. When injustice is reduced to pain, then it also has access to the interiority of the feelings of others, which is called the "sociality of pain."[7] This shared emotion of pain moves into other bodies, transforming the pain into their sadness. Emotions are not simply located in the individual but move between bodies, producing the so-called emotion of contagion. It is the emotion per se that passes on to others, and what passes on to others is considered to be the same emotional feeling. However, the passed emotion may not necessarily be the same emotion felt by the other subject. Instead, it is the objects of emotion that circulate rather than emotion as such. The emotion is thus not always felt the same from one person to the next when it navigates across bodies.[8] In the petitioning activity of the Chosŏn, the emotional pain of the wronged carried into the family members' bodies, but whether the pain they shared was the same seems to have not been a significant matter. More critical was how petitioners as family members understood, embraced, and represented the pain of the victims in the search for justice. When petitioners appealed for their family members, they first sympathized with the *wŏn* felt by those family members, and this shared feeling of *wŏn* was what led them to travel to the capital.

Through representation, petitioners not only addressed the grievances of the absent but also expressed their own empathy in order to persuade the Neo-Confucian officials. To effectively express the degree of painful sentiment, petitioners devised various strategies. For example, in written petitions, they often showed the pain of having lost their beloved family members by cutting a finger and writing the petition with blood.[9] In addition, during the king's procession, some held a banner written in blood to express their *wŏn*. To display grievance in such a way was to express internal pain on an outer surface. Although such petitions were illegal, petitioners used these tactics to achieve their aims. An act of writing a petition with blood expressed the true sincerity of the petitioners' grievance.[10] In some cases, those petitions were successful in arousing the sympathy of the authorities, which led to a thorough investigation of the case. I do not mean to suggest that the case itself was adjudicated based on represented emotion or evoked commiseration; these cases demonstrate that emotions expressed by petitioners influenced the authorities to investigate further.


PETITIONING ON BEHALF OF FAMILY MEMBERS:
BEFORE AND AFTER THE NEW FOUR CATEGORIES

During the Chosŏn, the state radically redefined the family, its internal dynamics, and its relationship to the state. As part of an attempt to re-create

subjects and build a more Confucian social structure, Neo-Confucian officials challenged long-standing domestic practices and infused politics into
the most intimate relationships. They disputed how the family should be
reformed to construct the new Neo-Confucian state. They debated how Neo-
Confucian ideals and institutions should transform the emotional bonds,
gender dynamics, legal customs, and economic arrangements that structured
the family. They discussed how to bring the principles of Confucian ethics,
the three bonds, and the five relationships into the home and community.
And as family members confronted one another in the home, they gradually
negotiated new domestic practices that balanced Koryŏ customs with Confucian innovations in law and culture. The Chosŏn bureaucrats were ambitious
in their attempts to transform the family, for they saw how profoundly politics
and the gendered matters of daily life were intertwined. Such a vision was thus
reflected in the legal codes and legal practice of the Chosŏn.

The codification of petitioning on behalf of family members first appeared
in the *Continuation of the Great Code*, which was compiled during Yŏngjo's
reign (r. 1724–76). Prior to this codification, however, the state limited petitionable categories to matters involving the petitioners themselves: one's corporal punishment, one's paternity, one's familial status as either legal wife or
concubine, and one's social status as commoner or slave. In addition to these
initial four categories, the *Continuation of the Great Code* stipulated a new
set of four ways to petition, that is, son for father, wife for husband, younger
brother for elder brother, and slave for master; these were first issued in the
edict of 1704 during Sukchong's reign (r. 1674–1720). The 1704 edict differed
slightly from the *Continuation of the Great Code* text in that it lacked the
category of slave for master. However, in Sukchong's edict of 1720, slaves were
allowed to represent masters, but only when their masters lacked offspring.
Not until twenty-six years later, when the *Continuation of the Great Code* was
compiled in 1746, were slaves unconditionally allowed to petition for their
masters.[11] The legalization of the new four categories reinforced not only the
cardinal familial relationships but also the three pillars of Confucian ethics—
filial piety, fidelity, and loyalty.

Although the new four categories were first stipulated in the legal codes
of the early eighteenth century, the practice of representing family members stretches far back to the early Chosŏn period, during T'aejong's reign (r.
1401–18). For example, in 1412, Pak Chŏsaeng's son struck the petition drum
and appealed on behalf of his imprisoned father. Pak was accused of taking
his own father's concubine after his death. In addition to Pak's son, his two

younger brothers, Pak Kangsaeng and Pak Sinsaeng, also appealed to complain about the misjudgment of their brother's case.[12] The outcome of the case is unknown, but it is clear that petitioners began to petition for family members as early as the fifteenth century.[13]

Women are no exception in that they also engaged in petitioning activity as early as the fifteenth century and also petitioned for family members. As early as 1409, the wife of the high official Ch'oi Kŭmgang beat the petition drum to present a grievance on behalf of her husband, who was imprisoned for making a false accusation. She petitioned to claim that her husband had been unfairly charged and held in custody.[14] In 1435, during Sejong's reign (r. 1418–50), a woman petitioned the king to plead mercy for her son, Kalju. Kalju was interrogated and tortured for receiving property from Yi Kyech'ung by forging a document. Because there was clear evidence of Kalju's crime, his mother's petition was disregarded by the court.[15] Slaves also represented their masters prior to the eighteenth century. For example, during King Injo's reign (r. 1623–49), Cho Chŏngnip, magistrate of Haenam, was imprisoned for embezzlement and ordered his slave to appeal his innocence on his behalf, but this action was in vain because there was clear evidence against Cho.[16]

As we can see from the case in which Kalju's mother petitioned for her son, not all cases adhered to the new four categories legislated in the early eighteenth century. For instance, during King Hyojong's reign (r. 1649–59) in 1653, a son petitioned for his mother, Hyodŏk, who was a concubine of the royal family. She was accused of murdering another concubine who was pregnant. Her son appealed on behalf of his mother to claim her innocence. The officials claimed that she should be sentenced to death, but the king reduced the sentence and banished her to the northern frontier; his reason was that the case was a matter of the royal family.[17]

Another deviant example can be found during Hyŏnjong's reign (r. 1659–74), in which a father petitioned on behalf of his daughter. In 1667, the father of Madam Yun, Yun Kukkyŏng, petitioned the king, representing his daughter's grievance.[18] Madam Yun was a wife of Yi Chŏng and lived together with his adoptive father, Yi Yuch'ŏng. Ch'oi Segyŏng, who was a grandson of Yi Yuch'ŏng, also resided with the family. One day, a rumor circulated that Madam Yun and Ch'oi were having an affair. This rumor eventually reached officials at the court, and Madam Yun and Ch'oi were both imprisoned for committing adultery. During interrogation, Madam Yun defended herself by saying, "Ch'oi Segyŏng sneaked into my room in the middle of the night and tried to rape me. I resisted unyieldingly and was able to escape the peril." In contrast, Ch'oi defended himself by stating that "Madam Yun was having an affair with another man; when her secret was disclosed, she used me as a pretext to protect herself."[19] In the course of interrogation, Madam Yun's father petitioned the king to complain about an official's unfair treatment of his daughter's case.[20] He claimed that Hong Chungbo, who was a minister of the Board of Punishments, abetted Ch'oi and failed to display impartiality. The father's petition ultimately led Hong to resign from his official post.[21] The outcome of the case, however, turned out to be unfavorable to both parties. Due to conflicting testimony and lack of evidence, it was difficult for officials to fairly adjudicate the case, and this unduly prolonged the interrogation. In issuing the ruling of the case, the king acknowledged the imbroglio nature of the situation and stated: "The testimonies made by both Ch'oe Segyŏng and Madam Yun are dubious. In such a case, inflicting torture is inevitable in order to make the suspects speak the truth. However, there is a possibility that one of the suspects might die unjustly during the torture. . . . Because this case is about public morals, the suspects cannot be easily exonerated."[22] The king then ultimately commanded that both Ch'oi and Madam Yun be exiled.[23]

These cases show not only that petitioners did not always abide by the hierarchical order stipulated in the legal codes but also that the state neither criticized nor restricted such practice. As a result, petitioners continued to petition on behalf of their family members in multifarious fashion. It seems that the four categories specified in the *Continuation of the Great Code* were grounded on the most frequently appealed cases that complied with Confucian hierarchical family relationships. Nevertheless, as long as petitioners were related by blood or marriage, or were extended family members, such as slaves, to the person they were representing, the state treated the petitioner and the absent as one equal subject even after the codification of the new four categories.

In order to analyze petitions on behalf of family members, I examined the *Records of Stating and Hearings* (Simnirok), which records criminal cases that took place during twenty-four years of Chŏngjo's reign in the late eighteenth century. Of the 1,112 cases in the *Records of Stating and Hearings*, there are 150 cases in which petitioners appealed on behalf of family members during the course of a murder trial. Although there are 150 cases, the actual number of petitions adds up to 180, because in some cases more than one petitioner was involved, and some petitioners appealed two to three times during a trial that lasted for several years (see table 4.1).[24]

TABLE 4.1. Petitions on behalf of imprisoned family members in *Records of Stating and Hearing* (Simnirok), vols.1–32.

|  | THE FOUR CATEGORIES |  | OTHER CATEGORIES |  | TOTAL |
|---|---|---|---|---|---|
| FEMALE | Wife for husband | 71 | Daughter for father | 1 | |
| | Female slave for master | 1 | Mother for son | 4 | |
| | | | Sister for brother | 1 | |
| | *Subtotal* | **72** | *Subtotal* | **6** | **78** |
| MALE | Son for father | 77 | Father for son | 4 | |
| | Younger brother for elder brother | 11 | Elder brother for younger brother | 2 | |
| | Male slave for master | 4 | Husband for wife | 1 | |
| | | | Relative for relative | 3 | |
| | *Subtotal* | **92** | *Subtotal* | **10** | **102** |
| TOTAL | | **164** | | **16** | **180** |

Of the 180 petitions, 78 were presented by women and 102 were presented by men. There were over 70 cases presented in each of the following two categories: "wife for husband" and "son for father." This implies that a woman's role as wife in a household preceded any other subject position, and that the primary role for a man was that of son. When it came to voicing grievances for family members in the late Chosŏn, the Confucianized society expected women to perform as faithful wives and men as filial sons. A woman's role as wife and a man's role as son were carried into legal space, which reinforced fidelity and filial piety in the petitioning practice of the late Chosŏn. Although wives and sons most actively petitioned for their husbands and fathers, respectively, petitioners did not always abide by the four categories, which were classified according to subordinates appealing for seniors. In practice, petitioning was executed in multiple patterns within familial relationships with one exception, and that was master's appealing for slaves.

As long as the grievances were adequately conveyed, the state did not take issue with senior family members petitioning for subordinate ones. For example, husbands even petitioned for wives and begged pardon on their behalf.[25] Instead of reproaching husbands for transgressing the four catego-

FIGURE 4.1. A wife visiting her imprisoned husband and giving him food. *Paintings on the Evolution of Legal System.* Call no. 5100–18. Courtesy of the Central Library of Seoul National University.

ries, the state was more concerned with the kinds of grievance they presented. Although the four categories were based on gender, age, and status hierarchy, the petitioning in such order empowered the petitioners to speak for superior family members in public space. The subordinate actors in the family spoke for their superiors by first publicizing their *wŏn* and expressing how grief-stricken they were due to the absence of beloved relatives. Only when the state officially recognized these emotions was there an investigation of the case to redress the grievance of the subject being represented. In this sense, gender, age, and status were intricately woven into shifting webs of familial relationality that at times enabled women and juniors to speak on behalf of men and seniors in the juridical domain.[26]

## PETITIONING ON BEHALF OF IMPRISONED HUSBANDS

When female petitioners made appeals on behalf of imprisoned or exiled husbands, the state's initial reaction was to investigate whether the men were wrongfully accused. When constructing a narrative to seek release on behalf of imprisoned husbands, women often relied on Confucian rhetoric to evoke authorities' compassion. Some women even exaggerated or distorted facts for the sake of saving the men. Whereas some female petitioners strategically chose to try to prove their husbands' innocence by fabricating, others acknowledged the men's crimes and candidly solicited remission. When women did not speak the truth, they endangered themselves by risking corporal punishment for deceiving the king. The cases discussed next illustrate how female petitioners sought the acquittal of their husbands and how the state was keen to verify the grievances they addressed.

During the Chosŏn, different kinds of virtues were attributed to women and men, and the state rewarded subjects who exemplified those separate virtues. Whereas men were generally honored for loyalty and filial piety, women were honored for fidelity.[27] A wife was expected to be morally obligated to the patriline into which she married, which demanded a woman's lifelong commitment not only to her husband but also to his parents and heirs. Although the state legally forced this virtue on elite women by indirectly restricting their remarriage through prohibiting secondary sons from taking the civil service examination, nonelite women were free from this restriction. However, due to the Confucianization in the late Chosŏn, social norms rather than laws pressured nonelite women into making a commitment to one patriline for their whole lifetime. Nevertheless, widows of the nonelite often chose to remarry for economic reasons even in the eighteenth century.[28] Among the three Confucian virtues most revered in the Chosŏn—loyalty, filial piety, and fidelity—it was filial piety that was most deeply ingrained in the minds of both genders and all societal statuses. Filial piety in a Confucian society was seen as the most essential virtue and as central in maintaining familial harmony and social order.[29] Women, regardless of their status, often appealed to this filial piety when petitioning on behalf of their husbands to the sovereign.[30]

Commoner woman Kim, wife of Yi Tŏksin, submitted a written petition to implore for a pardon for her husband in the second month of 1786. Her husband had been exiled for illegally trading tobacco. She stated in her appeal that his grandfather, who was eighty-eight years old, wished to see his grandson before his death. Officials, however, stated that it was not possible to easily discharge Tŏksin's crime, and the king agreed.[31] A year later, when Tŏksin's grandfather and his mother had both passed away, Kim presented a written petition for the second time to plead for her husband's acquittal so that he could attend their funerals. However, the state's response was the same.[32]

In 1786, another commoner woman, Yi, submitted a written petition stating that her husband, Yi Myŏnggyu, was falsely accused and banished to Posŏng county of Chŏlla province. According to her statement, her father-in-law, who was eighty years old, cried day and night yearning for his son's return, and his health had seriously deteriorated as a result. She therefore begged for her husband's exoneration. Officials suggested that since Myŏnggyu was originally banished for the crime he had committed, it was not feasible to acquit him out of pity.[33] A similar petition was made by commoner woman O in 1787. Her husband, Im Ch'ŏbŏn, was exiled to Yongch'ŏn county of P'yŏng'an province; she beseeched the king to exonerate her husband because his eighty-year-old mother's death was imminent. Officials criticized the wife for being imprudent because her husband was not so distantly removed from his residence. They likewise proposed that the king disregard the petition.[34]

In these three petitions, the king and his officials all refrained from showing leniency toward husbands despite their wives' efforts that relied on the rhetoric of filial piety to arouse authorities' sympathy. If the crimes the husbands had committed were deemed unpardonable, then it was likely that the state would show no mercy despite the wives' appeals. Contrary to the cases of these three petitions, there was a female petitioner who succeeded in exonerating her husband by appropriating the same rhetoric. In the second month of 1786, a commoner woman Kang presented a written petition entreating the king to acquit her husband, who had been charged with attempted rape. He had been banished to Yŏnggwang county of Chŏlla province after receiving one hundred blows. Kang stated in her petition that her husband was unjustly accused by a widow, and that her parents-in-law, who were both septuagenarian, hoped to see their son again. She pleaded for her husband to be redeemed monetarily so that he could return home to fulfill his parents' wish. The king ordered that her husband be acquitted because the law permitted monetary redemption on certain occasions such as when the offender's parents passed away or were aged and needed care.[35] In this case, it is possible to surmise that the king and his officials regarded Kang's husband's crime to be pardonable because it was an attempted rape, which may have been considered a less serious crime than those of the previous cases. Moreover, Kang was willing to pay a fine for the release of her husband instead of merely using his aged parents as an excuse. The state was cognizant of the fact that wives often relied on the Confucian rhetoric of filial piety in seeking pardon, but their rhetoric was persuasive only when the husband's crime was deemed pardonable.

Since petitions for imprisoned or exiled husbands were primarily self-interested pleadings, the state was cautious about determining the truth. In the second month of 1786, another commoner woman named Kang petitioned the king for her husband's release by similarly appealing to his parents' age; they were both seventy. In this particular case, the king ordered that the husband be released.[36] However, before executing the order, officials investigated to confirm the ages by examining the census register. It turned out that the father was sixty-three and the mother was fifty-eight. Officials reported to the king that petitioners had recently become more cunning and had even tried to deceive him. They proposed to nullify the release of the petitioner's husband because her crime of presenting a false statement before the king could not be overlooked. The king assented and ordered that Kang be reprimanded.[37]

The rhetoric of filial piety was one common strategy female petitioners used to implore that their husbands be pardoned. In other cases, women intentionally made up stories to place their husbands in a good light. For example, in 1781, Yi Ch'ŏnbong, a resident of Seoul, assaulted and murdered No Han'gŏl. Yi's wife, commoner woman Pak, presented an oral petition to the king stating that Han'gŏl's death stemmed from falling down and breaking a bone while he was chasing her husband. The king ordered the case be investigated, and the Board of Punishments reported to the king that Pak was faking a grievance because her husband had already confessed his crime and therefore her petition should be disregarded. Her husband's sentence, however, was reduced from death to banishment.[38]

In a similar vein, commoner woman Kim used false statements in her petition presented to the king in 1780. Yun Tongp'il, who was Kim's husband and a resident of P'yŏngyang county, battered Sin Tongi to death. When Tongp'il was imprisoned, Kim appealed, defending her husband. Her claim was that Tongi's life was not taken by her husband's assault but by a festering wound on his back. Chŏngjo ordered the provincial governor of P'yŏng'an to investigate the case. The minister of the Board of Punishments, Yi Sŏngwŏn, memorialized to the king using the provincial governor's report and stated that what Kim had claimed in her petition to vindicate her husband turned out to be false. They then proposed to punish the petitioner for conveying false statements to the king.[39]

Although it was mostly commoner women who arrived at the capital to appeal on behalf of imprisoned husbands, slave women also headed to Seoul to defend their husbands. Fights involving two individuals did not always occur between equal parties. Often times, a fight was between subjects of different statuses. The following case is an example of a female slave petitioning for her husband, who was murdered by a commoner man. Chŏng Panbong, a resident of Seoul, was accused of killing Hwang Honggon in the second month of

1786. Hwang's wife, whose name was Yŏnni and who was a public slave of the Royal College (*Sŏnggyungwan*), made the initial move to petition the king in the same month Panbong was incarcerated. She stated in her written petition, "Chŏng Panbong murdered my husband. Without receiving a single blow, he already confessed his crime. Please let the Board of Punishments punish him according to law." The Board of Punishments reported to the king that it was imprudent of Yŏnni to appeal prematurely because the investigation of Panbong's case had just been initiated. They proposed that her petition should be not taken seriously, and the king agreed.[40] As the victim's wife, Yŏnni petitioned at this stage to prevent Panbong from receiving a light punishment for having confessed quickly. Yŏnni's complaint expressed her dissatisfaction that the offender had not suffered enough from judicial torture.

About a year later, in the fourth month of 1787, Panbong's wife, commoner woman Kim, appealed orally to the king regarding her husband's murder trial.[41] She explained that Honggon, her cousin, had visited her house while her husband was away and sexually harassed her. When her husband returned and chided him, Honggon began to act as if he were drunk and fell down on the floor, hurting himself; he died a few days later. In the petition, she implored that her husband be pardoned. After investigating the case, the Board of Punishments reached the conclusion that Panbong was the offender but there was an accessory, Kim Kwangdŭk, who had assisted Chŏng in assaulting Honggon and absconded as the case underwent investigation. They claimed that Panbong's wife was shifting the blame onto Honggon, who was already dead. They proposed that the petition be disregarded and that she be punished for presenting a false statement. The king ordered Kwangdŭk be captured immediately in order to clarify the case. The king further commanded the Board of Punishments to punish the head of the Constabulary if Kwangdŭk was not arrested. In order to reach a verdict in Panbong's murder trial, it was imperative to arrest Kwangdŭk.[42]

Four months later, Kwangdŭk was detained. When he was under interrogation, during the same month he was captured, his wife, Sunnae, who was also a slave, presented an oral petition, pleading for a fair investigation. The Board of Punishments criticized the petitioner for indiscreetly petitioning immediately after the arrest of her husband, who had been in hiding for ten months. The king also reprimanded her and stated, "Although the appeal was made on behalf of her husband, it was indeed very imprudent of her to petition when he had been imprisoned for such a short period of time." The king then ordered her petition be disregarded.[43] According to the record of Panbong's trial, which lasted for more than two years, there seems to have been another accessory besides Kwangdŭk who assisted with the murder but had not been captured. Chŏngjo concluded that it was not possible to fairly adjudicate the case without this missing accessory. Under such a circumstance, he deemed it unfair to continue to detain Panbong. The king stated, "Unless the accessory is captured, it is not possible to collect complete facts of the case. Chŏng Panbong's interrogation cannot be further pursued when there is not enough evidence to charge the offender with murder. . . . Law should be fair under Heaven." Chŏngjo then sentenced Panbong to blows and released him according to the amnesty declared in that year.[44]

Elite women were no different from nonelite women in exaggerating their appeals in defense of their husbands. During Sukchong's reign, in 1715, Yi Ton's wife, Madam An, presented a written petition to the king on behalf of her exiled husband, who was charged with malfeasance while conducting the civil service examination in 1712. Yi's grandson, Yi Sihyŏng, initially petitioned on behalf of his grandfather, claiming that the charge against him was unjust. The Board of Punishments reinvestigated the case based on the petition but came to the conclusion that there was no sign of grievance. Three years later, Madam An appealed on behalf of Yi again. The king, however, was disturbed by her petition because the case had already been reexamined and it was verified that there was not a grievance to be redressed. The king ordered that the petition be disregarded.[45]

In addition to crimes of homicide, attempted rape, malfeasance, and illegal trading, husbands were also detained for forgery, stealing from the state treasury, and violating moral principles. Further, it was not uncommon for husbands to get into disputes with others of different classes and statuses. In commoner woman Chin's case, her slave husband was imprisoned for cursing his owner. She pleaded to the king for mercy and requested her husband's release.[46] Commoner woman Min, wife of the private scholar Chŏng Igwŏn,[47] appealed for her husband's acquittal; he had been banished for making a false accusation against Yun T'aep'yŏng.[48] Commoner woman Pak similarly implored for the release of her husband, who had been exiled for cursing at a county official while intoxicated. In this case, the Board of Punishments suggested to the king that it was not possible to easily acquit him because the crime he had committed was not light and he had served only one year of his three-year sentence.[49]

Women actively petitioned on behalf of imprisoned husbands, especially when the men were likely to receive the death penalty. On the one hand, for practical purposes, a wife had to plead for her husband's release in order to protect the family's well-being regardless of whether he was innocent or guilty. On the other hand, society recognized women's petitioning for their husbands as a wifely virtue when husbands were unjustly killed or imprisoned. The emotion that stemmed from a grievance against a husband was perceived as "natural" for a wife and in line with human feelings, and the state took this into consideration when listening to women petitioning for their husbands. Unlike petitions presented to seek rectification for unjust death, petitions in which wives begged pardon for or tried to vindicate imprisoned husbands were cautiously filtered by the state. The state sought to determine to what extent the claims women made were true or false. Although the state expected women to act and speak for their husbands, their words influenced the adjudication process only after the case had been verified through thorough investigation.

When women petitioned to vindicate or beg pardon for imprisoned husbands, the ruling authorities had to sift through their words so as not to be deceived by fake statements. The state's primary aim of listening to women's grievances was to prevent miscarriage of justice if their husbands had been wrongfully accused. However, at the same time, the state was keen on executing proper punishment so that justice was served for those who were wronged because of the men. While the state took a rigorous approach toward the petitions presented for imprisoned husbands who were convicted of crimes, the state, as we shall see in the next chapter, tended to be more lenient toward the grievances addressed on behalf of a dead victim. The cases analyzed here show that the state, in most cases, disregarded women's petitions when the reinvestigation only confirmed the husbands' crimes. Using the narrative of filial piety and showing fidelity toward husbands, women sought to save their spouses by underlining the importance of sustaining the patrilineal family. This narrative, however, was not persuasive enough for the king to exercise discretionary justice. From the state's point of view, executing laws and administering justice were far more critical than releasing guilty husbands in order to stay in line with the patrilineal system.


CONCLUSION

The petitioning activity that began with addressing a personal grievance to the sovereign gradually shifted to include petitions that were made on behalf of family members in the late Chosŏn. The practice of representing family members preceded the legalization of the new four categories in the early eighteenth century. As the petitioning process evolved through continuous interaction between the state and society, the meaning of personal *wŏn* changed accordingly. The construction of legal subjects broadened to include intersubjectivity as the judicial practice came to depend on collaborative and reciprocal petitioning in the late Chosŏn. When the petition system was first institutionalized, the state defined *wŏn* as emotions that were confined to petitioners and thus allowed them to appeal on personal *wŏn*. However, as people increasingly appealed to relieve the *wŏn* they felt through sympathy with their family members, the state eventually came to recognize the practice of appealing on others' behalf.

As the emotions of *wŏn* navigated from family members to petitioners, the state legalized the new four categories based on Confucian familial relationships. A woman's domestic role as wife was carried into her legal role as a representative of fidelity in the juridical domain of the late Chosŏn. When a woman acted as her husband's legal agent, her sense of self was intimately linked with her husband and engaged with him in shaping her emotions and identities. Through petitioning for family members, women were able to enhance their own moral authority within the household, and their petitioning relied on cross-subjective and familial connectivity that considerably empowered the relationships and subjectivities involved.

Although it was the state that conferred the legal capacity to petition, the petitioners took on the role of actively petitioning according to their needs. Under the Confucian gender system, the state's authorization of women's capacity to petition generated leeway for women to become defenders of husbands in public space. While petitioning reinforced official gender norms by enabling women to perform such a legal and wifely duty, it simultaneously empowered them to represent husbands who had no choice but to depend on wives' narratives and performance in seeking rectification or pardon.

*Chapter Five*

# IN SEARCH OF JUSTICE
# ON BEHALF OF THE DEAD

Subjects are aggrieved when the channel to convey their words is blocked. A virtuous governor is one who allows his subjects to comfortably walk into his office as if they are entering their house.

— Chŏng Yagyong, *Mongmin simsŏ*

ON THE TWENTY-SEVENTH DAY OF THE TENTH MONTH OF 1771, a commoner woman, surnamed Kim, cross-dressed as a man and struck a gong placed in front of the palace gate. She cried out to appeal on behalf of her father, who had been unjustly tortured to death by a county magistrate. In order to express her state of grief and pain, she cut her finger and wrote the petition in blood. The Board of Punishments received her petition and reported it to the king. After hearing Kim's case, Yŏngjo ordered that it be investigated thoroughly. When the case was verified as one of injustice, he imprisoned the county magistrate and relieved him from his official post. Yŏngjo then awarded Kim with grain as an expression of his sympathy.[1] By exercising her legal capacity to petition, Kim was able to penalize the magistrate and rectify the injustice against her father.

With the magistrate relieved from his official post and imprisoned, was the injustice toward Kim's father fully rectified? How are the emotions of *wŏn* related to the sense of injustice? What kinds of grievances did petitioners present on behalf of the dead? What is the implication of a petitioner's representing an injury and *wŏn* on behalf of his or her dead family member? To what extent did such petitioning influence adjudication? How did the state endeavor to prevent the miscarriage of justice? Two major types of injustice that family members brought before the court during the late Chosŏn period illustrate these inequities: one was county magistrates' abusive use of judicial torture, as illustrated in the preceding brief anecdote, and the other was powerful subjects' enslaving manumitted slaves or destitute commoners, which was known as "oppressing commoners as slaves."

These two kinds of injustices appealed by family members in the late Chosŏn show how laws related to magistrates' abusive usage of torture and "oppressing commoners as slaves" were newly codified in the early eighteenth century. The two injustices became officially recognized as grievances in the late Chosŏn. This implies that the two injustices, which people thought of as "unjust" or "unfair," were previously neglected in the state's definition of grievance. However, as people complained about these two injustices by adding their private experiences of suffering to the "public" discourse, the state eventually came to endorse the two types of injustice as legitimate grievances. Petitioning practice negotiated between the state and the society thus defined the meanings of grievance and *wŏn*.

During the initial phase of the petition system, there was a disparity in the understanding of "injustice" between the government and the subjects. In other words, demarcating the line between the state's recognition of injustice and the people's sense of injustice was never an explicit matter. In the Chosŏn, the petition system was a site to negotiate the meaning of grievance through the very practice of petitioning. Instead of remaining passive to injustice, people actively filed complaints to right wrongs. Not all cases brought before the court were rectified. However, by voicing grievances, petitioners were successful in broadening the meaning of grievance that the state had narrowly defined. The two injustices discussed in this chapter exemplify the negotiation between the state and society in the late Chosŏn. The two grievances, which were previously treated as subjectively felt injustices, eventually came to be recognized by the state in the early eighteenth century as objective injustices. Although it was the state that both created and executed laws, both the government and its people shaped the process of administering justice. Throughout the Chosŏn, the multifarious issues people addressed to the state shaped the modes of petitioning and the meanings of grievance. Conversely, expressing emotions of *wŏn* through either written or oral petitions was a powerful device that reflected social change in the late Chosŏn. The two injustices represent the changes that took place as a result of people's display of *wŏn* in public space.

Petitioners made efforts to represent family grievances in order to exert their influence in the adjudication process. Unlike personal grievances, where petitioners appealed to seek their own emotional satisfaction, petitioners who appealed family grievances emphasized the sentiment of pain they *shared* with the family members who had been wronged. In order to enhance the merit of the appeals, petitioners addressed vicarious suffering in addition to the pain that was personified in the wronged. They spoke on behalf of their dead family members, becoming "inventors of language," and communicated the reality of family members' suffering to government authorities.[2] Because the dead remained silent, it was their family members who used the language for pain of the dead, enabling their experiences to enter the realm of public discourse.

Appealing on behalf of the dead cannot be treated in the same way as speaking on behalf of imprisoned family members. Those who were imprisoned were at least able to either defend themselves or confess during the interrogation process, whereas the dead permanently lost the ability to speak for themselves. Thus, in order for grievances of the dead to be redressed, family members had to seek legal remedies for their bodily suffering and communicate the physical pain to ruling authorities and the sovereign.[3] The burden of representation was much greater in this case because petitioners had to reconstruct the pain the dead suffered by "imagining" how their beloved family members were brutally murdered by villagers or county magistrates.[4] The sense of injustice was amplified when a county magistrate who was supposed to prevent injustice killed an innocent victim, but in his official capacity instead committed the gravest act of injustice. Although the appeals presented by family members might not have necessarily altered the outcomes, they at least highlighted the need for the authorities to implement fair adjudication by generating reinvestigations. The petitions analyzed here demonstrate how they prolonged the adjudication of trials in order for fair investigation to be conducted, and how they carried weight in seeking justice on behalf of dead family members.

The two injustices discussed in this chapter were identified through the narrating of grievances regarding the unjust deaths of family members. The petitioners' loss of family members in the two cases was certainly different from the type of loss caused by such events as natural death. The victims' unjust deaths were reflected in relationship to others, especially when their family members petitioned to authenticate the victims' suffering and the pain they felt as family. The display of pain and grief in courts transformed those emotions into a condition that could be quantified as the basis for rectification. Although subjects normally had an unequal relation to entitlement according to status differences, it was not necessarily the case that the more privileged had a greater recourse to narratives of grievance in the public domain. This is precisely because it was the oppressed subjects who were most vulnerable to injustice.

## THE NEXUS OF INJUSTICE AND *WŎN*

In the Confucian worldview, the spheres of man and nature were thought to be inextricably interwoven to form a single continuum. The cosmic harmony in the Confucian universe was considered to be damaged when appropriate punishment had not been introduced to redress the grievances of either the living or the dead. In order to maintain equilibrium, it was imperative for the state to properly administer justice. If the state failed to right a wrong, it was thought that the spirits of the wrongfully dead might wreak havoc on the living, which further reinforced interdependence. This idea was embedded in the two proverbs "a woman's grievance can bring on three years' drought" and "the grievance of a woman can bring late spring frost," which were often cited in court. The proverbs imply that the grievances of the people, especially women, should not be overlooked if the state sought to sustain social and cosmic harmony.[5] In Neo-Confucian legal thought, misfortune caused by natural disaster was deeply related to injustice. When natural calamities such as drought occurred and caused the general public to suffer, the state either pardoned prisoners or ordered local officials to adjudicate unresolved lawsuits without any delay.[6]

From the state's point of view, it was critical to relieve the *wŏn* of not only the living but also the dead because the emotion was perceived to interfere with the harmonious order of nature. Homicide cases recorded in the *Records of Stating and Hearings* show that the state was reluctant to execute anyone involved in a murder in order to fulfill the idea of cosmic balance. Furthermore, there was a great potential to create additional grievance by executing the wrong person. No more than 2 percent of the nearly one thousand cases recorded in the text were sentences of death.[7] The state was less concerned with redressing the grievances of the dead by taking another's life than with relieving the negative emotions of survivors and the potential further grievances such feelings might create.

The difference between injustice and misfortune can depend on our willingness and capacity to act on behalf of victims. What begins as a natural disaster can turn into a public injustice, depending on how victims are treated. The line of separation between injustice and misfortune is a political judgment, and it is necessary to draw the line in order to enhance responsibility and avoid random retaliation.[8] In the Chosŏn, where the rhetoric and ideas of the sage king were paramount, it was crucial for the ruler to be responsible for providing his people with livelihoods and to be fair and just to each and all. The discourse of *wŏn* and its relation with natural disaster show not that the injustice per se disturbed nature's harmony but rather that people's *wŏn* and their general well-being must be addressed. In times of crisis caused by natural disaster, the government paid extra attention to people's livelihood. Out of concern and compassion, the king focused on people's suffering and any unjustness that was generated by the misjudgment of lawsuits, unfair punishment, abuse of judicial torture, or corrupt magistrates.[9]

A victim's family suffered to the greatest degree when a death was caused by a magistrate's unfair punishment. Because the magistrate represented the sovereign at the county level, he was supposedly a father figure to his people, as the king was to all of his subjects. Because the ruler's image was damaged when magistrates exercised injustices on his people, it was even more imperative for the king to rectify these wrongs and restore his subjects' trust in him. According to the state's foundational Neo-Confucian ideology, if the ruler failed to win the hearts of his people, then his legitimacy would be lost and society would be in disorder. The ruler's tasks were to relieve his people's emotions of *wŏn* that stemmed from injustice and to assure the safety of his people. Thus, for a sage ruler to maintain social harmony, it was critical to continuously check whether justice had been properly administered.

The state was especially concerned with the unjust treatment of subordinate subjects. The state often referred to this group as *somin*, which literally means "small people." The *Veritable Records* include many instances in which it was the state's duty to redress *somin*'s grievance that stemmed from elites' unjust treatment. If the state abandoned the *somin*, then there would be no place for them to express their grievances. If the *somin*'s emotions of *wŏn* heightened, then social and cosmic disorder would ultimately result.[10] Based on this rationale, the judicial system of the Chosŏn was constructed to allow each individual to seek redress. Because women were recognized as subordinate subjects, along with the lower strata of society, it was crucial for the state to redress women's grievances, whether their own or those of their family members.

Although various issues addressed at lower courts overlapped with capital appeals, there was one conspicuous grievance that was predominantly appealed in search of royal justice. When innocent family members lost their lives due to judicial torture, petitioners often bypassed intermediate courts and headed directly to the capital. When a beloved family member was killed by a public figure whose primary duty was to protect his people, the offender's act evoked in the victim's family emotions of *wŏn* such as grief, anger, pity, and suffering, which inevitably led them to seek redress. The family members grieved when they thought about the loss of a relative who was vital in their daily presence; they felt angry at the damage that was wrongfully inflicted; and they pitied and shared the victim's significant suffering.[11] The role of law in a society can be seen as protection of people against death and bodily injury so that they may live safely and without fear.[12] Did the Chosŏn law protect its people from death and bodily injury? If it did, then was law applied differently according to social status?

The state's protection of authority at the local level engendered one side effect, that is, county magistrates' abuse of power in administering penal justice. They sometimes wrongfully accused innocents and inflicted severe torture intentionally as well as unintentionally. Despite the state's effort to protect authority, people would not tolerate county magistrates' punitive practices at the county courts and eventually petitioned the king in search of justice. For example, in the seventh year of Hyŏnjong's reign (r. 1659–74), a son of a functionary appealed to the king about his father's death, which resulted from heavy corporal punishment inflicted by a county magistrate.[13] The state initially applied the prohibition law and banished the functionary's son, but he was soon released because his father's death was in fact unjust.[14] When similar petitions were ceaselessly presented, the state had to weigh protecting authority and rectifying injustice against subjects.

By the early eighteenth century, the prohibition law initially stipulated in the *Great Code of Administration* was amended with a new statute in the *Continuation of the Great Code* that authorized subjects to accuse magistrates, but only when their family members died from excessive torture.[15] With this newly codified law, subjects were legally allowed to accuse county magistrates but only when family members had died from harsh torture. Nevertheless, even subordinate actors such as women and slaves were able to exercise power over corrupt officials by utilizing their capacity to petition. By reporting the miscarriage of justice at the local level, they could depend on the sovereign's power to punish county magistrates and redress grievances of the dead as well as those of family members.

## A Female Entertainer's Appeal on Behalf of Her Dead Daughters

One summer day in 1705, Konsaeng, a registered female entertainer (*kisaeng*) who lived on Cheju Island, took a long journey across the sea to reach Chŏlla province.[16] As soon as she landed, she headed to the provincial office to appeal the unjust deaths of her three daughters. The provincial governor, Sŏ Munyu, permitted Konsaeng to present her verbal petition. Having lost three of her innocent daughters concurrently, Konsaeng was extremely grief stricken and cried complaining how the county magistrate of Cheju, Yi Hŭit'ae, had killed her daughters by inflicting severe corporal punishment merely out of his personal grudge against them.

When Yi was assigned to Cheju county, he brought his concubine along with her ex-husband's son to the island. Wishing to conceal the son's identity, Yi introduced the son as his wife's nephew to people around him. However, this lie did not last long; people soon found out who the son really was and began to gossip about the magistrate's family. As the gossip widely spread, Yi lost his tolerance and decided to take revenge on Konsaeng's three daughters—Kyejŏng, Ch'ajŏng, and Samjŏng—whom he believed first spread the gossip.

Yi schemed against the daughters to make a groundless accusation. In order to find a pretext to arrest the daughters, he selected five female entertainers who felt animosity toward Konsaeng's daughters and covertly ordered them to make accusations so that he could legally arrest the three women. After capturing them, he deliberately interrogated the accused in the presence of two magistrates of other counties in order to disguise his vicious intention.[17] He wreaked vengeance via inflicting severe corporal punishment and ultimately tortured the three daughters to death. He then drafted a false report about the victims' supposed crime and sent it to the Border Defense Command (Pibyŏnsa) at the capital.

Konsaeng, having lost her three daughters unjustly, was determined to relieve their aggrieved souls. Due to her lowborn status, the only way she could take revenge against the magistrate without violating the law was through the petition system. Whereas Yi had abused his power to punish the daughters,

Konsaeng, who had no such power, appropriated a higher appellate system to punish him. During the Chosŏn, the provincial office of Chŏlla was responsible for reporting all the cases of Cheju Island to the capital; thus, Konsaeng appealed to the provincial governor of Chŏlla.

After hearing Konsaeng's verbal petition, Sŏ Munyu sent a letter to the State Council to report the case to Sukchong. After the king heard the report, the third state councilor, Yi Yu, defended Yi Hŭit'ae by stating: "Since the interrogation took place in the presence of two other magistrates and the case was reported to the Border Defense Command, there is no evidence that Yi Hŭit'ae intended to kill and further masked his deed. An ignorant petitioner from the island accused the magistrate of murder, and this cannot be overlooked. She must be interrogated for making a false accusation."[18] Despite Yi Yu's defense, Sukchong ordered the case be thoroughly investigated.

By the time the case was reported to the capital, a new county magistrate, Song Chŏnggyu, had been assigned to Cheju county. This suggests that Konsaeng was well aware of two things. First, she knew that the replacement was going to take place; she intentionally made the appeal only when Yi Hŭit'ae's term neared its end. Two, she probably knew that Song Chŏnggyu was not close enough with Yi Hŭit'ae to draft a false report to defend him. When Song arrived at the island, he conducted a thorough investigation of the case and sent a report to the king notifying him of Yi's misdeed of having killed the innocents because of his personal grudge against them.

After reading the memorial, Sukchong lamented how insignificantly Yi had treated the people of Cheju county and further deplored how meticulously he had planned to hide his vicious intention. He then commanded the arrest and interrogation of Yi. Sukchong further commented by saying, "If an official such as Yi Hŭit'ae is allowed to escape his crime without punishment, then those with power will continuously find a way to escape their crimes and victimize innocents."[19] When Yi was captured and interrogated, he denied his crime. However, when the king ordered the infliction of harsher punishment, Yi finally confessed that he did intend to harm Konsaeng's daughters.

After the confession, the court discussed the type of punishment that Yi should receive. The chief magistrate of the State Tribunal, Cho T'aech'ae, suggested that all the existing laws were inappropriate to apply to his case. The provision in the *Great Code of Administration* on the improper usage of corporal punishment stipulated: "If an official unreasonably inflicted corporal punishment, then he should receive one hundred beatings and be exiled for three years. If he killed the victim, then he should receive one hundred beatings and be permanently banned from the office."[20] However, this provision was unsuitable to apply to Yi because he had the "intention" of harming the victims. In addition, the punishment stipulated in the *Great Ming Code* for "one person murdering three people" was also inapplicable because it was intended for private individuals. Since Yi was a public figure and Konsaeng's daughters were officially registered female entertainers, this punishment was unsuitable to apply to the case. As there was a lack of appropriate law, Cho asked the king to discuss with officials and then decide Yi's sentence. Having discussed the matter with Sŏ Munjung, P'yŏn Ch'ŏn'gun, and Sin Wan, the king decided to banish Yi to the farthest frontier of the peninsula, which was the heaviest sentence besides capital punishment.[21]

According to the *Great Code of Administration*, it was against the law for functionaries and private individuals to accuse a magistrate except when the matter concerned the royal court, administration, or homicide.[22] If petitioners violated the law, then they would receive one hundred beatings and three years of exile.[23] Although it was still illegal to accuse magistrates during Sukchong's reign, petitioners persistently appealed to the central government when their family members died from unjust corporal punishment. In the eighteenth century, the situation reached a point where it was imperative for the state to revise the law in order to rectify injustice that was exercised by public officials. Konsaeng's case well illustrates the shift in the state's attitude toward the power of authority. This shift was vividly manifested during Yŏngjo's reign when the *Continuation of the Great Code* was compiled to add to the *Great Code of Administration*. From 1746 on, the state authorized petitioners to accuse magistrates when their family members died from unjust corporal punishment.[24]

Due to Konsaeng's appeal, Yi was exiled to the farthest frontier. However, he was not exiled for life, as he should have been according to the original sentence. The *Veritable records of Sukchong* records that Yi was criticized by a special emissary, Yi Ikhan, whom Sukchong had dispatched to investigate corrupt officials in Ch'ungch'ŏng province in 1708; Yi was serving as county magistrate of Haemi in the same province at the time.[25] If the name appearing in the record of 1708 refers to the same person as the one in Konsaeng's case, then his exile did not last for more than three whole years and he was reassigned shortly thereafter. To what extent, then, was injustice rectified in Konsaeng's case? The *Veritable records of Sukchong* states Konsaeng's case as follows: "Yi Hŭit'ae is senseless in nature and loses his temper easily. He committed a grave crime by killing innocents mercilessly. It is normally difficult to conduct a thorough investigation of a case in a far distant region. However, due to Song Chŏnggyu's report, the king was able to punish Yi Hŭit'ae and relieve Konsaeng's *wŏn* at least to a certain degree." [26] Although the state made concerted efforts to relieve the grievances of victims, it seems to have shown some leniency to the accused after righting a wrong through retribution.

*Elite Women's Appeals on Behalf of Their Dead Husbands*

Although the elite *yangban* group possessed the most social and economic privileges in Chosŏn society, they were not spared the injustices exercised on the lower strata. In the eighth month of 1794, Madam Song went to the capital, Seoul, from Changdan, Kyŏnggi province, to appeal her husband's unjust death. Her husband, Kwŏn Chinsŏng, had been killed by a magistrate through excessive use of torture. Kwŏn was involved in a legal dispute with his neighbors over the location of an ancestral gravesite. [27] When Kwŏn's father passed away, his neighbors Chŏng Sun and Chŏng Sik gathered a number of men and disrupted the funeral claiming that the gravesite Kwŏn had selected was in close proximity to their ancestral gravesite. Enraged by their cruelty, Kwŏn reported them to the county magistrate of Changdan, Sŏ Yuhwa, and filed suit against them. The magistrate accepted the suit but was slow in adjudicating the case. Wishing to hear the outcome of the case before returning home, Kwŏn lodged near the county office.

Before initiating the suit, Kwŏn had set another date for his father's funeral. However, it happened that he was unable to return home by the date of the funeral and ordered his half-brother to carry on with it in his absence. When the magistrate was later informed that the funeral had taken place, he imprisoned Kwŏn for having conducted the funeral without waiting for his judgment. The county magistrate sent a false report to the provincial governor, and the provincial governor responded by proceeding with the punishment. The county magistrate needed the provincial governor's permission in order to inflict a beating by heavy stick. When Sŏ received permission from the provincial governor, he punished Kwŏn by beating and further incarcerated him. Having heard about Kwŏn's situation, his seventy-year-old mother and ninety-year-old grandmother headed to the county office and pleaded to the magistrate for his release, but these actions were in vain. Kwŏn was finally released when a prison warden reported to the magistrate about his severely ill condition. However, Kwŏn died soon after he was released. Kwŏn's mother and wife once again cried out their grievances, but the magistrate showed no mercy. Instead, he instructed his underlings to send them away. Madam Song was then determined to go to the capital to appeal to the king.[28] When she arrived in the capital, she struck a gong to present an oral petition. Once she had completed her verbal appeal, Yi Uje sent a memorial to Chŏngjo regarding the injustice addressed in the petition. After reading the report, Chŏngjo commanded the provincial governor of Kyŏnggi, Sŏ Yongbo, to investigate the case thoroughly. When Sŏ Yongbo substantiated the case, Chŏngjo ordered the Board of Punishments to immediately imprison the former magistrate of Changdan, Sŏ Yuhwa, and sternly interrogate him.[29]

When Madam Song's husband died shortly after his release, she and her mother-in-law appealed to the county office about the unjust death. However, as the magistrate neglected her appeal and was unsympathetic about her husband's death, she decided to petition to a higher authority about the magistrate's misdeed. Utilizing the higher appellate system was the only legitimate way Madam Song could seek retributive justice. However, Madam Song refused to abide by the proper procedure of the appellate system. According to the legal codes, petitioners should initially appeal their grievance to the provincial governor; if they are unable to relieve their grievance at that stage, then they should appeal to the Office of the Inspector General in the capital; if they are still unable to assuage their grievance, only then they should beat the drum to appeal to the king.[30] Instead of petitioning the provincial governor, Madam Song bypassed the intermediate court and made the capital appeal directly. Skipping the intermediate court was not uncommon especially when the petitioning matters demanded grave emotional appeal.[31]

Although bypassing the intermediate court was illegal and the state punished those who did so, this did not stop petitioners from appealing directly to the king. As there was a mushrooming of such capital appeals, the state tolerated the practice when it officially recognized the grievances of petitioners. If the state regarded a case as without merit, then it punished the petitioner for misappropriating the system and disturbing the king by presenting a frivolous petition. Despite the risk petitioners took by making direct appeals to the king, in their minds, the sovereign was "a father, judge, and reference point of justice and fairness" on whom they could rely.[32] Although there was distrust of delinquent officials at the local level, the relationship of trust with the king was always to be preserved and confirmed.

Having that trust in the king, Madam Song claimed in her petition that the magistrate handled the case in a way favorable to the Chŏng brothers because one of them was a teacher of the magistrate's child. Due to this intimate rela-

FIGURE 5.1. Beating with light sticks. *Paintings on the Evolution of Legal System.* Call no. 5100–18. Courtesy of the Central Library of Seoul National University.

tionship, she argued that the magistrate unfairly treated her husband. She made specific statements concerning the magistrate's improper usage of the punishment:

> The magistrate and the Chŏng brothers co-schemed to punish my husband. My husband was cudgeled thirty-nine times consecutively with a heavy stick (fig. 5.2) and was further incarcerated and confined in a cangue. Because he was not treated properly after the severe beating and bleeding, my husband was in critically ill condition. My husband's seventy-year-old mother and ninety-year-old grandmother pleaded to the magistrate for his release, but this was in vain. My husband was released only after a prison warden reported to the magistrate about his severe condition. However, he died shortly after his release.[33]

Yi Uje, who made the initial report to the king, made three further comments on Madam Song's petition. First, he wrote, the county magistrate vio-

FIGURE 5.2. Beating with heavy sticks. *Paintings on the Evolution of Legal System.* Call no. 5100–18. Courtesy of the Central Library of Seoul National University.

lated the law by using a heavy stick, which was prohibited for use at the county level. The purpose of the stick was to punish perpetrators of robberies and military offenses. Second, the magistrate committed another violation by beating Kwŏn thirty-nine times. The law restricted the beating to thirty consecutive times.[34] Finally, Yi criticized the magistrate for not releasing Kwŏn immediately when he was well aware that Kwŏn was in a seriously bad condition. Yi lamented the fact that the magistrate had neglected to comply with the rules for inflicting corporal punishments.[35]

Chŏngjo had promulgated special laws in 1777, a year after he succeeded the throne, on the standardization of instruments of punishment and the procedures to be used in the interrogation of suspects. These laws were compiled in a volume called *Codes for the Treatment of Prisoners* (Hŭmhyul chŏnch'ik), which functioned as a guidance text for local officials. The central government had been concerned about local officials' improper usage of punishment since early in the dynasty and punished officials who killed suspects in the midst of their punishment.[36] However, subjects continued to be victimized during punishment, and Chŏngjo considered it imperative to compile more standardized rules for using instruments of punishment. The rationale behind promulgating the related laws was to force local officials to treat suspects cautiously during interrogation. Such an implication was manifested in the title with the word *hŭmhyul*, which implies alleviating the suffering of suspects.[37]

When Madam Song's petition was verified, Chŏngjo particularly regretted the magistrate's misdeed, because her husband's case was not an unpardonable crime. The king pitied Kwŏn even more because he was the sole heir of the family and had a widowed and aged mother and grandmother to support. What Chŏngjo deemed incomprehensible about the magistrate was his intention of incarcerating the prisoner during the torrid season of the year for more than one month. The law prohibited imprisoning prisoners during either the torrid or frigid seasons of the year, that is, from the eleventh through the first months and the fifth through the seventh months, unless the sentence was more than sixty beatings for a man and one hundred beatings for a woman. For beatings of less than one hundred strokes, the prisoners were all made to pay redemption unless they preferred to be punished via beating.[38] The purpose of this law was to prevent prisoners from dying in prison. Kwŏn was imprisoned for more than a month sometime between the fifth and the seventh months. Chŏngjo deplored not only the magistrate's failure to abide by the laws that were intended to protect prisoners but also his lack of mercy toward the victim's family. The king criticized the magistrate's wickedness in handling the matter, stating:

> Although the magistrate may not have intentionally killed Kwŏn Chinsŏng, how dare he be pardoned for his crime? The magistrate was well aware of the victim's innocence, but he inflicted punishment and further incarcerated him. This ultimately led the victim to die, which is even worse than intentional killing. If officials are easily acquitted in such cases, then the alienated subjects will harbor grudges against the government. The Board of Punishments should immediately capture the former magistrate of Changdan, Sŏ Yuhwa, and rigorously interrogate him. The Board of Punishments should then report his interrogation. Sŏ Yuhwa should be stringently treated by the law so that it will succor in redressing the injustice of the aggrieved.[39]

By making an emotional appeal to the king, Madam Song succeeded in punishing the magistrate. Although she was from an elite *yangban* family, she presented a verbal petition, which was the form most frequently used by illiterate, commoner women. According to Han Sang-gwŏn's statistics, commoner women participants outnumbered elite women participants in petitioning the king during the reign of Chŏngjo, and commoner women were more likely than elite women to present an oral petition.[40] Nevertheless, literate elite women occasionally used the verbal mode when petitioning matters related to injustice. Presenting an emotional appeal verbally was often more persuasive than the written mode because of the accompanying visual and sound effects. The petitioners could cry agonizingly in front of the authorities and thereby invoke commiseration. Another merit in presenting verbal petitions was that the number of times the petitioners were allowed to present was unlimited, whereas written petitions were limited to three submissions.

Despite these merits, petitioners had to risk undergoing an interrogation when presenting oral petitions; they were initially treated as criminals; this process was instituted to help deter abuse of the system by petitioners. In order to seek legal justice, Madam Song risked interrogation. However, she was well aware that using a heavy stick and beating thirty-nine times consecutively were both illegal; in addition, she was also cognizant of the fact that it was unjust of the magistrate to neglect the appeal she and her mother-in-law had made. The investigating officials and the king determined to punish the magistrate precisely based on these three factors. Through her emotional appeal, Madam Song not only succeeded in arousing sympathy but also persuasively conveyed constructed speech to the authorities. Using the highest appellate system, Madam Song was able to seek justice on behalf of her husband and ultimately have the offending magistrate punished.[41]

## Nonelite Women's Appeals on Behalf of Their Dead Husbands

Elite women's petitions illustrate that their husbands suffered from injustices exercised by magistrates, but it was men of lower strata who were most vulnerable to undergoing such experiences. For example, in the seventh month of 1777, the wife of Yi Chinsin struck a gong and petitioned the king during the royal procession. She appealed the unjust deaths of her husband, mother-in-law, and brother-in-law, whose lives were deprived all at once. Yi was an underling of Kim Sumuk, who was magistrate of Koryŏng county, Kyŏngsang province. One day, Yi cursed at the magistrate after the magistrate had reproached him bitterly. Kim became furious and punished Yi by beating him with a heavy stick used for punishing those who had committed a serious crime. When the beating of Yi was not enough to assuage his outrage, he then captured Yi's mother and brother. They were brought to the magistrate's courtyard and beaten relentlessly. The beating ultimately took the lives of all three family members. When Chŏngjo heard of the wife's grievance, he lamented the magistrate's abuse of punishment. He compared the case with that of Yu Sinil, who had committed a similar injustice in 1699 during the reign of Sukchong. Yu had killed the innocent Yi Wubaek, a student scholar, via excessive beating. Yu was captured but died before he was actually sentenced due to judicial torture during his interrogation.[42] Citing Yu's case as legal precedent, Chŏngjo ordered that the magistrate be arrested and that a rigorous interrogation be conducted in order to obtain his confession.[43]

Similarly, in 1795, a commoner woman, the wife of Chŏng Chun, struck the gong and petitioned the king to make an accusation against a magistrate for unjustly killing her husband. Due to her oral petition, the state became aware of the ruthless murder perpetrated by Yi Yŏjŏl, who was magistrate of Ch'angwŏn, Kyŏngsang province. The king ordered the provincial governor to conduct an interrogation of Yi, but the governor attempted to conceal the magistrate's crime because of his ties with the magistrate. The king was enraged that the provincial governor not only failed to keep an eye on the magistrate's conduct but also dared to protect him by improperly interrogating the criminal. The king thereby ordered the former provincial governor of Kyŏngsang province, Cho Chint'aek, to carry out the investigation to adjudicate fairly. When Cho made a thorough report on Yi's abuse of authority, the king was appalled that he had taken away the lives of not one but several. When the report corroborated the appeal of Chŏng's wife, the king commanded that all the offenders who were implicated in the crime be arrested. The king firmly set Yi's case as a legal precedent to warn bureaucrats who dared not to take royal orders seriously and made a mockery of state law.[44]

When husbands were victimized in a group, wives who shared the resulting grievance sometimes collectively headed to the capital in search of royal justice. For example, when Min Ch'isin, magistrate of Sakju county, Pyŏng'an province, deprived the lives of three bothers in 1796, their wives were determined to seek rectification on behalf of their aggrieved husbands by making an accusation against the corrupt magistrate. They thereby set off on a long journey from the northern region to the capital to strike the gong to address their grievances to the king. When they arrived, they cried day and night, advertising their painful sentiments in front of the State Tribunal. Chu Chungong memorialized to the king concerning these women and stated that "the three women's grievances were transgressing heaven and likely to produce frost in May." He then proposed that the king give an order to arrest the magistrate. Chŏngjo issued such an order and also commanded that an emissary be dispatched to conduct an investigation in Sakju county to find out the details of the magistrate's misdeeds.[45]

Through women's active petitioning on behalf of dead husbands, the state was informed of local authorities who failed to administer justice at county and provincial courts. In addition to dispatching secret emissaries, the state was able to monitor officials who abused power in their jurisdiction via petitioners' voices. This allowed the state to seize hold of its legitimacy by regulating those who infringed on the laws or social norms, thereby preserving peace and social harmony. Through an appeals system that functioned as a safety valve, there was constant interaction between the sovereign and women engaging in dialogue, either textually or verbally, regarding corrupt officials. This interactive dialogue conducted in the judicial realm was an important social site for rectifying social injustice.

Women's petitions to redress the unjust deaths of their husbands reveal that local authorities victimized elites as well as nonelites. They were killed by magistrates, often through beatings with a heavy stick that was meant for punishing those who had committed a military offense or grand larceny. Besides violating the law by using the heavy stick, magistrates transgressed by striking the victims beyond the legally limited number of times. Among various kinds of grievances addressed, the state perceived the unjust deaths of family members to be in most extreme need of rectification. When it came to redressing grievances, Chŏngjo stated, "even the *wŏn* of the lowborn was sufficient to transgress harmony and damage moral transformation."[46] It was thus crucial for the state to embrace the voice of every subject to maintain social harmony and equilibrium.


PRIVATE ACTS OF INJUSTICE:
EXPLOITATION OF MANUMITTED SLAVES

The social order in the Chosŏn was organized and sustained by the hereditary status system. However, toward the late Chosŏn, especially from the eighteenth century until the demise of the dynasty, the composition of status groups underwent changes that brought confusion to the social hierarchy. For example, the percentage of *yangban* in the Taegu district increased from 18.7 percent in 1727 to 70.2 percent in 1858. In contrast, the commoner and slave population continually decreased, such that the commoner population went from 54.6 percent in 1727 down to 28.2 percent in 1858, and slaves decreased from 26.7 percent in 1727 to 1.6 percent in 1858.[47] This trend was displayed in other districts of Kyŏngsang province as well. Although these statistics are somewhat questionable and cannot be generalized to the Chosŏn population as a whole, they nevertheless demonstrate the increased social mobility of the late Chosŏn.[48] Subjects' social status could also go downward depending on their socioeconomic situation. For example, in the eighteenth and nineteenth centuries, many destitute commoners chose to sell themselves as slaves to evade heavily levied taxes.[49]

Although the hereditary status system had lost much of its function by the nineteenth century, the state strove to maintain the system throughout the Chosŏn dynasty via various mechanisms, one of which was control of intermarriage between commoner and slave.[50] Unlike in the preceding Koryŏ dynasty, when the state explicitly legislated the prohibition of intermarriage between different social statuses, the representative volumes of legal codes in the Chosŏn, that is, the *Great Code of Administration* and the *Continuation of the Great Code*, lacked such a prohibition. These two codes indirectly approved the practice of intermarriage by stipulating the regulation of off-springs' social status.[51] It was vital to determine offsprings' social status, since this was correlated to the population growth of commoners and slaves due to the hereditary factor. Mothers played the key role in defining a child's social status, especially in the case of intermarriage between different statuses.

The matrifilial succession law was applied to sustain the hereditary status system; the status of offspring was to be defined by the mother's status, with two exceptions. First, the child of a public official and a concubine of slave status would be recognized as a commoner if the father reported the child to the government and paid for the manumission fee. Second, the offspring of a slave father and a commoner mother inherited slave status. Despite the matrifilial succession rule, the child of a commoner mother had to have slave status due to the father's status. In other words, when either of the parents was a slave, then the child inherited the slave status. Because of this second exception, the population of slaves gradually increased as intermarriage between com-moners and slaves became more common. By sustaining the hereditary status system, the Chosŏn state seems to have politicized the category of "the female sex" to serve the purposes of reproductive sexuality and to fulfill economic needs by controlling the slave population. The state regulated status mobility via women's bodies in order to maintain social status distinctions.

Although the prohibition of intermarriage between commoner and slave was never explicitly codified in the law, during the early years of the dynasty, T'aejong promulgated the prohibition in order to secure the commoner population. In July 1401, Kwŏn Chunghwa sent a memorial to the king, raising the issue of intermarriage between slave man and commoner woman, stating that slave owners manipulated such marriages in order to increase their wealth. He proposed that intermarriage between slave man and commoner woman be prohibited, and that those already married be divorced. He further suggested that slave owners who violated the state's order by inducing intermarriage be strictly punished.[52] T'aejong approved this memorial and, in September 1405, promulgated the prohibition of intermarriage by defining such marriage as equal to having illicit sexual intercourse (*sanggan*) and stating that the offspring born from such intermarriage would be regressed to "public slave."[53] Furthermore, in June 1414, T'aejong proclaimed that offspring between a slave woman and a commoner man would inherit the father's commoner status.[54] This proclamation was epochal in the sense that it challenged the long tradition of inheriting the mother's status and elevated the offspring of slave woman to commoners. T'aejong's original aim was to strictly implement the patrilineal rule in intermarriage, but this policy was reversed when Sejong took the throne.

Sejong's initial goal was to maintain his predecessor's policy on intermarriage. However, officials such as Maeng Sasŏng persistently sent memorials to request the king to abolish the law, based on the rationale that it was disrupting the social status distinction. One of the reasons they provided was that if a slave woman claimed that the child's father was a commoner when the father was actually a slave, then it was impossible to discern who the father was. Female slaves were thereby causing social disorder by changing their husbands' status from slave to commoner. Officials at the court supported the matrifilial succession rule to prevent the children of female slaves from gaining commoner status. Aside from the reasons they provided to the king, it seems they also had their own practical reasons. If T'aejong's policy on intermarriage continued, then it would bring two specific consequences. First, there would be an increase in the commoner population due to the offspring of commoner fathers and slave mothers. Second, there would be an increase in the number of public slaves because offspring of a slave woman and a commoner man were to be regressed to public slave status. What these two consequences implied for the ruling class was that the number of private slaves would decrease dramatically, thereby affecting the economic wealth of the rulers. Therefore, bureaucrats continuously lobbied Sejong to nullify T'aejong's promulgation of 1414. Sejong rescinded the promulgation in 1432 and reestablished the policy of inheriting the mother's status for the children of slave women and commoner men. By 1455, during King Tanjong's reign (r. 1452–55), the children of a slave father and a commoner mother were no longer regressed to public slaves and instead inherited their father's slave status. Thus, by 1454, the state's policy toward intermarriage between commoner and slave had settled to maintaining slave status for the children.[55] The government had attempted to prevent slave owners' exploitation of intermarriage, but this effort had come to an end.[56]

Due to intermarriage practices, the commoner population gradually decreased toward the middle of the Chosŏn. According to Kim Sŏng-u, the "decrease of commoner and increase of slave" phenomenon in the sixteenth century was based on three factors: first, powerful *yangban* families took advantage of impecunious commoners and coercively made them their slaves; second, destitute commoners, who did not have a means of survival, voluntarily became dependants of wealthy *yangban* families; third, *yangban* families attempted to produce slaves by inducing impoverished commoners to marry their slaves.[57] There was already a sign of a decrease in the commoner population in the sixteenth century, but the situation deteriorated in the seventeenth century as the Chosŏn faced invasions by Japan (1592–98) and the Manchus (1627 and 1637–38).[58]

After the two devastating sets of wars, controlling intermarriage practice was one measure Chosŏn rulers used to balance the population that had wobbled as a result. During Hyŏnjong's reign, in 1669, the state revised the policy of intermarriage by abolishing the exception that applied to the offspring between a slave father and a commoner mother; the offspring now inherited the mother's commoner status. However, this decision underwent several changes during Sukchong's reign due to officials' opposition, and it was ultimately settled in 1731, during Yŏngjo's reign, by the reinstitution of Hyŏnjong's promulgation of 1669.

While the discussion of intermarriage continued at the court for several decades, a confrontation between masters and slaves was germinating outside the court.[59] When Hyŏnjong first announced his promulgation, slaves born from commoner mothers wished to be manumitted from their lowborn status. Prior to the promulgation, the only channel provided to slaves for their manumission was through purchase. This practice began as early as 1485, but not many slaves were wealthy enough to afford the manumission fee. As a result, there was an increase in the number of runaway slaves, which caused conflicts with their owners. When slave owners reported runaway slaves to the government, the Board of Slaves (Changyewŏn) would conduct an investigation and search for slaves for their owners. However, finding runaway slaves was difficult. Hyŏnjong's promulgation provided another legitimate channel for slaves to legally achieve manumission. The slaves manumitted, especially during this period, had to struggle with their masters because the policy underwent several changes over more than six decades until it was finalized. This confusion generated arguments between former slaves and their masters, because the masters did not easily renounce their ownership of the slaves' bodies.[60]

The kernel of conflict between former slaves and their masters was in the slave owners' attempt to exploit their former slaves' labor. Former slaves, in order to protect their freedom as commoners, petitioned to complain about these masters. By the eighteenth century, the state was well aware of such oppression by former owners and stipulated in the *Continuation of the Great Code* under the statute of "Purchase of Commoner Status" (*Songnyang*) the punishment of those who oppressed commoners as slaves (*amnyangwich'ŏnryul*).[61]

It was not only manumitted slaves that suffered from such oppression but also destitute commoners or commoners whose spouses were slaves. For example, in the second month of the year *ŭlmi*, a commoner woman surnamed Chŏng, a resident of Yŏnch'ŏn, petitioned the provincial governor concerning her granddaughter, who had been unjustly treated as a slave.[62] Chŏng's daughter, an officially recognized commoner, married a slave owned by a *yangban* with the surname Kang and had one daughter, whose name was Yungŭm. Unfortunately, she and her husband both died at an early age, and Chŏng raised the child. However, when Yungŭm reached the age of eight, Kang coercively exploited her labor. Chŏng initially appealed to the county office stating that her granddaughter was a commoner but was unfairly being treated as a slave by Kang. Chŏng petitioned to protect her granddaughter's right to live as a commoner. The magistrate ordered Kang to return the granddaughter to her grandmother. However, as Kang continued to treat Yungŭm as his slave, Chŏng appealed to the provincial government concerning the matter. The provincial governor responded to Chŏng by giving an order to investigate the case and punish Kang accordingly.[63]

Chong's petition is a typical example of the "oppressing of commoners as slaves" phenomenon that was prevalent in the late Chosŏn. The following case similarly represents this phenomenon, but it accompanied a murder, which was also not uncommon. In this particular case, the son of the victim first petitioned to appeal the grievance of his dead father, and the wife of the offender counterpetitioned in order to claim innocence on behalf of her imprisoned husband.

In 1777, during Chŏngjo's reign, a homicide took place in Chinju county of Kyŏngsang province. At the outset of the case, Sŏng Yongsŏk demanded 10,000 *nyang* from Hŏ Ch'ae and Kim Yŏhu for their manumission money. However, Ch'ae reported Yongsŏk's unreasonable demand to the county office. The next day, Yongsŏk and his brother Kwisŏk bludgeoned Ch'ae to death for his reporting. It is uncertain whether Ch'ae's ancestors were from slave status and he was recently manumitted. Regardless, Ch'ae was an officially recognized commoner. His wife, however, was a slave of Yongsŏk's, and this was one of the reasons that Yongsŏk tried to treat Ch'ae as his slave. There was a tendency among the masters of female slaves to also treat their commoner husbands as slaves. Shortly after Ch'ae's death, his son, Hŏ Kyŏng, presented a written petition to the king regarding his father, who he felt had been unjustly treated and murdered. The Board of Punishments reported to the king about the son's petition stating that Yongsŏk oppressed a commoner by inappropriately demanding money for manumission and went beyond the limits of acceptable violence. They concluded their report by proposing to investigate the case in detail. The king agreed and ordered the provincial governor to proceed with the investigation. However, Chŏngjo ordered that the investigation await the appointment of the new provincial governor. This was to prevent the confusion and delay that would occur when the current provincial governor was replaced. As soon as the new provincial governor was assigned to Kyŏngsang province, he initiated the investigation and verified the case to the king in the ninth month.[64]

When the case was substantiated to the king, Yongsŏk's wife, the commoner Chŏng, struck the drum to counterpetition the king. Her story entirely differed from that of Kyŏng and conveyed that his statements were untrue. She went even further to claim that the county magistrate's investigation was unfairly conducted and therefore the submitted report was untrustworthy. After going over her petition, the king commented: "Is it truly the provincial governor's report that is unfair or is it the folk custom that has become evil in blaming the governor? It will be clear who is lying when the murder case is further clarified. . . . This homicide case should be distinguished from murder without intention. If the accused is lightly punished, then the deceased soul cannot be solaced. Therefore, it must be reinvestigated thoroughly."[65]

In the fifth month of 1778, Yongsŏk's wife struck the drum for the second time, and this time she presented a verbal petition to appeal on behalf of her

husband. In her petition, she claimed that Ch'ae's death was due to an illness and not from the beating. She stated, "During the first inquest investigation, the county magistrate recorded seven beatings based on the physical
examination of the body. Thus, it is clear that the death was not caused by the
beating. However, when the second inquest investigation was conducted, it
reversed the first investigation. This was because functionaries who attended
the second investigation were relatives of a former slave who had betrayed
his master, and a man named Sŏ Poksu bribed them to overrule the initial
investigation."[66]

The kernel of her claim was that Ch'ae's death was not caused by her husband's beating him but from a disease. She also claimed that there was a plot
against her husband that reversed the initial investigation, and she provided
evidence in order to exonerate her imprisoned husband. After having read the
board memorial of her petition, the king stated the following:

> As the inquest official stated, the punishment for a slave owner killing the
> husband of a female slave is indeed the death penalty. Although Hŏ Ch'ae
> was suffering from a disease, it was Sŏng Yongsŏk who solely caused his
> death. Whether he was beaten seventeen or seven times does not matter.
> Six people have testified about Sŏng Yongsŏk's beating. There are two evil
> customs in this country. One is ill-natured slaves betraying their masters and
> the other is powerful landowners in the countryside oppressing commoners.
> Law must strictly regulate these two evil customs in order to prevent their
> practice. According to the wife's petition, the case should be further inves-
> tigated because there are still traces of doubt. The report suggests that Hŏ
> Ch'ae was beaten simultaneously by both Sŏng Yongsŏk and Sŏng Kwisŏk. If
> that is the case, then it is unfair to impose different kinds of punishment on
> the brothers.[67]

The king's statement implies that Chŏng's petition caused the case to be
reinvestigated and the punishment of Yongsŏk to be reconsidered. Not only
was Chŏngjo considerate of the victim's grievance, but he was also cautious
about preventing potential grievance from the offender's side. Thus, in adjudicating the case, the king made every effort to redress the grievances of both
parties. The king finally ruled to reverse Yongsŏk's punishment from the
death penalty to banishment in May 1777.[68]

When Yongsŏk's punishment was reduced to banishment, Kyŏng appealed
for the second time to protest his father's unjust death. After the appeal was

made, the king took the petition into serious consideration and sent a special emissary to the county to reinvestigate the case.[69] After conducting the investigation, the special emissary memorialized to the king stating that Yongsŏk's case should be reconsidered because the grievance of the victim was not fully redressed. The king then ordered the provincial governor to reinvestigate the case. The provincial governor reported to the king, asking him to disregard the son's petition, but the Board of Punishments proposed to reinterrogate Yongsŏk. The king followed the board's proposal. The case then underwent another round of investigation due to Kyŏng's petition. Chŏngjo finally adjudicated the case and stated the following:

> I previously banished the accused but ordered to imprison him once again to conduct another round of interrogation. This is not because I had doubts about his statement but because even the minutest detail in a homicide case should be cautiously investigated. Furthermore, when Hŏ Ch'ae's son cried extremely agonizingly, I was even able to hear it from the royal chariot.[70] After having witnessed such a scene, I could not help but pity him and thought his grievance had not been properly redressed. Finally, I also had the intention to suppress the powerful and support the weak. . . . Since nothing new was revealed during the second round of interrogation, it would be unfair to impose different kinds of punishments on the Sŏng brothers, where one received banishment and the other capital punishment. Therefore, according to the initial adjudication, send back Sŏng Yongsŏk to his location of banishment.[71]

Based on Chŏngjo's comments, it is possible to know how close Kyŏng approached the king to petition during his procession. The king was even able to hear Kyŏng's voice from his royal chariot and was able to sympathize with him. One salient aspect of Chosŏn legal culture was that the legal channel was relatively open and accessible to the sovereign. Although it was the state that allowed people to approach the king during his royal procession, this practice came to be legitimized based on the petitioners' mode of petitioning. As shown in chapter 2, people began petitioning during the royal procession and attempted to approach the king in various ways as early as the fifteenth century.

The practice of petitioning during the royal procession allowed the king to easily empathize with people's sense of injustice. When Chŏngjo stated that he was able to grasp the son's grief, we can see an example of the contingent

FIGURE 5.3. Hŏ Kyŏng's petition would have been addressed in a procession such as this one. As King Chŏngjo proceeds to his father's tomb, men and women of different statuses are gathered together to watch. Since they are sitting and standing not far from the king's presence, it is possible that the officials or even the king could hear when people struck the gong and approached to address their grievances. H: 46.7cm. Deoksu 2507. Courtesy of National Museum of Korea.

attachment of the sociality of pain, which begins with the victim's pain and moves toward others so that they can feel the trace of the pain on the surface of the victim's body. When the pain of the victim is expressed through his or her body, this ethically demands that the person who witnesses the pain act on behalf of the victim and empathize with the victim's pain. The assumption here is that the petitioners know how the victims feel, which allows them to transform the other's pain into their own and to feel moved to seek justice on the victims' behalf.[72] When the petitioners represented the victims' pain to the king, the pain first navigated to the petitioners and then on to the sovereign as the petitioners narrated the victims' pain as theirs. In this particular case, Kyŏng successfully represented not only his but also his father's *wŏn*. Through his performance, he was able to invoke Chŏngjo's pity and led the king to understand that his grievance had not been fully redressed.

As shown in this case, petitions addressed by the son and the wife prompted the reinvestigation of a case. To what extent, then, did the petitions in a murder trial exert influence on the ruling? According to Sim Chae-u's study of *Records of Stating and Hearings*, there were 150 cases in which petitioning activities were involved in homicide cases.[73] Of these 150 cases, the sentences of 66 cases (44 percent) were reduced from the death penalty, 57 cases (38 percent) were exonerated, 10 cases (6.6 percent) were ruled to be false accusations, and 2 cases (1.3 percent) received the death penalty; there were 13 "other" cases (8.6 percent).[74] These statistics seem to demonstrate that the petitions did have an impact on the verdicts.

The investigation of Yongsŏk's case lasted from autumn 1777 to spring 1781. During the course of the murder trial, the victim's son and the offender's wife each petitioned twice on behalf of their families. The petitions from both sides caused the case to be reinvestigated, thereby prolonging the murder trial. Chŏngjo carefully took into consideration all of the petitions regardless of whether the appeals were made on behalf of the victim or the accused. It was important for Chŏngjo both to redress the injustice of the victim and his family and to avert potential grievance on the offender's side. In order to execute rectificatory justice, Chŏngjo distinguished "victim-centered rectification" and "wrongdoer-centered rectification."[75] The aim of rectificatory justice is to set right any unjust states of affairs by using punishment that is usually ordered by the authorities to inflict pain or suffering upon the person who has infringed a right. Although it is crucial to consider what ought to be done for the benefit of the victim of an injustice, it is similarly necessary to discuss what the wrongdoer deserves as retributive punishment.[76] To rectify injustice in this case, it was important for Chŏngjo to not only redress the victim's injustice but also prevent potential grievance through unfair execution of punishment.

## CONCLUSION

The state's response to the two major injustices of the late Chosŏn discussed in this chapter demonstrates how the petitioning activity by victims' and offenders' family members influenced the adjudication process. Although petitioners' grief was naturally expressed to a certain degree, on behalf of their imprisoned or unjustly murdered family members, petitioning also required them to articulately craft grievances in order to effectively persuade the authorities. Their petitions may not have necessarily altered the rulings, but the petitions certainly reinforced the need for the authorities to execute fair adjudication by conducting reinvestigations whenever necessary.

It was never an easy task for the king or investigating officials to discern the truth of petitioners' stories. For example, in the anecdote introduced in the beginning of this chapter, the magistrate was suspended from his official duty for three years and the provincial governor was relieved from his official post. However, two months after the case was closed, Yu Hun memorialized to the king stating that there were testimonies that contradicted Kim's petition and the case needed to be reinvestigated.[77] The king approved the reinvestigation, but the *Veritable Records of King Yŏngjo* does not provide further information. Although it is difficult to glean all the ins and outs of the case from the records, what is certain is that Kim's father died from excessive torture and that she petitioned on his behalf. There is the possibility that Kim exaggerated her father's innocence; nevertheless, she was seeking justice for her dead father.

When petitioners appealed to the sovereign in order to seek justice, the central government commanded local officials to investigate. If the case was verified, then the state proceeded with determining a punishment to redress the grievance of the victim. However, the state was also cautious not to generate potential grievances from the offender's side. Although it was the state that held the power to define injustice, subjects were empowered to redefine it via petitioning; they could persuade the state to recognize their experience of injustice, which the state had previously neglected to rectify.

When petitioners sought justice on behalf of their dead family members, they not only represented the pain of the wronged but also their own feelings of empathy, which effectively enhanced the merit of their appeals. In addition, two laws regarding "making an accusation against a magistrate" and "oppressing commoners as slaves" were legislated in the early eighteenth century to regulate social injustices; these laws were the result of petitioners' efforts to redress grievances from earlier in the dynasty. Records of petitions show how the petitioning practice developed through constant interaction and negotiation between the state and society and how women along with their male counterparts actively participated as legal agents questioning social injustices during the late Chosŏn.

# CONCLUSION

If people's *wŏn* is not relieved, how could it be the Way
[K. To; Ch. Dao] of politics?

—King Sejong, *Sejong sillok* 51 (13/1/19)

DURING THE CHOSŎN, PEOPLE WHO WENT TO COURT PRE-sented grievances related to various civil and criminal matters. Through their performance of petitioning the state, the meanings of *wŏn* were defined and redefined throughout the dynasty. Although the emotions of *wŏn* that people expressed in their petitions were perceived as "natural" feelings, the meanings attached to *wŏn* were culturally constructed through a discussion of what aroused *wŏn*. The emotions of *wŏn* that people expressed eventually transformed the reality and functioned as a powerful device of social change.

In examining Chosŏn legal practice, we find that the society was far more complex than we might assume. Every subject was conferred with the legal capacity to petition and air grievances to the state. In the minds of Chosŏn bureaucrats, the emotions of *wŏn* endangered social, legal, and cosmic harmony if they were not relieved appropriately. The state considered that suppressing either individual or collective *wŏn* would be counterproductive, and the accumulation of such emotions had the potential to cause rebellion. In order to relieve people's emotions of *wŏn*, the state empowered every subject to file a complaint against a private individual or even a public authority when necessary, with the exceptions being when the two parties were bound by a father-son, husband-wife, or master-slave relationship. However, in practice, some cases of these supposed exceptions did occur.[1]

The Chosŏn legal system functioned in a contradictory fashion. While applying unequal laws and punishments according to different social statuses, the state's recognition of *wŏn* as an egalitarian sentiment allowed every subject to petition. By embracing the voice of every subject, the state built a stronghold of legitimacy and also was able to maintain social harmony by regulating those who transgressed the laws or social norms. However, subjects concurrently utilized the appeals system to pursue their own interests and even manipulated the system to achieve some form of emotional satisfaction regardless of the legal results.

Aside from personal and family grievances, people also petitioned on collective grievances; these petitions were known as *tŭngjang*, or joint petitions, and were pertinent to social issues such as tax. The rebels who participated in the Hong Kyŏngnae Rebellion of 1812 appropriated the Confucian discourse of the state having the mandate to listen to people's grievances. It was said that if the state failed to heed people's complaints and neglected to relieve their suffering, then people would eventually rise up against the state.[2] This discourse can similarly be detected in the Tonghak Rebellion of 1894, which led to the start of the first Sino-Japanese War in the seventh month of the same year. Chŏn Pongjun, the leader of the Tonghak Rebellion, after he was captured in the twelfth month of 1895, stated in his interrogation that joint petitions were made several times addressing grievances regarding misgovernment and corruption of local officials. However, those petitions were disregarded, and the petitioners were arrested.[3] When taking the Tonghak Rebellion into consideration, we find that the state that was so concerned with listening to people's grievances actually witnessed a rebellion that demonstrated the risks of failing to relieve the *wŏn* of enraged people.

It is worth mentioning here that one of the aims of establishing the petition drum in 1401 was to prevent people from rising up against the state by providing a sanctioned way for them to articulate their concerns. Throughout the Chosŏn, Neo-Confucian bureaucrats emphasized the importance of listening to people's grievances not only to relieve their *wŏn* and maintain social harmony but also to monitor those who were suspected of planning to rebel against the state. By failing to embrace people's voices, the state witnessed small- and large-scale rebellions in the nineteenth century.

Emotions similarly played a powerful role in medieval Marseille France, where the courts provided a space for people to invest in a transaction of emotions, a stage on which to advertise hatreds, humiliations, and social sanctions. The law courts of medieval Europe functioned efficiently and became venues for the pursuit of emotional satisfaction. The suppression of emotions such as anger and hatred would have generated adverse effects and damaged one's legal rights, in this case.[4]

Interesting from a comparative aspect is that while members of unfree and marginalized groups, such as domestic servants, serfs, Muslims, and Jews, in medieval Europe had to restrain themselves from showing anger in public, free and autonomous individuals were allowed to publicly exhibit the legitimate emotions of anger and hatred.[5] Women of free status were allowed to publicize their anger in law courts, but subjects of unfree status had to subdue their emotions because it was too dangerous for the state to allow them to vent their anger in public. This is precisely opposite of the Chosŏn case, that is, those of unfree status were allowed to publicize the emotions of *wŏn* because suppressing such feelings was perceived to have been too perilous to the state.

Although the public expression of emotions varies depending on temporal and spatial circumstances, medical and scientific research indicates that emotions as sets of neurophysiological patterns are essentially identical in all human cultures.[6] In this regard, the Chosŏn judicial system provides useful insights into how emotions played a role in a legal institution to sustain social harmony by recognizing *wŏn* horizontally as well as vertically. The sui generis feature of the Chosŏn legal system was displayed in the judicial culture where it functioned in a contradictory manner.

The legal transformations from the premodern to the modern judicial system that took place during the Japanese colonial period (1910–45) divested women of legal capacity as colonial subjects, which meant that female subjects were no longer empowered to speak in the legal realm except on certain occasions. What is intriguing is that this contradictory mode continued to exist under the modern legal system, but was manifested in a different manner. Although the hereditary status system was officially abolished in 1894, gender hierarchy was reinforced when the *Japanese Civil Code*, with little revision, was instituted in Korea in 1921.[7]

When Korea was annexed by Japan in 1910, there was a fundamental reconfiguration of legal policy in the new colony. The Japanese colonial authorities collected the Chosŏn customs and declared in the *Chosŏn Ordinance on Civil Matters* (K. Chosŏn minsaryŏng, J. Chōsen minjirei) of 1912 that Korean customary rules would be applied to colonial subjects in civil matters. Article 11 of the *Chosŏn Ordinance on Civil Matters* stipulated that Korean custom was to be followed in matters of "capacity, family, and succession" among Koreans.[8] However, in an investigation report on the Chosŏn custom, the Japanese had misinterpreted a wife's legal capacity and specified that a wife had to "absolutely" depend on her husband in order to exercise legal capacity, as women were subjugated to men in that state.[9]

Later, in 1921, the colonial government applied the restrictions on a wife's legal capacity in the *Japanese Civil Code* to colonial subjects. While single women were authorized to exercise legal capacity, a wife had to rely on her husband to enter the legal space due to the concept of legal guardianship. The *Japanese Civil Code* stipulated a wife's legal "incapacity" regarding the following eight acts: acquiring or using an acquisition, borrowing or giving security for an estate, exercising rights on real estate, filing civil litigation, making a gift or settling a dispute concerning property rights or entering into a contract to arbitrate, recognizing or renouncing the right of succession, recognizing or rejecting an amount stated in an will or gift, and binding one's freedom of body or entering into such a contract. Exceptions to these restrictions allowed women to exercise legal capacity in the following cases: when a husband was imprisoned, when a husband was hospitalized due to mental illness, when it was uncertain whether the husband was alive, and when the interests of husband and wife conflicted.[10]

Due to the misinterpretation of the *Chosŏn Ordinance on Civil Matters*, it has been understood that a wife's legal capacity stipulated in the *Japanese Civil Code* was elevated from "absolute" to "limited" dependence on her husband, despite the fact that the *Japanese Civil Code* officially deprived women of their legal capacity. Whether actual practice corresponded to or contradicted the law is a different matter and can be determined only by probing into how women were represented in social practice under the colonial judicial system by examining actual legal cases.

Scholars of the post-Liberation period have generally accepted the Japanese investigation report on the Chosŏn customs that were included in the *Chosŏn Ordinance on Civil Matters* without a critical lens and have continued to discuss women's legal "incapacity" during the Chosŏn as a fact,[11] stating, for example, that it was necessary for a wife to have her husband's permission to enter court during the Chosŏn,[12] or claiming that the *Japanese Civil Code* actually advanced the legal status of women because the Confucian gender system demanded wife's absolute subjugation to men and therefore wives were not able to exercise legal capacity without their husband's permission.[13]

Women's legal position in the Chosŏn has often been incorrectly related by scholars of the post-Liberation period because of their presumption that women's legal existence was subjugated to men. It is thus critical to illuminate women's legal capacity as it was actually practiced during the Chosŏn. Women of the Chosŏn dynasty were recognized as legal subjects and exercised legal capacity that was not inferior to that of their male counterparts. Furthermore, women petitioned to air grievances on behalf of themselves as well as family members, especially husbands, in courts. Their petitioning practice enabled them to challenge the domestic patriarch by reversing the power relationship when they spoke on behalf of husbands. By capitalizing on the legal capacity to petition, women were empowered to negotiate with authorities to pursue their interests, seek rectification, and plead pardon or favor. Chosŏn legal space was utilized as a site of negotiation between the state and society that generated new types of grievances that needed to be redressed in order to maintain social harmony. If we situate women at the center stage when examining the legal culture of the Chosŏn, we can not only restore their voices but also bring attention to the complex interrelation between gender and status in the domain of law. Furthermore, by exploring the intersection of gender, status, emotions, and law, it is possible to uncover how women's legal capacity was misrepresented under the Japanese colonial rule as well as how that misperception continued through the post-Liberation period.

Emotions of *wŏn* were deeply entwined with the search for justice in the Chosŏn. People of different genders and statuses experienced injustice when they were legally violated. More specifically, the emotions of *wŏn* were aroused when ordinary people were violated of something they were legally entitled to. In order to rectify injustice, they petitioned the state to seek emotional satisfaction and protection of privilege they were able to enjoy within their social status.[14] For example, if an elite man coercively exploited a commoner woman's labor, this was enough to trigger *wŏn* and provide sufficient grounds for her to bring a lawsuit against him. The Chosŏn state envisioned a just society by expecting people to play their role according to their social status but simultaneously protecting what every subject regardless of gender or status was legally entitled to such as life, property, and the capacity to engage in legal transactions. Relieving people's *wŏn* or their sense of injustice by executing fair punishment was the crux of performing justice in the Chosŏn.

If filing legal petitions was perceived as a pursuit of individual self-interest, could the petitions have been dismissed by the Confucian state? Were they acceptable only when they were seen as seeking the objective good of a family or a community rather than an individual? It is true that the fundamental goal of Neo-Confucian society was to seek the common good of a family or a community rather than an individual.[15] Although this study demonstrated the construction of intersubjectivity and the importance of the relational self, it also showed that an individual's experience of *wŏn* was as equally important as the family or collective *wŏn*. When people presented petitions that raised frivolous or petty grievances, the state was determined to punish them. In these cases, the authorities dismissed their petitions thinking that their intention stemmed from selfish act. However, when dealing with such unjust cases, it is clear that the state did not perceive seeking the redress of individual *wŏn* to be selfish behavior in itself. The petitioning practices illustrate that the state was concerned with relieving individual *wŏn* as much as family or collective *wŏn*. In the end, it was the individual that constructed family and community and it was necessary to relieve individual *wŏn* to prevent even greater *wŏn*. If the state did not value individual *wŏn*, it would have made more sense for them to have applied legal guardianship for women and allowed men to represent women in courts. Also, lowborn such as slaves would not have been recognized as legal subjects capable of raising their independent voices directly to the state.

This is of course not to suggest that modern construction of "individual rights" or "human rights" as we understand them today existed in the Chosŏn. It is clear that the Chosŏn society was organized hierarchically according to gender and status and the notion of equality was absent. However, the Chosŏn legal system, although not always efficient, at least provided measures for people to seek judicial protection and the grievances they addressed were certainly more than "obligations and privileges" that their social status entailed. The judicial system protected even a female slave's capacity to exercise legal activities such as petitioning, buying and selling, borrowing and lending, entering into contracts, and making bequests. This means that she was able to independently sign a contract to buy land from her neighbors. The very fact that every subject regardless of gender or status was conferred with autonomous capacity to engage in legal transactions complicates the meaning of the individual in a hierarchical and gender-segregated society as the Chosŏn. In other words, the significance of legal capacity shown in this study complicates our understanding of individual in a premodern context. This certainly warrants further in-depth study on the trajectory of the individual before the rise of modernity.

Although the notions of "equality," "inalienable rights," and "human rights" are embedded in our modern legal system, social inequality and the sense of injustice are still very much prevalent today in almost any society. Every legal system has its own distinctive features but simultaneously shares some common legal practices that provide useful insights across temporal and spatial boundaries. I hope that this book, the first to discuss the role of emotions in judiciary practice of the Chosŏn, might bring the Korean case into global historical and interdisciplinary dialogues on justice.

*Notes*



1   The year *kyŏngo* stated in Malgŭm's petition could have been 1750, 1810, or 1870, depending on which sixty-year cycle the year fell in.

2   Malgŭm's petition does not mention which county or province she was from; she identifies herself only as a resident of "northern district."

3   *Komunsŏ*, 22: 149–51.

4   Ibid.

5   Rockhill, "Notes on Some of the Laws, Customs, and Superstitions of Korea," 180.

6   Pak Pyŏng-ho, *Kŭnse ŭi pŏp*, 63–68, and Chŏn Hyŏng-t'aek, *Chosŏn hugi nobi sinbun yŏn'gu*, 14–39.

7   For a discussion of the slavery system in Korean history, see Salem, "Slavery in Medieval Korea"; Hong Sŭng-gi, *Koryŏ kwijok sahoe wa nobi*; Palais, *Confucian Statecraft*, 208–70 and "A Search for Korean Uniqueness"; Chŏn Hyŏng-t'aek, *Chosŏn hugi nobi sinbun yŏn'gu*; Chi Sŭng-jong, *Chosŏn chŏn'gi nobi sinbun yŏn'gu*; and Joy S. Kim, "Representing Slavery."

8   There was a small group of governing aristocrats at the top of the society known as the *yangban*. During the Chosŏn, this group enjoyed most socioeconomic privileges. Due to status instability during the late Chosŏn, *yangban* no longer immediately represented the ruling class, whereas *sadaebu* referred specifically to the ruling group. There was another small group known as the "middle people" (*chungin*) that consisted mostly of technical specialists and functionaries. Under the middle class, there were the commoners, most of whom were peasants known as *yangin* or *sangmin*. These people made up the majority of the population and carried most of the burden of taxation, military service, and corvée labor. Lastly, the lowborn, known as *ch'ŏnmin*, were mostly slaves but also included those with debased occupations such as butchers, tanners, shamans, and female entertainers.

9   For a study of "middle people" (*chungin*) published in English, see Hwang, *Beyond Birth*, and Park, *A Family of No Prominence*.

10  For a discussion of Neo-Confucianism and other religions in Korea, see de Bary and Haboush, *Rise of Neo-Confucianism in Korea*; Haboush, *The Confucian Kingship in Korea*; Deuchler, *Confucian Transformation of Korea*; Buswell, *Religions of Korea in Practice*, 163–230; Walraven, "Popular Religion in a Confucianized Society"; and Baker, "A Different Thread."

11  For a discussion of the transition from Koryŏ to the Chosŏn dynasty, see Duncan, *The Origins of the Chosŏn Dynasty*, and Deuchler, *The Confucian Transformation of Korea*, 29–87.

12  For a discussion of law and emotion in the early Chosŏn, see Jisoo M. Kim, "Law and Emotion," 203–39. For a discussion of *qing* and the rise of public sympathy in Republican China, see Lean, *Public Passions*.

13  Solomon, *A Passion for Justice*, 243.

14  Pak Pyŏng-ho, *Chŏnt'ongjŏk pŏpch'egye*, *Han'guk pŏpchesago*, and *Kŭnse ŭi pŏp*; Chŏng Kŭng-sik, *Han'guk pŏpchesago* and "Chosŏn sidae ŭi kwŏllyŏk pullip"; Cho Yun-sŏn, *Chosŏn hugi sosong yŏn'gu*; Sim Chae-u, *Chosŏn hugi kukka kwŏllyŏk* and "Chosŏn malgi hyŏngsa pŏp ch'egye"; and Im Sang-hyŏk, "Sosong kip'i ŭi munhwa chŏnt'ong" and "Chosŏn chŏn'gi minsa sosong."

15  Marie S. Kim, "Law and Custom," 1068.

16  By examining actual legal practice at the local level, some scholars of Chinese legal history have argued that "civil law" was present in local judicial procedures and in custom. See Huang, *Civil Justice in China*, and *Code, Custom, and Legal Practice in China*; and Bernhardt and Huang, *Civil Law in Qing and Republican China*.

17  Marie S. Kim, *Law and Custom in Korea*, 1.

18  Ibid., 1–40.

19  Ibid., 24

20  Marie S. Kim's study focuses primarily on the issue of customary law during the Japanese occupation period (1910–45). The discussion of Chosŏn legal practice is thus limited in her study.

21  *T'aejong sillok,* 18 (9/7/19).

22  For Korean legal history published in English, see Hahm, *The Korean Political Tradition and Law*; Shaw, *Legal Norms*, "The Neo-Confucian Revolution of Values," and "Traditional Korean Law"; Chŏn, Shaw, and Choi, *Traditional Korean Legal Attitudes*; and Marie S. Kim, *Law and Custom in Korea*.

23  Solomon, "Justice v. Vengeance," 128.

24  Santangelo, *Sentimental Education*, 7, cited in Choe Key-Sook, "A Weeping Man and the Mourning Ritual," 149.

25  The modern Korean translation of emotions is *kamjŏng*. However, the term *kamjŏng* was rarely used during the Chosŏn. As usage of the term "emotions" grew with the rise of modernity in the West, the word *kamjŏng* seems to have been used in Korea since the turn of the twentieth century. Further research will be required to trace the usage of *kamjŏng*.

26  Choe Key-sook, "A Weeping Man and the Mourning Ritual," 149.

27  The Four Beginnings are from the famous quote from Mencius about a child

falling down a well: The disposition of compassion is the beginning of humanity, the disposition of shame and dislike is the beginning of righteousness, the disposition of yielding and deference is the beginning of propriety, the disposition of approving and disapproving is the beginning of wisdom (Mencius 2A6). The translation comes from Kalton, *The Four-Seven Debate*, xxvii.

28  Kalton, *The Four-Seven Debate*.

29  Palais, *Confucian Statecraft*, 11–3.

30  Kalton eds., *The Four-Seven Debate*, xxxiv.

31  For an examination of how male literati controlled and expressed emotions in their writings, see Choe Key-sook, "A Weeping Man and the Mourning Ritual"; "Kamsŏngjŏk in'gan"; "Chosŏn sidae kamjŏngnon"; and "Hyonyŏ Simch'ŏng."

32  Solomon, *A Passion for Justice*.

33  Nussbaum, *Upheavals of Thought*.

34  Damasio, *Descartes' Error*.

35  For different frameworks for studying the history of emotions, see Stearns and Stearns, "Emotionology"; Reddy, *The Navigation of Feeling*; and Rosenwein, *Emotional Communities in the Early Middle Ages*.

36  Reddy, *Navigation of Feeling*, 1–137.

37  Previous studies on the topic of petitioning have examined the establishment of the petition drum and its practice but have not questioned how people of different genders and statuses were empowered to utilize the system. See Han U-gŭn, "Sinmun'go ŭi sŏlch'i"; Han Sang-gwŏn, *Chosŏn hugi sahoe wa sowŏn chedo*; and Kim Kyŏng-suk, "Chosŏn hugi yŏsŏng ŭi chŏngso hwaldong."

38  Recent scholarly discourse on emotions in medieval European courts is rather complex. People in the West have often perceived emotions as the antithesis to reason, especially since the Enlightenment period. Kathleen Wallace has challenged this perception and describes how it has distorted our understanding of moral judgment and the subject as moral agent. Also, in another recent study, Daniel L. Smail argues that emotions such as anger and enmity continued to play a significant role even after the medieval period in Marseille, and men and women chose to invest money and emotions in the law in order to broadcast their hatreds to a wider audience. He brings emotions back into the histories of law, and claims that it is critical to understand the role of emotions in both medieval and modern society. For a discussion of emotion and law, see Wallace, "Reconstructing Judgment," and Smail, *The Consumption of Justice*. For the European phenomenon of utilizing courts to pursue grudges as the "publicization" of vendetta, see Zorzi, "The Judicial System in Florence."

39  Shaw, *Legal Norms in a Confucian State* and "Traditional Korean Law and Its Relation to China."

40  Shaw, "Traditional Korean Law and Its Relation to China," 310–13.

41  In the case of early modern Japan, John W. Hall claims that it was a "container society." The "containers" that refer to status group can be perceived as secure within each given status, because they could expect equal treatment under the law. See Howell, *Geographies of Identity*, 31.

42  Sommer, *Sex, Law, and Society in Late Imperial China.*

43  *Continuation of the Great Code,* 309.

44  For a discussion of Chosŏn bureaucracy, see Wagner, *The Literati Purges*; Palais, *Confucian Statecraft,* and "Confucianism and the Aristocratic/Bureaucratic Balance in Korea"; Duncan, *The Origins of the Chosŏn Dynasty*; and Park, *Between Dreams and Reality.*

45  See Heerma van Voss, *Petitions in Social History,* 15.

46  For a discussion of the Hong Kyŏngnae Rebellion in early nineteenth-century Korea, see Sun Joo Kim, *Marginality and Subversion in Korea,* "Taxes, the Local Elite, and the Rural Populace," and "Fragmented: The *T'ongch'ŏng* Movements"; Karlsson, "The Hong Kyŏngnae Rebellion, 1811–1812" and "Challenging the Dynasty."

47  Davis, *Fiction in the Archives,* 1–6.

48  Yasuhiko Karasawa, also inspired by Davis's "crafting of narrative," explores the issue of orality and textuality in legal documents of Qing China. See Karasawa, "Between Oral and Written Cultures."

49  See Stacey, *Dark Speech,* 4.

50  While we do find evidence of scriveners during the Chosŏn, relying on them was discouraged by the state as they were thought to have instigated legal disputes. The role of scriveners, however, seems to have been far more active in Qing China. See Macauley, *Social Power and Legal Culture.*

51  Dudley, "In the Archive, in the Field," 163.

52  My reading of petitions is influenced by Dudley's approach to oral history; see, for example, "In the Archive, in the Field," 162.

53  Dudley, "In the Archive, in the Field," 165.

54  In making this argument, I was influenced by how oral history has been defined as genre. See Chamberlain and Thompson, *Narrative and Genre,* 1–45.

55  I borrow Roger Shrank's definition of "script" to mean "a predetermined, stereotyped sequence of actions that defines well-known situations" (Shrank and Abelson, *Scripts, Plans, Goals, and Understanding,* 41).

56  Shaw, *Legal Norms in a Confucian State*; Sim Chae-u, *Chosŏn hugi kukka kwŏllyŏk*; Sun Joo Kim and Jungwon Kim, *Wrongful Deaths*; and Kim Ho, "Kyujanggak sojang 'kŏman.'"

57  Smail, *The Consumption of Justice,* 92.

58  Ibid.

59  Besides the records of women's petitions, legal codes such as the *Great Code of Administration* (Kyŏngguk taejŏn), *Continuation of the Great Code* (Sok taejŏn), and *Comprehensive Great Code* (Taejŏn hoet'ong) are used to investigate the evolution of the appeals system. I also examine legal discourse using sources such as *Collected Writings of Sambong* (Sambongjip), *A Compendium to Warn the People* (Kyŏngminp'yŏn), *New Writings on Circumspection in Judicial Decisions* (Hŭmhŭm sinsŏ), and *A Book for the Heart of the Magistrate* (Mongmin simsŏ).

60  For women of the Chosŏn in English, see Mattielli, *Virtues in Conflict*; Kendall and Peterson, *Korean Women*; Deuchler, *The Confucian Transformation of Korea*

and "Propagating Female Virtues in Chosŏn Korea"; Peterson, *Korean Adoption and Inheritance*; Haboush, *The Memoirs of Lady Hyegyŏng*, 1–36, "Versions and Subversions: Patriarchy and Polygamy in Korean Narratives," and "Gender and the Politics of Language in Chosŏn Korea"; Duncan, "The *Naehun* and the Politics of Gender"; Jungwon Kim, "Negotiating Virtue"; and Kim and Pettid, *Women and Confucianism.*

61  Many of the records in these different sources overlap. For example, a number of women's petitions recorded in the *Simnirok* can be traced in the *Sillok* as well as the *Ilsŏngnok*. In Han Sang-gwŏn's meticulous research on petitions of the late Chosŏn, there are detailed statistics based on the *Ilsŏngnok*'s records during the reign of Chŏngjo. Han shows that there are 108 petitions of elite women and 310 petitions of commoner women but does not mention the lowborn. Further, his statistics lack women's petitions from other periods and other regions. Although he provides raw numbers of women's petitions, he does not analyze them, because he focuses on the petitions of men, not women. My study not only complements his data but also fills the lack of voices from the other half of the population. For statistics on women's petitions, see Han Sang-gwŏn, *Chosŏn hugi sahoe wa sowŏn chedo*, 110–11, 120–21.

62  For memorial-type petitions, see Koo, "Origins of the Public Sphere and Civil Society." Also, for a discussion of private academies and the writings of mass petitions or circular letters (*t'ongmun*), see Hwisang Cho, "The Community of Letters."


CHAPTER ONE. THE CONFUCIAN STATE, LAW, AND EMOTIONS

1  Im Sang-hyŏk , "Chosŏn chŏn'gi minsa sosong"; and Cho Yun-sŏn, *Chosŏn hugi sosong yŏn'gu.*

2  Shaw, *Legal Norms in a Confucian State*, 85–92, and Marie S. Kim, *Law and Custom*, 33.

3  Shaw, *Legal Norms in a Confucian State*, 91–2.

4  Huang, *Civil Justice in China.*

5  For studies on the community compact, see Tadao, "Yi Yulgok and the Community Compact"; Palais, *Confucian Statecraft*, 705–61; Deuchler, "The Practice of Confucianism"; and Chŏng Chin-yŏng, *Chosŏn sidae hyangch'on sahoesa.*

6  Ch'oe, Lee, and de Bary, *Sources of Korean Tradition*, 2: 151.

7  Marie S. Kim, *Law and Custom in Korea*, 24–29.

8  Huang, *Civil Justice in China*, 15. On the issue of property, see also Buoye, *Manslaughter, Markets, and Moral Economy*; Bernhardt, *Women and Property in China*; and Zelin, Ocko, and Gardella, *Contract and Property in Early Modern China.*

9  Han'guk komunsŏ hakhoe, *Chosŏn ŭi ilsang pŏpchŏng e sŏda*, 36.

10  In the case of Tokugawa Japan, where the legal system was similarly merged with the administrative apparatus, Herman Ooms discusses the coexistence of order and justice. *Tokugawa Village Practice*, 312–49.

11  *T'aejo sillok*, 1 (1/7/20). The translation comes from Lee, de Bary, Ch'oe, and Kang, *Sources of Korean Tradition*, 1: 274.

12  *T'aejong sillok*, 18 (9/7/19).

13  Ibid., 18 (9/7/19).

14  Ibid., 11 (6/3/20).

15  Ibid., 28 (14/8/13).

16  *Sejong sillok*, 7 (2/yun1/29).

17  Smail, *The Consumption of Justice*, 1–28.

18  Most of the scholarship that deals with the legal channel to petition as a major or minor theme emphasizes the Confucian politics of treating the people as the basis of the state stemmed from Mencian thought. See Han U-gŭn, "Sinmun'go ŭi sŏlch'i"; Pak Pyŏng-ho, *Kŭnse ŭi pŏp*; Han Sang-gwŏn, *Chosŏn hugi sahoe wa sowŏn chedo*; and Yi T'ae-jin, "Chosŏn sidae 'minbon' ŭisik."

19  During the Chosŏn, it was not uncommon for people to forge documents to try to win civil lawsuits. See Im Sang-hyŏk, "1583 nyŏn Kim Hyŏp Ko Kyŏnggi sosong."

20  The three representative lawsuits, especially in the late Chosŏn, were land, slave, and gravesite disputes. Gravesite disputes (*sansong*) were about the usage of a mountainside or gravesite that often involved illegal burials (*t'ujang*) due to various reasons such as economic profits, filial piety, and geomantic beliefs. For more details on gravesite disputes, see chapter 3.

21  For further details, see Shaw, *Legal Norms in a Confucian State*, 43–69; Sŏ Il-gyo, *Chosŏn wangjo hyŏngsa chedo ŭi yŏn'gu*; Sim Chae-u, *Chosŏn hugi kukka kwŏllyŏk*; To Myŏn-hoe, "1894–1905 nyŏn hyŏngsa chaep'an chedo yŏn'gu"; and Pak Pyŏng-ho, *Kŭnse ŭi pŏp*, 329–92.

22  *T'aejo sillok*, 1 (1/7/28). The translation is from Lee, de Bary, Ch'oe, and Kang, *Sources of Korean Tradition* 1:274.

23  Shaw, *Legal Norms in a Confucian State*, 46.

24  The Chosŏn dynasty divided their territory into eight provinces, which they subdivided into counties (*pu, taedohobu, mok, tohobu, kun*, and *hyŏn*). Within these units, officials and their different ranks were selected by the central government. Each county was further subdivided into districts (*myŏn* or *pang*), which comprised subdistricts (*li* or *ri*). For more details on how local administration was divided, see Sun Joo Kim and Jungwon Kim, *Wrongful Deaths*, 10–12.

25  *T'aejo sillok*, 1 (1/7/28).

26  The *Koryŏsa* states, "When beautiful women came to make claims, Sin Ton would outwardly show sympathy and entice them to his house, where he would seduce them. Their appeals would then certainly be redressed. Thereupon petitions from women increased, while officials ground their teeth in disgust." *Koryŏsa* 132: 3a–7a, cited in Lee, de Bary, Ch'oe, and Kang, *Sources of Korean Tradition*, 1:208. Also, for the petitioning activity of the Koryŏ, see Pak Chae-u, "Koryŏ hugi soji."

27  Unlike the *Great Code of Administration*, the *Continuation of the Great Code* specifies, in the beginning of its penal law section, that the two Korean codes

apply before the *Great Ming Code*. This shift in the application of the *Great Ming Code* shows how Korean legal codes had developed over the course of more than two centuries.

28 For a discussion of Confucian sage kingship, see Haboush, *The Confucian Kingship in Korea*, 29–82.

29 *T'aejong sillok*, 2 (1/11/16).

30 Ibid., 3 (2/1/26).

31 The *Kyŏngguk taejŏn* was the dynasty's first comprehensive set of legal codes; it was compiled during Sŏngjong's reign (r. 1469–94). According to the statute entitled "*Sowŏn*," the petitioner must present a grievance in person, and it must concern the petitioner personally. The petitioner was allowed to appeal to the king only after all other legal measures had been exhausted through the lower courts. See *Kyŏngguk taejŏn*, 473–74.

32 Han U-gŭn, "Sinmun'go ŭi sŏlch'i."

33 For a discussion of the lowborn in the Koryŏ dynasty, see Shultz, *Generals and Scholars*, 110–30.

34 *T'aejong sillok*, 17 (9/*yun*4/18). The Office of the Censor General strongly recommended that the king punish Yu and Kim for improperly handling the petition. The Censor General claimed that the Office of the Inspector General is the eyes and ears of the bureaucracy and is responsible for listening to people's grievances and reporting them to the king. Because Yu and Kim unfairly treated the petition, they caused Kŭmnok to beat the drum, and they should be punished for their failure in duty.

35 *Sejong sillok*, 40 (10/5/24).

36 *Sejo sillok*, 2 (1/8/7).

37 For a discussion of Chinese legal cosmology, see Jiang, *The Mandate of Heaven and the Great Ming Code*, 22–69. Also, for Chosŏn-era legal discourse on the importance of human feeling and how it played a crucial role in the adjudication of civil and criminal cases, see Jisoo M. Kim, "Law and Emotion."

38 Bodde and Morris, *Law in Imperial China*, 43–48.

39 *Sŏnjo sillok*, 4 (3/5/18).

40 For an explanation of Kwŏn Kŭn's (1352–1409) "Heaven and Man, Mind and Nature, Combined as One," see Kalton, "The Writings of Kwŏn Kŭn," 89–123.

41 *T'aejong sillok*, 13 (7/5/22).

42 Ibid., 13 (7/5/22).

43 Ibid., 4 (2/7/2).

44 Ibid., 6 (3/8/21).

45 Ibid., 31 (16/5/20).

46 *Sejong sillok*, 23 (6/1/16).

47 Ibid., 36 (9/6/14).

48 My examination of the usage of *tansong* corroborates the view that it should not be read literally to mean "to end lawsuits." Hankuk komunsŏ hakhoe, *Chosŏn ŭi ilsang, pŏpchŏng e sŏda*, 37–40.

49 *Sŏngjong sillok*, 125 (12/1/12).

50  For a discussion of civil lawsuits and *wŏn* during the reign of T'aejong, see
    *T'aejong sillok*, 4 (2/7/2), 6 (3/8/21), 6 (3/*yun*11/29), 10 (5/8/23), 11 (6/3/20), 12 (6/
    *yun*7/2), 13 (7/5/22), 14 (7/7/2), 17 (9/*yun*4/18), 18 (9/7/19), 24 (12/8/1), 24 (12/12/11), 26
    (13/9/7), 26 (13/11/11), 27 (14/2/10), 27 (14/4/16), 27 (14/5/21), 27 (14/6/6), 28 (14/8/13),
    30 (15/7/8), 31 (16/5/20), and 32 (16/7/28).

51  *T'aejong sillok*, 8 (4/10/28).

52  *Sejong sillok*, 32 (8/4/28).

53  For a discussion of penal benevolence during the Chosŏn, see Han Sang-gwŏn,
    "Sejongdae ch'idoron"; Cho Yun-sŏn, "Yŏngjodae namhyŏng, hokhyŏng p'yeji
    kwajŏng"; Sim Chae-u, "Chŏngjo dae hŭmhyul chŏnch'ik," and "Chosŏn sidae
    nŭngji ch'ŏsahyŏng chiphaeng," 153–54; and Karlsson, "Law and the Body."

54  *Sejong sillok*, 28 (7/6/17).

55  Ibid., 28 (7/6/23). For similar discussions, also see *T'aejong sillok*, 8 (4/10/28), 22
    (11/11/22), 28 (14/7/8), and 34 (17/9/19); *Sejong sillok*, 2 (0/11/3), 7 (2/*yun*1/29), 21
    (5/7/3), 28 (7/6/17), 28 (7/6/23), 32 (8/4/28), 32 (8/5/4), 38 (9/11/11), 39 (10/1/20), 48
    (12/6/10), 48 (12/4/28), 48 (12/5/15), 49 (12/7/5), 52 (13/5/16), 52 (13/6/2), 52 (13/6/13), 54
    (13/11/8), and 55 (14/1/15).

56  *T'aejong sillok*, 27 (14/4/16).

57  *Sejong sillok*, 37 (9/8/29).

58  Munro, *The Concept of Man in Early China*, 1–116.

59  *T'aejo sillok*, 1 (1/7/20).

60  *Sejong sillok*, 21 (5/7/3).

61  Cho Yun-sŏn, "Chosŏn hugi kangsang pŏmjoe," 63–68.

62  *T'aejong sillok*, 19 (10/4/8); *Sejong sillok*, 51 (13/1/26) and 52 (13/6/20); and
    *Myŏngjong sillok*, 11 (6/7/13).

63  *Sejong sillok*, 51 (13/1/19).

64  *Sejong sillok*, 52 (13/6/20). For similar discussions, see *Sejong sillok*, 53 (13/7/4), 60
    (15/4/24), and 61 (15/7/26).

65  Chŏn Pong-dŏk, *Han'guk pŏpchesa yŏn'gu*, 21–49, cited in Shaw, *Legal Norms in a
    Confucian State*, 57.

66  For a discussion of the use of special emissaries during Chŏngjo's reign, see Han
    Sang-gwŏn, *Chosŏn hugi sahoe wa sowŏn chedo*, 288–337.

67  *Sejong sillok*, 56 (14/4/12).

68  Ibid., 58 (14/11/3).

69  Ibid.

70  *Sejong sillok*, 62 (15/10/20). See also ibid., 77 (19/6/1).

71  *Sok taejŏn*, 295. See chapter 5 for further discussion on making accusations
    against unjust magistrates.

72  Cho Yun-sŏn, *Chosŏn hugi sosong yŏn'gu*, 287–302.

1   Rockhill, "Notes," 177–88.

2   The literal meaning of *kyŏkchaeng*, "to strike a gong," signified presenting a petition during the royal procession.

3   The petition drum was institutionalized following the practice of Song China. The usage of the drum seems to have appeared in the Song, but appeals were made from a much earlier period. See *T'aejong sillok*, 2 (1/11/16). According to Jonathan Ocko, the Qin (221–206 BCE) legal system recognized the right of appeal, but the practice of carrying appeals to the capital existed from at least the Sui (589–626). Nevertheless, it was during the Qing that the appellate system most actively functioned. For a discussion of capital appeals in China, see Ocko, "I'll Take It All the Way to Beijing."

4   Ocko, "I'll Take It All the Way to Beijing," 294.

5   Hara, *Chikso wa wanggwŏn*, 106–26.

6   It is not certain when the appeals system first began to be practiced, but extant sources show that the Koryŏ dynasty maintained the system. For the petitioning activity of the Koryŏ, see Pak Chae-u, "Koryŏ hugi soji ŭi ch'ŏri chŏlch'a." See also Lee, de Bary, Ch'oe, and Kang, *Sources of Korean Tradition*, 1:208.

7   *Kyŏngguk taejŏn*, 473–74.

8   *T'aejong sillok*, 17 (9/2/17).

9   *Sejong sillok*, 18 (4/11/28). The Chosŏn state attempted to circulate paper money in the early period but failed due to its continuous decrease in value. The court ceased using it by 1512, the seventh year of Chungjong's reign. The grain loan was one of the government loans provided to peasants at a specified amount of interest. Peasants would normally receive it in the spring and pay it back in the fall. See Palais, *Confucian Statecraft*, 50–60 for paper money, and 689–704 for the grain-loan system.

10  *Sejong sillok*, 40 (10/5/24).

11  *Sŏngjong sillok*, 264 (23/4/28). A gong was a musical instrument used by peasants for playing farm music.

12  *Sŏngjong sillok*, 264 (23/4/28).

13  For more on the Confucianization of Korean society, see Deuchler, *The Confucian Transformation of Korea*; Haboush, "The Confucianization of Korean Society"; and Peterson, *Korean Adoption and Inheritance*.

14  Whereas *sangŏn* and *kyŏkchaeng* were specifically used to mean petitions addressed to the sovereign, the term *soji* was used for petitions and legal documents in general that were presented at local and provincial levels. For further details of *sangŏn* and *kyŏkchaeng*, see Han Sang-gwŏn, *Chosŏn hugi sahoe wa sowŏn chedo*, 19–28.

15  *Yŏngjo sillok*, 9 (2/5/27).

16  *Yŏngjo sillok*, 81 (30/2/7).

17  *Yŏngjo sillok*, 3 (1/1/16).

18  *Simnirok*, 1:35.

19 The practice of blood writing in China was perceived to have given numinous power. The ritual of blood writing was more than a symbolic behavior that had practical effect of establishing their sanctity. See Yu, *Sanctity and Self-Inflicted Violence*, 37–61.

20 *Yŏngjo sillok*, 95 (36/4/20) and 117 (47/10/27), and *Ch'ugwanji*, 2:29–30.

21 *Yŏngjo sillok*, 2 (0/12/17).

22 Yu, *Sanctity and Self-Inflicted Violence*, 60–61.

23 *Sŭngjŏngwŏn ilgi*, Kojong, 5/3/19.

24 The Korean-script petition, formally approved by an official's red-seal stamp, was not questioned at the local level.

25 Haboush, "Gender and the Politics of Language," 243–55.

26 During this study, which examined *Old Documents*, vols. 16–26, and *Compilation Volume of the Old Documents*, vols. 1–76, I could not find a single vernacular petition written by men.

27 Kim Kyŏng-suk, "Chosŏn hugi yŏsŏng ŭi chŏngso hwaldong."

28 Unfortunately, the role of scriveners is almost invisible from the extant sources. However, it is possible to find scant writings about them in literary works. For the role of scriveners in the Chosŏn, see Pak Pyŏng-ho, *Han'guk pŏpchesa go*, 257; and Han Sang-gwŏn, "Chosŏn sidae sosong kwa woejibu," 284–89.

29 For the significant role of scriveners in the crafting of plaints in late imperial China, see Macauley, *Social Power and Legal Culture*; and Karasawa, "Between Oral and Written Cultures."

30 For a discussion about reading "fictional" elements in pardon letters in sixteenth-century France, see Davis, *Fiction in the Archives*.

31 Han Sang-gwŏn , *Chosŏn hugi sahoe wa sowŏn chedo*, 137–50. According to Han's statistics, commoners numbered higher than elite *yangban* in using oral petitions when addressing grievances.

32 Haboush states: "the interrogation procedure, which often accompanied physical torture, was as if petitions were writ on the petitioners' bodies." "Gender and the Politics of Language," 245.

33 *Chŏngjo sillok*, 35 (16/9/11).

34 For further description of the royal procession, see Bishop, *Korea and Her Neighbours*, 47–58.

35 Slaves were included in this category, because they were regarded as extended family members.

36 *Sok taejŏn*, 294–95. All the ad hoc edicts and special laws promulgated after the *Kyŏngguk taejŏn* were compiled in the *Sok taejŏn*.

37 This study does not include petitions requesting official commendation of virtuous conduct by an ancestor or another individual, because my focus is on the search for corrective justice through a petitioner's display of *wŏn*.

38 *Ilsŏngnok*, Chŏngjo, 10/9/7.

39 Haboush, "Gender and the Politics of Language in Chosŏn Korea," 246.

40 *Myŏngjong sillok*, 26 (15/5/2, 15/6/10, and 15/6/25).

41 *Wŏn sinbo sugyo chimnok sasong yuch'wi*, 155.

42 Han Sang-gwŏn, *Chosŏn hugi sahoe wa sowŏn chedo*, 48–83.

43 Ibid., 110–11. According to Han's reckoning, in the *Ilsŏngnok* of Chŏngjo's reign, there are 310 petitions by commoner women, 108 by *yangban* women, and 79 by slaves. Han does not distinguish the gender of slaves, so the last number includes both male and female slaves.

44 For further discussion of elite women's petitioning activity, see Jisoo M. Kim, "Crossing the Boundary of Inner Quarters."

45 Butler, "Performative Acts and Gender Constitution," 187–99.

46 Although the official language of legal documents was Classical Chinese, it must be mentioned that it was mixed with "clerk's writing" (*idu*). This form of clerical writing was a device in which Chinese characters were used to write down colloquial Korean, especially to indicate verb endings and other rules of Korean language that were essentially different from Chinese. When examining vernacular Korean petitions, it is sometimes difficult to read without knowing the Chinese characters, because we find transliteration of Classical Chinese and the clerk's writing.

47 For this study, I primarily examined the petitions in the *Komunsŏ chipsŏng*, vols. 1–76, which were collected by the Changsŏgak Archives of the Academy of Korean Studies, and *Komunsŏ*, vols. 16–26, which were collected by the Kyujang-gak Archives of Seoul National University. In these compiled volumes, I was unable to find a single petition written in vernacular Korean by men, whereas I found 25 vernacular Korean petitions submitted by women, out of a total of 147 petitions in both archives. Men began to submit petitions in a mixed script of classical Chinese and vernacular Korean only in the late nineteenth century. For a discussion of language reform at the turn of the twentieth century, see King, "Western Protestant Missionaries," and "Nationalism and Language Reform in Korea."

48 At the Association of Korean Studies in Europe conference in 2013, I organized a panel entitled, "Diglossia and the Linguistic Culture of Chosŏn Korea—In Memory of JaHyun Kim Haboush." Marion Eggert, Choe Key-sook, and I examined the usage of classical Chinese and vernacular Korean in the genres of poetry, novel, and legal petition. There was a consensus among panelists that the usage of the two languages in Chosŏn literary culture was far more complex than what previous studies have shown. The term "diglossia," which tends to divide into high and low culture, cannot be applied to the Chosŏn due to the heavy interaction between the two languages. For example, examining the interaction between *sijo* and *hansi*, Eggert suggests that "the notion of literary co-evolves with the entanglement of the classical Chinese and vernacular Korean literary spheres." Through an analysis of the *Namwŏngosa* novel in the nineteenth century, Choe shows how upper and lower cultures converged through vernacular usage. The writing in vernacular-Korean petitions is closer to a transliteration of classical Chinese than a representation of the sounds of spoken language. Although the panel was organized to discuss diglossia in the Chosŏn, we concluded that the framework of diglossia does not apply to that era. Thus, it is nec-

essary to further investigate the usage of two written languages in the Chosŏn and come up with an alternative framework. The term "diglossia," despite its limitations, is used here in the sense that the classical Chinese was recognized as the official "high" language, whereas the vernacular Korean was treated as the "low" language when drafting legal petitions.

49  For further discussion of dual literary culture in the Chosŏn, see Haboush, *Memoirs of Lady Hyegyŏng*, 1–36; "Gender and the Politics of Language"; "Versions and Subversions"; "Private Memory and Public History"; and *Epistolary Korea*, 1–16.

50  The increase of literacy among Chinese elite women during Ming dynasty enabled them to enjoy a far more active role in social and cultural life. See Dorothy Ko, *Teachers of the Inner Chambers*, 29–114.

51  *Chungjong sillok*, 8 (4/4/16), 9 (4/9/11). The record does not mention the crime she had committed.

52  *Chungjong sillok*, 12 (5/12/12).

53  The two versions of the *Kwanghaegun ilgi* both record the discussion about whether the Korean-script petition submitted by Madam Kim, wife of Yi Hongno (1560–1610), should be accepted. See *Kwanghaegun ilgi* (Chungch'o pon and Chŏngch'o pon; 2/5/5, 2/5/10, and 2/5/16). Also cited in Haboush, "Gender and the Politics of Language," 250.

54  For example, Madam Yi, wife of the private scholar (*yuhak*) Cho Chinsŏng, submitted a Korean-script petition, but the state did not question its written language (*Ilsŏngnok*, Chŏngjo, 11/4/4).

55  In addition to 147 women's petitions in *Komunsŏ chipsŏng*, vols. 1–76, and *Komunsŏ*, vols. 16–26, four additional elite women's petitions can be found in *Munhŏn kwa haesŏk* [Sources and interpretation]. Four additional petitions, submitted by an elite woman, Madam Cho, can also be found in different scholarly journals, which published her original petitions in full. I was able to find a total of 155 petitions that were submitted to county and provincial courts.

56  Kim Kyŏng-suk, "Chosŏn hugi yŏsŏng ŭi chŏngso hwaldong," 97.

57  In the Chosŏn dynasty, a ritual heir received two kinds of property: property for an individual and property for the entire descent group. The latter property was specifically used for serving ancestor worship. This was again divided into two kinds of property: land and slaves for the services dedicated to the direct lineal antecedents (*chewijo*), and land and slaves for collateral members of the descent group who died without heirs (*panbujo*). A ritual heir controlled all of this land and could not divide it among his siblings; law also forbade him to sell this portion of property. The fourth question Madam Im raised is related to her husband's official rank. "Prebendary" ranked land, meaning land given by the state, had to be returned to the state upon the recipient's death. However, in some cases, the state allowed the family to keep the land and made them pay tax for all or portions of the land. Thus, in this case, it seems that Madam Im had kept the land after her husband's death and then was concerned with how much of it should be returned to the state. See An Sŭng-jun, "1652 nyŏn O Sinnam ŭi ch'ŏ Im ssika kyehu," 63.

58  Ibid.

59  An Sŭng-jun, "1652 nyŏn O Sinnam ŭi ch'ŏ Im ssika kyehu," 66–67.

60  Hong Ŭn-jin first introduced Madam Cho's vernacular-Korean-script petition in her article "Kurye munhwa yussiga."

61  Madam Yi's petition and will can be found in Kim Yong-gyŏng, "Pyŏnghae Hwang ssi ga Wansan Yi ssi," 82–87. It must be noted that the contents of original sources, either in classical Chinese or vernacular Korean, are all included in this journal, along with interpretations.

62  The petition sent to the king, like the petition written in 1656, no longer exists but is mentioned in Madam Yi's will.

63  The will was first introduced in Yi Chŏng-ok, "Wansan Yi ssi yuŏn ko." It was reintroduced in Kim Yong-kyŏng , "Pyŏnghae Hwang ssiga Wansan Yi ssi," 79–82.

64  Kim Yong-kyŏng, "Pyŏnghae Hwang ssiga Wansan Yi ssi," 82–87.

65  *Yŏngjo sillok*, 6 (1/5/9).

66  Im Hyŏng-t'aek, "Charyo haejae," 362–65. Madam Kim's second petition is also presented in this article. Im primarily focuses on the political aspect of the petition and admits that he does not extend his analysis to gender aspects, such as the role of Madam Kim within the context of the Confucian patriarchal family. The second petition exists in an unedited version written in vernacular Korean.

67  Haboush, *Confucian Kingship*, 122.

68  Kim wrote *Madam Sa's Conquest of the South* while he was in exile; the novel metaphorically criticizes Sukchong's love triangle at the court. Kim, a supporter of Queen Inhyŏn, depicts her as the ideal Confucian woman.

69  The Chosŏn court's customary method of executing scholar-officials was to give them a cup of poison to drink. However, Yi Kŏnmyŏng was beheaded, which was a humiliating way to die. Two of his sons committed suicide after burying their father's body. Yu Suk-ki, *Kyŏmsanjip*, 14:30, cited in Haboush, *Confucian Kingship*, 274, note 17.

70  *Yŏngjo sillok*, 5 (1/4/25).

71  When Yŏngjo ascended the throne, Noron members initially thought that the times had shifted favorably to their side. However, because Yŏngjo was determined to overcome a factional schism that had deepened during his predecessor's reign, he tried to embrace both Noron and Soron under his *t'angp'yŏng* (magnificent harmony) policy, which sought to achieve grand harmony through impartial rule. In the year that Yŏngjo ascended the throne, the political climate was on Noron's side, but it gradually shifted to Soron's side as the king tried to embrace both factions. For details, see Haboush, *Confucian Kingship*, 117–65.

72  *Yŏngjo sillok*, 4 (1/3/2).

73  Ibid., 7 (1/8/16). Yi Imyŏng's tablet was ordered to be enshrined in Namhae, where the tablet of Admiral Yi Sunshin (1545–98) was located. Yi Sunshin was the hero who led Chosŏn forces to victory in a battle against the Japanese during the Imjin War (1592–98).

74 After Kyŏngjong's death, there was a rumor that he had died from eating pre-
   sumably poisoned pickled crab sent by Yŏngjo. This claim was never verified.
   However, Yŏngjo had to suffer severe consequences for his suspected fratricide
   during his reign.

75 After Pongsang fled, he hid somewhere in the mountains. One day, a wealthy
   man named Yi Mandŭk met Pongsang and decided to help him after listening to
   his pitiful situation. Yi Mandŭk provided him with shelter, food, and clothes.

76 *Yŏngjo sillok*, 5 (1/4/25).

77 Ibid., 5 (1/4/28).

78 Unlike Madam Kim's second petition, this initial petition is not extant; however,
   it is recorded in the *Yŏngjo sillok*. It is not certain what language Madam Kim
   used to write the first petition, but it is possible that she wrote it in the vernacular Korean script, which was the language she used in her second petition. See
   *Yŏngjo sillok*, 6 (1/5/9).

79 During the Kyŏngjong period, Yi Kiji and his father were accused of treason
   and imprisoned in the State Tribunal prison. Yi Kiji was tortured to death four
   days after his father was executed. Nine of Yi Imyŏng's family members died
   in this incident, and many scores of people were sent into exile. Madam Kim,
   Yi Kiji's wife, and Yi Pongsang's wife were all banished to Puan, in Chŏlla
   province, where they lived for three years. When Yŏngjo ascended the throne
   after Kyŏngjong's death, Yi Imyŏng's honor was restored and all three women
   returned to their home in Puyŏ. This petition was presented to Yŏngjo after
   Madam Kim was released from exile.

80 *Yŏngjo sillok*, 6 (1/5/9). After reading Madam Kim's petition, Yŏngjo sent an official to the palace gate, where she and Pongsang knelt, awaiting their punishment.
   The official conveyed the message that they need not wait for any punishment.
   Yŏngjo also commanded that the family of the slave boy who had sacrificed his
   life for Pongsang be rewarded. The king later summoned Pongsang to an audience and consoled him. I use the translation of Madam Kim's two petitions in
   Jisoo Kim, "Individual Petitions," cited in Haboush, *Epistolary Korea*, 71–74.

81 *Yŏngjo sillok*, 6 (1/5/9).

82 Im Hyŏng-t'aek, "Charyo haejae," 359.

83 *Yŏngjo sillok*, 13 (3/9/12).

84 The *Yŏngjo sillok* does not mention what kind of punishment the Office of the
   Inspector General suggested. However, Madam Kim, in her petition, mentions
   that the office recommended that Pongsang receive capital punishment and Yi
   Ingmyŏng suffer punishment for committing a felony.

85 *Yŏngjo sillok*, 5 (1/4/20). Several officials suggested to Yŏngjo that Yi Imyŏng's
   wife be provided a monthly provision because she was suffering from starvation.
   Since she was the only surviving wife among those of the four Noron ministers,
   Yŏngjo told the officials to take especially good care of her.

86 Im Hyŏng-t'aek, "Charyo haejae," 362–67.

87 *Yŏngjo sillok*, 4 (1/3/2).

88 Im Hyŏng-t'aek, "Charyo haejae," 362–67.

89  Ibid., 381–83.

90  I would like to thank one of my anonymous reviewers for suggesting this point.

91  I would like to thank Choe Key-sook for helping me to clarify my ideas about women's usage of vernacular Korean petitions.

## CHAPTER THREE. WOMEN'S GRIEVANCES AND THEIR GENDERED NARRATIVE OF *WŎN*

1  Smail, *The Consumption of Justice*, 94.

2  Ibid., 89–132.

3  For the petitioning practice at the capital level in the late Chosŏn, see Han Sang-gwŏn, *Chosŏn hugi sahoe wa sowŏn chedo*.

4  Joseph, "Brother/Sister Relationships," 55.

5  The petitions presented at the capital level is explored in the next two chapters, where I discuss how women were active agents petitioning the king when appealing grievances on behalf of family members.

6  "Incapable husbands" are those who were unable to petition because they were ill, imprisoned, or absent from home.

7  For discussions of widows in the Chosŏn, see Kim Ki-hyŏng, "Kubi sŏrhwa e nat'anan kwabu"; Chŏng Chi-yŏng, "Chosŏn hugi kwabu,"; and Jungwon Kim, "Negotiating Virtue," 137–65.

8  The Chinese character for "wang" connotes that those emotions were suppressed within one's body. Toward the end of petitions, it is common to find the expression *sinwŏn*, which means to release *wŏn*. In the Chosŏn, it was thought that negative emotions such as grievance and anger had to be released from one's body, as these negative emotions, which were considered harmful energy, could bring disorder to society.

9  For the sources of petitions submitted to county and provincial courts, see chapter 2, note 55.

10  For the role of "fictional" elements in pardon letters in sixteenth-century France, see Davis, *Fiction in the Archives*.

11  In addition to 147 women's petitions found in the *Komunsŏ chipsŏng* (vols. 1–76) and *Komunsŏ* (vols. 16–26), I also examined four additional elite women's petitions found in *Munhŏn kwa haesŏk* and four petitions submitted by an elite woman and introduced with the full original petitions in different scholarly journals. In total, I examined 155 women's petitions that were submitted to county and provincial courts. According to Han's statistics, of 418 women's petitions submitted at the capital during the reign of Chŏngjo, 310 were by commoner women and 108 by elite women. Also, there were 56 petitions submitted by slaves, but this figure includes both female and male slaves. For the statistics, see Han Sang-gwŏn, *Chosŏn hugi sahoe wa sowŏn chedo*, 110–11.

12  For further description of this text, see Chŏn Kyŏng-mok, *Yusŏp'ilji*, 367–405.

13  Based on the petitions examined, the term *sosa* or *choi* denoted a commoner woman's status, whereas *ssi* denoted an elite woman. Such a term did not

accompany the names of female slaves because they were referred to merely by their first (given) name. The *Yusŏp'ilji* reflects how the state recognized commoner women as the most active legal agents petitioning the government. In order to avoid confusion, I do not use the terms *sosa* or *ssi*; instead, I use the title "Madam" for elite women, and refer to commoner women by their surname and specify their status. For female slaves, I use their name as stated in the petitions.

14  Preface to the *Yusŏp'ilji*. The first woodblock print edition of this text, printed in Chŏnju in 1872, is located in the Kyujanggak Archive of Seoul National University, no. 6700 (1872). Also see Chŏn Kyŏng-mok, *Yusŏp'ilji*, 41.

15  Ibid., 41.

16  For the usage of *min* in petition documents, see Chŏn Kyŏng-mok, "Komunsŏ yong'ŏ puri."

17  Chŏn Kyŏng-mok, *Yusŏp'ilji*, 173.

18  Ibid., 199.

19  Song and Chŏn, *Chosŏn sidae Namwŏn Tundŏkpang ŭi Chŏnju Yi ssi wa kŭ tŭl ŭi munsŏ*, 65, cited in Chŏn Kyŏng-mok, "Komunsŏ yong'ŏ p'uri," 143–44.

20  Kim Yong-mu, "Chosŏn hugi sansong yŏn'gu."

21  Kim Sŏn-kyŏng, "Chosŏn hugi sansong"; Han Sang-gwŏn, *Chosŏn hugi sahoe wa sowŏn chedo*; Chŏn Kyŏng-mok, "Chosŏn hugi sansong yŏn'gu"; and Cho Yun-sŏn, *Chosŏn hugi sosong yŏn'gu*.

22  Chŏn Kyŏng-mok, "Sansong ŭl t'onghae pon Chosŏn hugi sapŏp chedo unyŏng silt'ae," 5–31. For further reference, see Chŏn, "Chosŏn hugi sansong yŏn'gu," and "Chosŏn hugi sansong ŭi han sarye"; and Kim Sŏn-kyŏng, "Chosŏn hugi sansong kwa sallim soyugwŏn."

23  See Kim Kyŏng-suk, "Chosŏn hugi sansong kwa sahoe kaldŭng yŏn'gu" and "18, 19 segi sajokch'ŭng."

24  Song and Chŏn, *Chosŏn sidae Namwŏn Tundŏkpang ŭi Chŏnju Yi ssi wa kŭ tŭl ŭi munsŏ*, 65, cited in Chŏn Kyŏng-mok, "Komunsŏ yong'ŏ p'uri," 143–44.

25  The date of the petition is unknown, except that it was submitted in the year *sinhae*, which could be 1731, 1791, or 1851.

26  *Komunsŏ*, 16: 200–1.

27  Ibid., 18: 438–39.

28  The year *ŭlmyo* could refer to 1735, 1795, or 1855.

29  Ibid., 18: 439–40.

30  Ibid., 18: 439–40.

31  Ibid., 18: 440–1.

32  Kim Kyŏng-suk, "18, 19 segi sajokch'ŭng," 75–83.

33  Haboush, "Confucianization of Korean Society" and Deuchler, *Confucian Transformation of Korea*, 231–82.

34  In the early years of the Chosŏn, daughters shared ritual duties and continued to receive equal shares of inheritance with sons. However, these practices gradually changed as society Confucianized by the mid-seventeenth century. For the practice of ritual heirship, see Deuchler, *Confucian Transformation*, 179–201, 231–82.

35 Deuchler, *Confucian Transformation*, 231–82 and Peterson, *Korean Adoption and Inheritance*.

36 Deuchler, *Confucian Transformation*; Peterson, *Korean Adoption and Inheritance*; and Ch'oe Chae-sŏk, *Han'guk kajok yŏn'gu*.

37 Chŏng Chi-yŏng, "Chosŏn hugi ŭi yŏsŏng hoju yŏn'gu"; Kim Kyŏng-suk, "Chosŏn hugi yŏsŏng ŭi chŏngso hwaldong"; and Jungwon Kim, "'You Must Avenge on My Behalf.'"

38 This petition was first introduced in Yi Chŏng-yŏp, *Kŭnjonaegansŏn*, 29–33. It was reintroduced in An Sŭng-jun, "1689 nyŏn Chŏng ssi puin."

39 Private scholars were those from the *yangban* class who did not hold positions in the bureaucracy due to their failure to pass the civil service examination.

40 For details on the deprivation of daughters' ritual rights, see Deuchler, *Confucian Transformation*, 129–78.

41 An Sŭng-jun, "1689 nyŏn Chŏng ssi puin," 93.

42 *Sukchong sillok*, 46 (34/8/20).

43 An Sŭngjun, "1689 nyŏn Chŏng ssi puin," 89–95.

44 Haboush, "Filial Emotions and Filial Values," 129–77.

45 Ibid.

46 Duncan, "The *Naehun* and the Politics of Gender," 43–7.

47 Regarding petitions related to seeking endorsements, see Chŏng Kŭng-sik, "Charyo: 16 segi iban."

48 The year *kyech'uk* could refer to 1733, 1793, or 1853. In this petition, Nam did not specify her status using either *ssi* or *sosa*. She identified herself only as a widow.

49 It is not certain whether the five paddies she inherited were from her husband or her natal parents. She stated only that these paddies were bought from a male slave of Mr. Cho in the year *chŏngmyo*.

50 *Ch'ŏk* was a unit used to measure length during the Chosŏn. There were *chi-ch'ŏk* and *yangjŏn-ch'ŏk* for measuring distance. The latter was used for land survey and registration. During the fifteenth century, one *yangjŏn-ch'ŏk* of first-grade land was equivalent to 99.296 centimeters in length. See Pak Hŭng-su, "Toryanghyŏng chedo," 617, cited in Sun Joo Kim and Jungwon Kim, *Wrongful Deaths*, xiii.

51 *Komunsŏ*, 20: 234–35.

52 The year *chŏngmyo* could refer to 1747, 1807, or 1867.

53 *Komunsŏ*, 20: 236.

54 The year *ŭllyu* could refer to 1705, 1765, 1825, or 1885.

55 *Komunsŏ*, 20: 360–61.

56 During the Chosŏn, slaves were divided into two categories: public or state-owned slaves (*kongnobi*) and privately owned slaves (*sanobi*). This petition was submitted in the second month of a year that cannot be ascertained due to the condition of the original document.

57 *Komunsŏ*, 20: 143.

58 The year *sinch'uk* could be 1721, 1781, 1841, or 1901.

59 *Nyang* was a unit of measurement for coins used as currency during the Chosŏn. Each *nyang* weighed approximately 37 grams.

60 *Komunsŏ*, 25: 126–27.

61 The year *chŏngmi* could be 1727, 1787, 1847, or 1907.

62 *Komunsŏ*, 25: 356–57.

63 Because many cases were delayed at county and provincial levels, some schol-ars suggest that petitioners often bypassed intermediate courts and directly petitioned the king to redress grievances. One scholar goes so far as to claim that such practice impeded the development of a modern legal system. See Cho Yun-sŏn, *Chosŏn hugi sosong yŏn'gu*, 287–302; see also Chŏn Kyŏng-mok, "Sansong ŭl t'onghae pon Chosŏn hugi sapŏp chedo unyŏng silt'ae," 5–31.

64 The year *musin* could be 1728, 1788, 1848, or 1908.

65 *Komunsŏ*, 22: 105–6.

66 Ibid.

67 For discussions of how nonelite women were relatively uninfluenced by Confucian chastity ideology in the late Chosŏn, see Chŏng Chi-yŏng, "Chosŏn hugi kwabu,"; see also Jungwon Kim, "Negotiating Virtue." For a discussion of chastity ideology and female moral agency in Qing China, see Theiss, *Disgraceful Matters*.

68 *Komunsŏ*, 25: 502–3.

69 Ibid., 17: 378.

70 For further discussion of how ruling authorities emphasized a married man's filiality toward his mother-in-law in a property dispute case, see Jisoo M. Kim, "Law and Emotion."

71 The year *sinsa* could refer to 1701, 1761, 1821, or 1881.

72 *Komunsŏ*, 25: 480–1.

73 Ibid., 25: 480–1.

74 *Komunsŏ chipsŏng*, 65: 281.


CHAPTER FOUR. SEEKING VINDICATION OR BEGGING PARDON
ON BEHALF OF THE LIVING

1 Chaedae died in prison during the course of the murder trial. The source does not mention the cause of Chaedae's death, but we can presume that it was due to judicial torture. See *Simnirok*, 9: 77 and *Ch'ugwanji*, 2: 164–72.

2 Jean-Klein, "Mothercraft, Statecraft, and Subjectivity," 100–27.

3 For a discussion of women petitioning for husbands in Japan, see Walthall "Devoted Wives/Unruly Women."

4 According to Sim Chae-u's research, out of 1,112 criminal cases recorded in the *Simnirok*, 150 cases involve petitions of appeal by family members of either the accused or the victim. Among these 150 cases, 142 (95 percent) are related to homicide; 2 were for economic offences; 3 were for violation of authorial power; and 3 were for the infringement of social customs. For details, see Sim Chae-u, "*Simnirok* yŏn'gu," 90–117, 175–216.

5 Chartier, *Cultural History*, 7.

6 Chartier, *On the Edge of the Cliff*, 91.

7 Ahmed, *The Cultural Politics of Emotion*, 193.

8   Ibid., 1–19.

9   *Yŏngjo sillok*, 95 (36/4/20) and 117 (47/10/27), and *Ch'ugwanji*, 2:29–30.

10   I would like to thank Clark Sorensen for pointing out that writing petitions in blood were used not only to arouse sympathy but also to express the true sincerity of plaintiffs.

11   *Wŏn sinbo sugyo chimnok*, 419.

12   *T'aejong sillok*, 24 (12/12/11). See also *Hyŏnjong sillok*, 1 (0/8/6), for a younger brother's represention of an elder brother.

13   Another example of a son's petition for his father can be found in a case dated 1418. In this case, Pak Sŭp ordered his son to petition on his behalf. It is not uncommon to find that junior family members were ordered by senior ones to convey their grievances to the king. See *T'aejong sillok*, 35 (18/1/30). Examples of a son's petition on behalf of his father prior to the eighteenth century can also be found in *Injo sillok*, 13 (4/yun6/6), 25 (9/8/11), and 34 (15/5/21); *Hyŏnjong sillok*, 13 (7/12/16); and *Sukchong sillok*, 6 (3/2/11).

14   *T'aejong sillok*, 17 (9/2/17).

15   *Sejong sillok*, 67 (17/1/14).

16   *Injo sillok*, 42 (19/7/20).

17   *Hyojong sillok*, 10 (4/5/29).

18   A *yangban* woman was usually referred to by her surname. However, the record also states Madam Yun's first name, Tanil.

19   *Hyŏnjong sillok*, 14 (8/11/14).

20   Madam Yun's father, Yun Kukkyŏng, held the *chinsa* degree. There were two tiers of civil service examination in the Chosŏn: the lower (*sokwa*) and the higher (*taekwa*). While the lower examination conferred the *saengwŏn* or *chinsa* degree, the higher bestowed the *munkwa* degree.

21   *Hyŏnjong sillok*, 14 (8/11/3) and (8/11/13).

22   Ibid., 14 (8/11/14).

23   For further details of the case, see *Hyŏnjong sillok*, 14 (8/7/29), (8/11/3), (8/11/13), and (8/11/14).

24   This finding matches Sim Chae-u's total of 150 criminal cases in the *Simnirok* that involved petitions. However, his study does not include the total number of petitions. See Sim Chae-u, "*Simnirok* yŏn'gu."

25   Although the *Simnirok* contains only one case of a husband petitioning on behalf of his wife, I found two more such cases in the *Sillok*. See *T'aejong sillok*, 32 (16/7/28) and *Sukchong sillok*, 8 (5/3/10).

26   Status cannot be included here because I could not find a single case of a master petitioning for a slave. On relationality, see Joseph, "Gender and Relationality."

27   Although illustrations of filial piety by sons held greater public value, this does not mean that illustrations by daughters were devalued. Married daughters continued to be filial toward their natal parents, and this was expected to a certain extent despite its irregularity. On women's filial piety, see Haboush, "Filial Emotions and Filial Values."

28  On widow remarriage, see Chŏng Chiyŏng, "Chosŏn hugi kwabu."

29  For a discussion of a son's filial piety and benevolent ruling in the homicide cases of Qing China, see Buoye, "Filial Felons," 109–24.

30  For a discussion about the hegemonic and popular discourses of filial emotions, see Haboush, "Filial Emotions and Filial Values."

31  *Ilsŏngnok*, Chŏngjo, 10/2/26.

32  Ibid., 11/2/6.

33  Ibid., 10/2/26.

34  Ibid., 11/3/9.

35  Ibid., 10/2/26.

36  It is uncertain why the king pardoned the husband; the record does not give further information.

37  *Ilsŏngnok*, Chŏngjo, 10/2/26.

38  *Ch'ugwanji*, 2:147–50.

39  Ibid., 2:69–72.

40  *Ilsŏngnok*, Chŏngjo, 10/2/26. This murder case is also recorded in *Simnirok*, 17:156–60. These page numbers are from the classical Chinese and not the translated version.

41  Whereas the *Ilsŏngnok* records the petitioner by her last name, Kim, the *Simnirok* records her first (given) name, Sŏngnyŏn (*Ilsŏngnok*, Chŏngjo, 11/4/4, and *Simnirok*, 16: 156–60).

42  *Ilsŏngnok*, Chŏngjo, 11/4/4.

43  Ibid., 11/8/18.

44  *Simnirok*, 16:159–60.

45  *Sukchong sillok*, 56 (41/9/18).

46  *Ilsŏngnok*, Chŏngjo, 13/4/27.

47  As this case shows, in the late Chosŏn, private scholars often married commoner women. It was not uncommon for a commoner man to identify himself as a private scholar. For a discussion about the usage of the term *yuhak*, see Ch'oe Sŭng-hee, *Komunsŏ rŭl t'onghae pon Chosŏn hugi sahoe*, 59–96.

48  *Ilsŏngnok*, Chŏngjo, 13/4/27.

49  Ibid., 13/4/27


CHAPTER FIVE. IN SEARCH OF JUSTICE ON BEHALF OF THE DEAD

1  *Yŏngjo sillok*, 117 (47/10/27).

2  Scarry, *The Body in Pain*, 10.

3  Scarry, *The Body in Pain*, 3–11.

4  On the relationship between pain and imagining, see Scarry, *The Body in Pain*, 161–80.

5  Although the two proverbs refer to women, they were often used in reference to men in the discourse about *wŏn*, and the state treated the *wŏn* of the genders equally. *Sejong sillok*, 48 (12/6/10).

6  *T'aejong sillok*, 1 (1/1/14), 2 (1/10/20), 10 (5/8/23), 24 (12/8/1), and 31 (16/5/20); *Sejong*

*sillok*, 7 (2/*yun* 1/29), 28 (7/6/17), 18 (7/6/23), 45 (11/7/2), and 48 (12/6/10).

7   Shaw, *Legal Norms*, 118–22.

8   Shklar, *The Faces of Injustice*, 1–14.

9   *T'aejong sillok*, 1 (1/1/14), 2 (1/10/20), 10 (5/8/23), 24 (12/8/1), and 31 (16/5/20); *Sejong sillok*, 7 (2/*yun* 1/29), 28 (7/6/17), 18 (7/6/23), 45 (11/7/2), and 48 (12/6/10).

10  For details about the state's consciousness of *somin* protection, see Yi T'ae-jin, "Chosŏn sidae 'minbon' ŭisik," 22–30.

11  Nussbaum, *Hiding from Humanity*, 27.

12  Ibid., 8.

13  *Sŭngjŏngwŏn ilgi*, Hyŏnjong, 7/11/11; Cho Yun-sŏn, "Chosŏn hugi kangsang pŏmjoe," 67.

14  *Sŭngjŏngwŏn ilgi*, Hyŏnjong, 7/12/17; Cho Yun-sŏn, "Chosŏn hugi kangsang pŏmjoe," 67.

15  *Sok taejŏn*, 295.

16  See *Sukchong sillok*, 42 (31/9/6); *Pibyŏnsa tŭngnok*, Sukchong, 31/7/13 and 31/9/19; and *Sŭngjŏngwŏn ilgi*, Sukchong, 31/7/13 and 31/9/19.

17  During the Chosŏn, Cheju Island was divided into three counties: Cheju in the middle of the island, Chŏng'ŭi in the west, and Taejŏng in the east. In total, there were three county magistrates on Cheju.

18  *Sukchong sillok*, 42 (31/9/6).

19  Ibid., 42 (31/9/6).

20  *Kyŏngguk taejŏn*, 459.

21  *Sukchong sillok*, 42 (31/9/6).

22  Here, the word *homicide* refers to a murder committed by a private individual.

23  *Kyŏngguk taejŏn*, 473–74.

24  *Sok taejŏn*, 295. The *Veritable Record* records two other cases during the Sukchong period in which magistrates were punished based on women's petitions; one is a petition by a *yangban* woman, Madam An, and the other is a petition by a commoner woman (*Sukchong sillok*, 33 [25/9/13] and 46 [34/2/5]).

25  *Sukchong sillok*, 46 (34/2/12).

26  Ibid., 42 (31/9/6).

27  Gravesite litigation was one of the three major litigations of the late Chosŏn, along with cases involving land and slaves. This particular case was understood as a dispute over the ownership of a mountain. For further details about gravesite litigation, see chapter 3.

28  *Chŏngjo sillok*, 40 (18/8/26).

29  In the record, Sŏ Yuhwa is referred to as a former magistrate of Changdan. Thus, it can be inferred that Sŏ's term as magistrate in Changdan had ended by the time the case was investigated. The central government appointed magistrates to counties for 1,800 days.

30  *Taejŏn t'ongp'yŏn*, 627–28.

31  Cho Yun-sŏn argues that petitioners utilized the petition system as a type of legal institution to resolve legal disputes. In the eighteenth century, people increasingly bypassed the intermediate courts and used the capital appeal in

order to bring immediate settlement. See Cho Yun-sŏn, *Chosŏn hugi sosong yŏn'gu.*

32  Nubola, "Supplications in the Italian States," 36.

33  *Chŏngjo sillok*, 40 (18/8/26).

34  *Taejŏn t'ongp'yŏn*, 589.

35  *Chŏngjo sillok*, 40 (18/8/26).

36  According to the legal code, if an official used punishment improperly, he would receive one hundred beatings and three years of exile. If a suspect died during that punishment, then the magistrate would receive one hundred beatings and be permanently expelled from his official post. *Taejŏn t'ongp'yŏn*, 601.

37  For details about the *Codes for the Treatment of Prisoners*, see Sim Chae-u, "Chŏngjo dae *hŭmhyul chŏnch'ik.*"

38  *Taejŏn t'ongp'yŏn*, 603.

39  *Chŏngjo sillok*, 40 (18/8/26).

40  Han Sang-gwŏn, *Chosŏn hugi sahoe wa sowŏn chedo*, 110.

41  In 1750, during Yŏngjo's reign, another elite woman petitioned in protest against her husband's unjust death. She stated that Kim Kwang'u, a former magistrate of Haeju, had assaulted and killed her husband. However, her effort was in vain, because the Board of Punishments neglected to convey her petition to the king. Kwŏn Kiŏn, who became aware of her appeal, reported it to the king and recommended relieving the official in charge of the petition and arresting the former magistrate. Yŏngjo issued the order as proposed. See *Yŏngjo sillok*, 72 (26/9/25).

42  *Sukchong sillok*, 33 (25/yun7/8); *Chŏngjo sillok*, 4 (1/7/20).

43  *Chŏngjo sillok*, 4 (1/7/20).

44  Ibid., 42 (19/6/11).

45  Ibid., 45 (20/8/29).

46  *Ilsŏngnok*, Chŏngjo, 3/8/13.

47  Hiroshi, "Richō jinkō kansuru mibun kaikyubetsuteki kansatsu [Observations on the status and class of the Yi dynasty population]," cited in Haboush, *Confucian Kingship*, 87.

48  For statistics, see Kim Yong-sŏp, *Chosŏn hugi nongŏpsa yŏn'gu*, 427; Chŏng Sŏk-chong, *Chosŏn hugi sahoe pyŏndong yŏn'gu*, 248–51; Susan Shin, "Social Structure of Kŭmhwa County"; and Wagner, "Social Stratification."

49  The *Komunsŏ* compiled by the Kyujanggak Archive of Seoul National University contains many original manuscripts of commoners' petitions requesting the government to endorse their contracts selling their bodies as slaves.

50  In this study, usage of the term "intermarriage" will be limited to marriage between a commoner and a slave.

51  For details about intermarriage, see Palais, *Confucian Statecraft*, 215–25; Han Sang-gwŏn, "15 segi noryangch'ŏ kyohon chŏngch'aek." Han compares intermarriage law in the *Koryŏsa*, the *Great Ming Code*, and the *Kyŏngguk taejŏn*. He claims that while China banned intermarriage between a slave man and commoner woman, the Chosŏn state tacitly approved such intermarriage in order to maintain the slave owners' interests.

52  *T'aejong sillok*, 2 (1/7/27); Han Sang-gwŏn, "15 segi noryangch'ŏ kyohon chŏngch'aek, 64.

53  *T'aejong sillok*, 10 (5/9/22); Han Sang-gwŏn, "15 segi noryangch'ŏ kyohon chŏngch'aek," 65. Slaves in the Chosŏn era were divided into two categories: public slaves who were owned by the state, known as *kongnobi*, and private slaves who were owned by individuals, called *sanobi*. Private slaves were subdivided into service slaves (*solgŏ nobi*) and outside-resident slaves (*oegŏ nobi*). Service slaves lived with their masters in the same house, whereas outside-resident slaves lived separately from their masters while providing their labor. For details about public and private slaves, see Chŏn Hyŏng-t'aek, *Chosŏn yangban sahoe wa nobi*, 193–450.

54  *T'aejong sillok*, 27 (14/6/27); Han Sang-gwŏn, "15 segi noryangch'ŏ kyohon chŏngch'aek," 66.

55  Intermarriage was frequently practiced in the fifteenth century. According to old privately owned documents, slave owners recorded the offspring of a slave man and a commoner woman as "co-produced children" (*pyŏngsan*). Slave owners explicitly stated ownership over these children in their property documents. According to Han Sang-gwŏn's statistics, which are based on fifteenth-century documents from several regions, a quarter or a third of the total number of slaves owned were offspring of a slave man and a commoner woman ("15 segi noryangch'ŏ kyohon chŏngch'aek," 72–82).

56  Han Sang-gwŏn, "15 segi noryangch'ŏ kyohon chŏngch'aek," 67–72.

57  Kim Sŏng-u, *Chosŏn chunggi kukka wa sajok*, 125–59.

58  After the two sets of wars, the Chosŏn landscape was devastated and the state's power was greatly undermined. Although the wars brought social and political turmoil, the state experienced the rise of a market economy that led to various forms of social transformation. One of the most conspicuous of these changes took place in the existing social hierarchy. Although the state maintained the basic structure of the status system until the late nineteenth century, social mobility between statuses at that time was relatively flexible compared with the early Chosŏn, and this caused social conflicts between different statuses as well as classes, for example, between weakened literati and rich commoners, affluent commoners and poor commoners, and masters and slaves. For details on social transformations of the late Chosŏn, see Chŏng Sŏk-chong, *Chosŏn hugi sahoe pyŏndong yŏn'gu*.

59  Cho Yun-sŏn, *Chosŏn hugi sosong yŏn'gu*, 175–249.

60  "Former slaves" are those who were born as slaves but legally attained commoner status later in life.

61  *Sok taejŏn*, 311–12.

62  Taking into consideration that most extant petitions are from the late Chosŏn, the year *ŭlmi* could be 1715, 1775, 1835, or 1895.

63  *Komunsŏ*, 19: 452–53. Another commoner woman, surnamed Kim, petitioned the provincial governor on behalf of her daughters, who were also unfairly treated as slaves by a *yangban* with the surname Sin (*Komunsŏ*, 25: 480–81).

64  *Simnirok*, 1: 33–36. This volume consists of both classical Chinese and translated

versions of original texts. The pages cited here are from the classical Chinese version. Sŏng Yongsŏk's case can also be found in *Ilsŏngnok*, Chŏngjo, 1/7/19, 1/10/16/, 1/10/17, 2/5/11, 2/5/28, 2/5/29, 3/1/6, and 10/11/7.

65  *Simnirok*, 1: 33.

66  *Ilsŏngnok*, Chŏngjo, 2/5/11. It is unclear who Sŏ Poksu was, but it seems that the former slave here was referring to the victim.

67  *Simnirok*, 1: 34; *Ilsŏngnok*, Chŏngjo, 2/5/29.

68  For a similar discussion of benevolent rulings on capital crimes in late imperial China, see Buoye, "Suddenly Murderous Intent Arose."

69  The king dispatched special emissaries to the provinces when there was royal suspicion that the local administration of justice was not up to par. The usage of special emissaries functioned as a system of surveillance over local administration. For special emissaries, see Chŏn Pong-dŏk, "Amhaeng ŏsa chedo yŏn'gu," 1–186; Shaw, *Legal Norms*, 56–59; Han Sang-gwŏn, *Chosŏn hugi sahoe wa sowŏn chedo*, 303–37; and Ko Sŏk-kyu, *Amhaeng ŏsa ran muŏsinga*.

70  Chŏngjo, during his reign, further systematized the petition system and allowed subjects to present either a verbal or written petition during the royal procession. The authorization of subjects to petition the sovereign directly seems not to have been practiced in either China or Japan. In the case of China, petitioners attempted to petition during the emperor's procession, but this was strictly restricted, and petitioners were punished for making such petitions. Acessibility to the king during the Chosŏn allowed subjects to present their petitions, and this added to the number of capital appeals. Petitioners in the city would have been aware of the dates of the royal procession and would appropriately time the submission of their petitions to it. Hŏ Kyŏng seems to have made his petition during Chŏngjo's procession. On China's capital appeals, see Ocko, "I'll Take It All the Way to Beijing."

71  *Simnirok*, 1: 35.

72  Ahmed, *Cultural Politics of Emotions*, 28–31.

73  William Shaw also conducted research using *Simnirok* records, but his statistics come from a selection of one hundred cases. Sim Chae-u conducted a more comprehensive study, basing his statistics on all 1,112 cases. I relied on Sim Chae-u's statistics.

74  Sim Chae-u, "*Simnirok* yŏn'gu," 197. Out of 150 cases, 142 were homicides. The other eight cases include the violation of an authority's power, infringement of social custom, and economic crime.

75  Roberts, "Justice and Rectification," 24.

76  Ibid., 21–28.

77  *Yŏngjo sillok*, 118 (48/1/16).


CONCLUSION

1  Although we cannot find sons filing complaints against fathers, it is possible to see examples of wives petitioning against husbands. For instance, Madam Sin,

the wife of Yu Chŏnggi, made an accusation against Yu to report his wrong-ful deed as a patriarchal authority. Yu initiated a suit for divorce when Madam Sin showed outright jealousy over a concubine and failed to perform her duty as a faithful wife. She then filed a counterplaint in which she defended herself and accusing her husband of being responsible for the conflict. After a long and heated debate of this case among central government officials, the king ultimately denied the divorce. *Sukchong sillok*, 40 (30/10/9 and 30/11/14) and 53 (39/1/25, 39/4/27, and 39/5/21). For an example of master-slave relationship, see Hŏ Kyŏng's case examined in chapter 5. It was often the family members of slaves who filed complaints against masters. Also see *Sejong sillok*, 79 (19/11/4).

2  Sun Joo Kim, *Marginality and Subversion*, 88.

3  Lee et al., *Sources of Korean Tradition*, 2: 270.

4  Smail, *The Consumption of Justice*, 242–46.

5  Ibid., 245.

6  Ibid. , 246.

7  In the context of Japan, it was during the Meiji restoration (1868–1912) that the government deprived women of some of the privileges they enjoyed during the Tokugawa period (1603–1868). I would like to thank one of my anonymous reviewers for making this point.

8  Chōsen Sōtokufu, *Chōsen minjirei*, 18.

9  Chōsen Sōtokufu, *Chōsen kyūkan seido chōsa jigyō gaiyō*, 16–17.

10  Hatoyama, *Nihon minpōsōron*, 89–106.

11  Chang Pyŏng-in, "Chosŏn sidae wa ilje sidae yŏsŏng," 230.

12  Kim Tu-hŏn, *Han'guk kajok chedo yŏn'gu*, 332–33, cited in Chang Pyŏng-in, "Chosŏn sidae wa ilje sidae yŏsŏng," 230.

13  Pae Kyŏng-suk, *Han'guk yŏsŏng sapŏpsa*, 90–92, cited in Chang Pyŏng-in, "Chosŏn sidae wa ilje sidae yŏsŏng," 230.

14  Daniel Smail discusses how ordinary people in Marseille made financial invest-ments in order to seek emotional satisfaction by bringing disputes with their neighbors to court. See Smail, *The Consumption of Justice*, 1–28.

15  I would like to thank two anonymous reviewers for encouraging me to delve further into the meaning of individual, family, and collective *wŏn*.

# Glossary

*amnyangwich'ŏn*　壓良為賤　oppressing commoners as slaves

Changyewŏn　掌隸院　the Board of Slaves
*ch'iljŏng*　七情　the Seven Emotions
*ch'ŏ*　妻　wife
*chŏhwa*　楮貨　paper money
*ch'ŏk*　尺　a unit of length
*chŏng* (Ch. *qing*)　情　emotions, feeling
*chŏngmi*　丁未　name of a year in the sixty-year cycle (1727, 1787, or 1847)
*chongmopŏp*　從母法　matrifilial succession law
*chŏngmyo*　丁卯　name of a year in the sixty-year cycle (1747, 1807, or 1867)
*ch'ŏlli*　天理　heavenly principle
*ch'ŏnmin*　賤民　lowborn
*ch'ŏnmin*　天民　Heaven's people
*ch'ŏnsim*　天心　the mind of Heaven
*ch'ŏp*　妾　concubine
*Chosŏn wangjo sillok*　朝鮮王朝實錄　Veritable records of the Kings of the Chosŏn dynasty
*Ch'u-an kŭp kug-an*　推案及鞫案　Records of Ch'u and Kuk Hearings
*Ch'ugwanji*　秋官志　Treatise on the Board of Punishments
*chungin*　中人　middle people

*gongŭi*　公義　public (or universal) justice, public righteousness

Hansŏngbu　漢城府　Capital Magistracy
*hyŏn*　縣　lesser prefecture or prefecture
*Hŭmhŭm sinsŏ*　欽欽新書　New writings on circumspection in judicial decisions
*humhyul*　欽恤　judicial prudence
*Hŭmhyul chŏnch'ik*　欽恤典則　Codes for the Treatment of Prisoners
*hunmin chŏngŭm*　訓民正音　correct sound for the instruction of the people
*hyangyak*　鄉約　community compact
*hyŏlsŏ*　血書　writing with blood

Hyŏngjo　刑曹　Board of Punishments
*hwanja*　換資　state loan grain

*iban*　入案　endorsement document
*idu*　吏讀　clerk's writing
*Ilsŏngnok*　日省錄　Records of daily reflections
*inchŏng*　人情　human feeling
*insim*　人心　human mind
*insŏng*　人性　human nature

*kabo*　甲午　name of a year in the sixty-year cycle (1714, 1774, 1834, or 1894)
*kamjŏng*　感情　emotion, feeling, and sentiment
*kapja*　甲子　name of a year in the sixty-year cycle (1744, 1804, or 1864)
*ki*　氣　(material) force
*kigang*　紀綱　rules and laws
*kisaeng*　妓生　female entertainer
*Komunsŏ*　古文書　old documents
*Komunsŏ chipsŏng*　古文書集成　Compilation volume of old documents
*kongnobi*　公奴婢　public slaves, state-owned slaves
*Koryŏsa*　高麗史　History of Koryŏ
*kukpŏp*　國法　state law
*kun*　郡　lesser county
*Kuun mong*　九雲夢　*Nine-Cloud Dream*
*kyech'uk*　癸丑　name of a year in the sixty-year cycle (1733, 1793, or 1853)
*kyemyo*　癸卯　name of a year in the sixty-year cycle (1903)
*kyohwa*　教化　moral transformation
*kyŏkchaeng*　擊錚　oral petition
*Kyŏngguk taejŏn*　經國大典　Great code of administration
*kyŏngo*　庚午　name of a year in the sixty–year cycle (1750, 1810, or 1870)

*li*　里　a measuring unit of distance approximately 3.3 miles
*li*　理　principle

*min*　民　people
*minbon*　民本　people as the basis of the state
*mok*　牧　special county
*musin*　戊申　name of a year in the sixty-year cycle (1728, 1788, or 1848)
*myŏn*　面　district

*Naehun*　內訓　Instructions for the inner quarters
*naejaejŏk palchŏnron*　內在的發展論　internal development theory
*Noron*　老論　Patriarch's Faction
*nyang*　兩　a unit of measurement for coins used as currency

*oegŏ nobi*　外居奴婢　outside-resident slaves

*oksong*　獄訟　criminal suits

*Ŏnmun*　諺文　vernacular Korean

*pang*　坊　district

Pibyŏnsa　備邊司　Border Defense Command

*Pibyŏnsa tŭngnok*　備邊司謄錄　Records of the Border Defense Command

*pirihosong*　非理好訟　those who love to initiate improper lawsuits

Poch'ungdae　補充隊　Supplementary Department

P'odoch'ŏng　捕盜聽　Constabulary

*pu*　府　special city

*pun*　憤　anger

*p'ungsu*　風水　geomancy

*punt'ong*　憤痛　anger and pain

*punwang*　憤枉　anger and grievance

*punwŏn*　憤冤　anger and grievance

*pyŏlgŭp mun'gi*　別級文記　"special gift writ," an inheritance document given to an individual on certain occasions such as a birth, wedding, examination success, etc.

*pyŏngsan*　幷産　co-produced children

*ri* or *li*　里　subdistrict

*sa*　士　scholars; scholar-officials; a name of official rank

*sadaebu*　士大夫　scholar-officials

*sadan*　四端　The Four Beginnings

*sadan ch'iljŏng*　四端七情　The Four Beginnings and Seven Emotions

Sahŏnbu　司憲府　Office of the Inspector-General

*Sambongjip*　三峯集　Collected writings of Sambong

*sanggan*　相奸　illicit sexual intercourse

*sangmin*　常民　commoner

*sangmyŏng*　償命　requital for a life

*sangŏn*　上言　written petition

*sangso*　上疎　memorial-type petitions

*sanobi*　私奴婢　private slaves, privately owned slaves

*sansong*　山訟　gravesite dispute

*sasong*　詞訟　civil suits

*Sasong yuch'wi*　詞訟類聚　Classification of Legal Proceedings

*Sassi Namjŏng Ki*　謝氏南征記　Madam Sa's Conquest of the South

*Sayok*　私慾　personal desire

*Sillok*　實錄　Veritable Records

*Simnirok*　審理錄　Records of Stating and Hearing

*sinch'uk*　辛丑　name of a year in the sixty-year cycle (1721, 1781, 1841, or 1901)

*sinhae*　辛亥　name of a year in the sixty-year cycle (1731, 1791, or 1851)

*Sinim sahwa*　辛壬士禍　literati purge of 1721–22
*sinmun'go*　申聞鼓　petition drum
*sinsa*　辛巳　name of a year in the sixty-year cycle (1701, 1761, 1821, or 1881)
*sinwŏn*　伸冤　redressing grievance
*soji*　所志　petitions in general that were submitted to county and provincial courts
*Sok taejŏn*　續大典　Continuation of the Great Code
*solgŏ nobi*　率居奴婢　service slaves
*somin*　小民　small people or marginalized people
*Sŏnggyungwan*　成均館　Royal College
*Songnyang*　贖良　purchase of commoner status
*Soron*　少論　Disciples' Faction
*sosa*　召史　title for a commoner woman
*sowŏn*　訴冤　appealing grievances
*ssi*　氏　Madam
*Sukchong sillok*　肅宗實錄　Veritable records of Sukchong
*Sŭngjŏngwŏn*　承政院　Royal Secretariat
*Sŭngjŏngwŏn ilgi*　承政院日記　Records of the Royal Secretariat

*taebu*　大夫　a name of official rank that was higher than *sa*
*taedohobu*　大都護府　greater county
*Taejŏn*　大典　Great Codes
*Taejŏn t'ongp'yŏn*　大典通編　Comprehensive Great Code
*Taemyŏngnyul*　大明律　Great Ming Code
*Taemyŏngnyul chikhae*　大明律直解　Directly interpreted *Great Ming Code*
*tanja*　單子　petitions submitted by ruling aristocrats
*tansong*　斷訟　stop suits
*tao* (Ch. *dao*)　道　the Way
tohobu　都護府　county
*tongnyŏ*　獨女　single woman
*t'ong*　痛　pain
*t'ongmun*　通文　circular letter
*tosim*　道心　the Way of the mind
*t'ujang*　偷葬　illegal burials
*tŭngjang*　等狀　joint petitions

*uguk mangga*　憂國忘家　worry about the state and forget about your family
*ŭi* (Ch. *yi*)　義　justice, righteousness, propriety
*Ŭigŭmbu*　義禁府　State Tribunal
*Ŭijŏngbu*　議政府　State Council
*ŭinyŏ*　矣女　"I" used to designate a woman
*ŭisin*　矣身　"I" used to designate a man
*ŭisong*　議送　petitions submitted to provincial court
*ŭllyu*　乙酉　name of a year in the sixty-year cycle (1705, 1765, 1825, or 1885)

*ŭlmi*　乙未　name of a year in the sixty-year cycle (1715, 1775, 1835, or 1895)
*ŭlmyo*　乙卯　name of a year in the sixty-year cycle (1735, 1795, or 1855)
*umin*　愚民　ignorant people
*ŭmyok*　淫慾　sexual desire

*wŏn*　冤　injustice or grievance
*wŏnjŏng*　冤情　grievous situation
*wŏnjŏng*　原情　petitions
*wŏnpun*　冤憤　grievance/anger
*Wŏn sinbo sugyo chimnok sasong yuch'wi*　原新補受教輯錄 詞訟類聚　Original
　　and supplementary compilation of royal edicts and litigation cases
*wŏnt'ong*　冤痛　grievance/pain

*yangban*　兩班　ruling aristocrats
*yangch'ŏn*　良賤　the good people and the lowborn
*yangin*　良人　commoner
*Yejo*　禮曹　Board of Rites
*yuhak*　幼學　private scholar
*Yullye yoram*　律例要覽　Conspectus of laws and precedents
*Yusŏp'ilji*　儒胥必知　Necessary knowledge for scholar-officials and functionaries

*Bibliography*

Abu-Lughod, Lila, and Catherine A. Lutz, eds. *Language and the Politics of Emotion.* Cambridge: Cambridge University Press, 1986.

Ahmed, Sarah. *The Cultural Politics of Emotion.* New York: Routledge, 2004.

Allee, Mark. *Law and Local Society in Late Imperial China: Northern Taiwan in the Nineteenth Century.* Stanford: Stanford University Press, 1994.

An Chŏngbok. *Imgwan chŏngyo* [Essentials for officials]. Seoul: Kyujanggak Collection, *kyu* no. 15445.

An Sŭng-jun. "1652 nyŏn O Sinnam ŭi ch'ŏ Im ssiga kyehu e kwanhayŏ kwanch'alsa ege ollin ŭisong [An appeal submitted by Madam Im, wife of O Sinnam, to the provincial government in 1652 on family succession]." *Munhŏn kwa haesŏk* [Sources and interpretation] 10 (2000): 56–73.

———. "1689 nyŏn Chŏng ssi puin i Yejo e ollin Han'gŭl soji [A vernacular Korean petition submitted to the Board of Rites by Madam Chŏng in 1689]." *Munhŏn kwa haesŏk* [Sources and interpretation] 8 (Autumn 1999): 83–95.

Austin, J. L. *How To Do Things with Words.* Cambridge: Harvard University Press, 2001.

Baker, Donald. "Rhetoric, Ritual, and Political Legitimacy: Justifying Yi Seong-gye's Ascension to the Throne." *Korea Journal* 53, no. 4 (2013): 141–67.

———. "A Different Thread: Orthodoxy, Heterodoxy, and Catholicism in a Confucian World." In *Culture and the State in Late Chosŏn Korea*, edited by Haboush and Deuchler, 199–230.

Bandes, Susan A., ed. *The Passions of Law.* New York: New York University Press, 1999.

Berlant, Lauren. "The Subject of True Feeling: Pain, Privacy and Politics." In *Transformations: Thinking through Feminism*, edited by Sarah Ahmed et al., 33–47. London: Routledge, 2000.

Bernhardt, Kathryn. *Women and Property in China, 960–1949.* Stanford: Stanford University Press, 1999.

Bernhardt, Kathryn, and Philip C. C. Huang. *Civil Law in Qing and Republican China.* Stanford: Stanford University Press, 1994.

Bial, Henry, ed. *The Performance Studies Reader.* 2nd ed. New York: Routledge, 2007.

Bishop, Isabella L. *Korea and Her Neighbours.* London: John Murray, 1898.

Blaine, Marcia Schmidt. "Women and the New Hampshire Provincial Government." In *Petitions in Social History*, edited by Heerma van Voss, 57–77.

Bloom, Irene. "Confucian Perspectives on the Individual and the Collectivity." In *Religious Diversity and Human Rights*, edited by Irene Bloom, J. Paul Martin, and Wayne L. Proudfoot, 114–51. New York: Columbia University Press, 1996.

Bodde, Derk, and Clarence Morris. *Law in Imperial China: Exemplified by 190 Ch'ing Dynasty Cases*. Philadelphia: University of Pennsylvania Press, 1967.

Bohnet, Adam. "Ruling Ideology and Marginal Subjects: Ming Loyalism and Foreign Lineages in Late Chosŏn Korea." *Journal of Early Modern History* 15, no. 6 (2011): 477–505.

Bol, Peter K. *Neo-Confucianism in History*. Cambridge: Harvard University Asia Center, 2010.

Botsman, Daniel V. *Punishment and Power in the Making of Modern Japan*. Princeton: Princeton University Press, 2005.

Bourdieu, Pierre. *Language and Symbolic Power*. Cambridge: Harvard University Press, 1994.

Breuker, Remco. *Establishing a Pluralist Society in Medieval Korea, 918–1170: History, Ideology and Identity in the Koryŏ Dynasty*. Leiden: Brill, 2010.

Brook, Timothy, Jérôme Bourgon, and Gregory Blue, eds. *Death by a Thousand Cuts*. Cambridge: Harvard University Press, 2008.

Buoye, Thomas. "Filial Felons: Leniency and Legal Reasoning in Qing China." In *Writing and Law in Late Imperial China*, edited by Hegel and Carlitz, 109–24.

———. *Manslaughter, Markets, and Moral Economy: Violent Disputes over Property Rights in Eighteenth-Century China*. New York: Cambridge University Press, 2000.

———. "Suddenly Murderous Intent Arose: Bureaucratization and Benevolence in Eighteenth-Century Qing Homicide Reports." *Late Imperial China* 16, no. 2 (1995): 62–97.

Buswell, Robert, ed. *Religions of Korea in Practice*. Princeton: Princeton University Press, 2007.

Butler, Judith. "Performative Acts and Gender Constitution: An Essay in Phenomenology and Feminist Theory." In *The Performance Studies Reader*, edited by Bial, 187–99.

———. *Gender Trouble: Feminism and the Subversion of Identity*. New York: Routledge, 1999.

———. *Excitable Speech: A Politics of the Performative*. New York: Routledge, 1997.

Buxbaum, David. "Some Aspects of Civil Procedure and Practice at the Trial Level in Tanshui and Hsinchu from 1789 to 1895." *Journal of Asian Studies* 30, no. 2 (1971): 255–79.

Chamberlain, Mary, and Paul Thompson, eds. *Narrative and Genre*. London: Routledge, 1998.

Chang Pyŏng-in. "Chosŏn sidae wa ilche sidae yŏsŏng ŭi pŏpchŏk chiwi pigyo [A comparison of women's legal status of the Chosŏn period and the Japanese colonial period]." *Hosŏ sahak* [Journal of Hosŏ history] 36 (December 2003): 201–34.

———. "Chosŏn sidae sŏngbŏmjoe e taehan kukka kyuje ŭi pyŏnhwa [The change in the state's regulations on sex crime in the Chosŏn period]." *Yŏksa pip'yŏng* [History and criticism] 56 (August 2001): 228–50.

———. *Chosŏn chŏn'gi honinje wa sŏngch'abyŏl* [The marriage system and gender discrimination in the early dynasty]. Seoul: Ilchisa, 1999.

———. "Koryŏ sidae honinje e taehan chaegŏmt'o [A reexamination of the marriage system in Koryŏ]." *Han'guk sahak yŏn'gu* [Journal of Korean history] 71 (December 1990): 1–30.

Chartier, Roger. *On the Edge of the Cliff: History, Language, and Practices*. Translated by Lydia G. Cochrane. Baltimore: Johns Hopkins University Press, 1997.

———. *Cultural History: Between Practices and Representations*. Translated by Lydia G. Cochrane. Cambridge: Polity Press, 1988.

Chen, Li. "Legal Specialists and Judicial Administration in Late Imperial China, 1651–1911." *Late Imperial China* 33, no. 1 (2012): 1–54.

Chi Sŭng-jong. *Chosŏn chŏn'gi nobi sinbun yŏn'gu* [A study of slave status in the early Chosŏn]. Seoul: Ilchogak, 1995.

Cho Chi-man. *Chosŏn sidae ŭi hyŏngsabŏp: Taemyŏngnyul kwa kukchŏn* [Criminal law in the Chosŏn: The Great Ming Code and the State Codes]. Seoul: Kyŏngin Munhwasa, 2007.

Cho, Hwisang. "The Community of Letters: The T'oegye School and the Political Culture of Chosŏn Korea, 1545–1800." PhD dissertation, Columbia University, 2010.

Cho Yun-sŏn. "Yŏngjodae namhyŏng, hokhyŏng p'yeji kwajŏng ŭi silt'ae wa hŭmhyul e taehan p'yŏngkka [A study of the abolition of excessive punishments and the treatment of prisoners during the Yŏngjo period]." *Chosŏn sidaesa hakbo* [Journal of Chosŏn history] 48 (2009): 211–53.

———. "Chosŏn hugi kangsang pŏmjoe ŭi yangsang kwa pŏpchŏk taeŭngch'aek [The phenomenon of ethical crimes in the late Chosŏn and its legal measures]." *Pŏpsahak yŏn'gu* [Journal of Korean legal history] 34 (2006): 39–72.

———. *Chosŏn hugi sosong yŏn'gu* [A study of litigation in the late Chosŏn]. Seoul: Kukhak Charyowŏn, 2002.

Ch'oe Chae-sŏk. *Han'guk kajok yŏn'gu* [A study of the Korean family]. Seoul: Minjung Sŏgwan, 1966.

Choe, Key-sook. "A Weeping Man and the Mourning Ritual: Literati Writing and the Rhetoric of Funeral Oration in Eighteenth-Century Korea." *Korea Journal* 53, no. 1 (Spring 2013): 143–71.

———. "Hyonyŏ Simch'ŏng ŭi sŏsajŏk t'ansaeng kwa todŏkchŏk tillema: Kamsŏngjŏk p'oyong kwa chŏnhyang ŭi maengnak [The birth of filial daughter Simch'ŏng's narrative and moral dilemma: Embracing emotions and the changing context]." *Kososŏl yŏn'gu* [Journal of premodern novels] 35 (2013): 65–103.

———. "Kamsŏngjŏk in'gan ŭi palgyŏn kwa kamjŏng ŭi pokhapsŏng, sunsusŏng, inyŏmhwa: 19 segi kungmun sosŏl *Namwŏngosa* ŭi sarang p'yosanghwa maengnak [The discovery of the affective human being and complexity, purity, and idealization of emotions: The representative context of love in the nineteenth-century vernacular novel *Namwŏngosa*].” *Kososŏl yŏn'gu* [Journal of premodern novels] 34 (2012): 217–49.

———. “Chosŏn sidae kamjŏngnon ŭi ch'wi wa kamjŏng ŭi munhwa kyuyak: Sadaebu ŭi kŭlssŭgi rŭl chungsim ŭro [Discourse on emotions and their metaphysics during the Chosŏn period: A focus on the Chosŏn literati's writings].” *Tongbang hakji* [Journal of Eastern studies] 59 (September 2012): 3–52.

Ch'oe Sŭng-hee. *Komunsŏ rŭl t'onghae pon Chosŏn hugi sahoe sinbunsa yŏn'gu* [A study on the history of social status in the late Chosŏn through the Komunsŏ]. Seoul: Chisik Sanŏpsa, 2003.

———. *Komunsŏ yŏn'gu* [Study of old documents]. Seoul: Chŏngsin Munhwa Yŏn'guwŏn, 1981.

Choi, Hyaeweol. *Gender and Mission Encounters in Korea: New Women, Old Ways.* Seoul-California Series in Korean Studies, vol. 1. Berkeley: University of California Press, 2009.

———. “Women's Literacy and New Womanhood in Late Chosŏn Korea.” *Asian Journal of Women's Studies* 6, no. 1 (2000): 88–115.

*Chŏllyul t'ongbo* [A conspectus of Chinese and Korean codes]. Seoul: Pŏpchech'ŏ, 1971.

Chŏn Hyŏng-t'aek. *Chosŏn yangban sahoe wa nobi* [Yangban society and slaves in Chosŏn]. Seoul: Munhyŏn, 2010.

———. *Chosŏn hugi nobi sinbun yŏn'gu* [A study of slave status in the late Chosŏn]. Seoul: Ilchogak, 1989.

Chŏn Kyŏng-mok. “Chosŏn hugi sansong ŭi han sarye [A case study of late Chosŏn grave-site disputes].” *Komunsŏ yŏn'gu* [Journal of old documents] 14 (1998): 69–98.

———. “Sansong ŭl t'onghae pon Chosŏn hugi sapŏp chedo ŭnyong silt'ae wa kŭ t'ŭkching [The function of the Chosŏn judicial system and its characteristics through a study of grave-site lawsuits].” *Pŏpsahak yŏn'gu* [Journal of legal history] 18 (1997): 5–31.

———. “Komunsŏ yong'ŏ p'uri: Chosŏn hugi sojiryu e nat'ananŭn ‘hwamin’ e taehayŏ [An interpretation of terms in the old documents: The usage of “*hwamin*” in petitions of the late Chosŏn].” *Komunsŏ yŏn'gu* [Journal of old documents] 6, no. 1 (1996): 143–58.

———. “Chosŏn hugi sansong yŏn'gu: 18, 19 segi komunsŏ chungsim ŭro [A study of gravesite lawsuits in the late Chosŏn based on eighteenth- and nineteenth-century old documents].” PhD dissertation, University of North Chŏlla, 1996.

Chŏn Kyŏng-mok et al., trans. *Yusŏp'ilji* [Essential knowledge for scholar-officials and functionaries]. Seoul: Sakyejŏl ch'ulp'ansa, 2006.

Chŏn Pong-dŏk. “Amhaeng ŏsa chedo yŏn'gu [A study of secret royal emissary system].” *Han'guk pŏpchesa yŏn'gu* [Studies on Korean legal history]. Seoul: Seoul taehak ch'ulp'anbu, 1968.

———. *Han'guk pŏpchesa yŏn'gu* [A study of Korean legal history]. Seoul: Seoul National University Press, 1968.

Chŏn, Pong-dŏk, William Shaw, and Dai-Kwon Choi, eds. *Traditional Korean Legal*

*Attitudes*. Korea Research Monograph 2. Berkeley: Institute of East Asian Studies, University of California, 1980.

Chŏn, Shin-yong, ed. *Legal System of Korea*. Seoul: International Cultural Foundation, 1975.

Chŏng Chi-yŏng. "Chosŏn sidae honin changnyŏch'aek kwa toksin yŏsŏng [The policy of encouraging marriage and single women in the Chosŏn]." *Han'guk yŏsŏnghak* [Korean women's studies] 20, no. 3 (2004): 5–38.

———. "Chosŏn hugi ŭi ch'ŏp kwa kajok chilsŏ [Concubines and family order in the late Chosŏn]." *Sahoe wa yŏksa* [Society and history] 65 (May 2004): 6–40.

———. "Chosŏn hugi kwabu ŭi tto tarŭn sŏnt'aek [A widow's alternative choice in the late Chosŏn]." *Yŏksa wa munhwa* [History and culture] 5 (May 2002): 225–61.

———. "Chosŏn hugi ŭi yŏsŏng hoju yŏn'gu [A study of women householders in the late Chosŏn]." PhD dissertation, Sŏgang University, 2001.

Chŏng Chin-yŏng. *Chosŏn sidae hyangch'on sahoesa* [History of rural society in the Chosŏn period]. Seoul: Hangilsa, 1998.

Chŏng Chong-hyu. *Kankoku minpōten no hikakuhō teki kenkyū* [A study of the Korean civil code from a comparative legal perspective]. Tokyo: Sobunsha, 1989.

*Chŏngjo sillok* (Veritable records of King Chŏngjo). In *Chosŏn wangjo sillok*.

Chŏng Kŭng-sik. "Charyo: 16 segi iban [Sources: Two endorsements from the sixteenth century]." *Seoul taehakyo pŏphak* [Legal studies of Seoul National University] 47, no. 3 (2006): 464–98.

———. *Han'guk kŭndaepŏp sago* [Thoughts on Korean modern legal history]. Seoul: Pagyŏngsa, 2002.

———. "Chosŏn sidae ŭi kwŏllyŏk pullip kwa pŏpch'ijuŭi: Kŭ sironchŏk koch'al [Separation of power and rule of law under the Chosŏn dynasty: A preliminary examination]." *Seoul taehakkyo pŏphak* [Legal studies of Seoul National University] 42, no. 4 (2001): 27–65.

Chŏng Sŏk-chong. *Chosŏn hugi sahoe pyŏndong yŏn'gu* [A study on the social transformation of the late Chosŏn dynasty]. Seoul: Ilchogak, 1983.

Chŏng Tojŏn. *Sambongjip* [Collected writings of Sambong]. Seoul: Kuksa P'yŏnch'an Wiwŏnhoe, 1961.

Chŏng Yagyong. *Mongmin simsŏ* [A book for the heart of the magistrate]. In *Chŏng Tasan chŏnsŏ* [Complete works of Chŏng Tasan]. 3 vols. Seoul: Munhŏn P'yŏnch'an Wiwŏnhoe, 1961.

———. *Hŭmhŭm sinsŏ* [New writings on circumspection in judicial decisions]. 4 vols. Seoul: Kwangmunsa, 1901.

Chōsen sōtokufu. *Chōsen minjirei* [Chosŏn ordinance on civil matters]. Pusan: Minjok Munhwa, 1984.

———. *Chōsen kyūkan seido chōsa jigyō gaiyō* [Summary report on investigations of the old Korean customary system]. Keijō [Seoul]: Chōsen Sōtokufu, 1910.

*Chosŏn wangjo sillok* [Veritable records of the kings of the Chosŏn dynasty]. 48 vols. Reprint, Seoul: Kuksa P'yŏnch'an Wiwŏnhoe, 1970.

*Chosŏn wangjo sillok* [Veritable records of the kings of the Chosŏn dynasty]. Translated and edited by Kuksa P'yŏnch'an Wiwŏnhoe. Accessed January 17, 2014. http://sillok.history.go.kr.

Ch'ü T'ung-Tsu. *Law and Society in Traditional China*. Paris: Mouton, 1961.

*Ch'uan kŭp kugan* [Records of *ch'u* and *kug* hearings]. 30 vols. Seoul: Asea Munhwasa, 1978–.

*Ch'ugwanji* [Treatise on the Board of Punishments]. Compiled by Park Irwŏn in 1781. 3 vols. Reprint, Seoul: Seoul Taehakkyo Kyujanggak, 2004.

*Chungjong sillok* (Veritable records of King Chungjong). In *Chosŏn wangjo sillok*.

*Chŭngsu muwŏllok ŏnhae* [Amplified and corrected coroner's manual for the elimination of grievances in vernacular Korean]. Originally compiled by Wang Yü, edited by Ku T'aekkyu, and translated by Sŏ Yurin. Translated and annotated by Song Ch'ŏl-ŭi, Yi Hyŏn-hee, Chang Yun-hee, and Hwang Mun-hwan. Seoul: Seoul Taehakkyo Press, 2004.

Clark, Donald N. "Sino-Korean Tributary Relations under the Ming." In *The Cambridge History of China*. Vol. 8, *The Ming Dynasty*, edited by Denis C. Twitchett, 272–300. Princeton: Princeton University Press, 1998.

Cline, Erin M. *Confucius, Rawls, and the Sense of Justice*. New York: Fordham University Press, 2013.

Crane, Elaine Forman. *Ebb Tide in New England: Women, Seaports, and Social Change, 1600–1800*. Boston: Northeastern University Press, 1998.

Damasio, Antonio. *Descartes' Error: Emotion, Reason, and the Human Brain*. New York: Putnam, 1994.

*Da Ming Lü* [Great Ming Code]. Translated by Jiang Yonglin. Seattle: University of Washington Press, 2005.

Davis, Natalie Zemon. *Fiction in the Archives: Pardon Tales and Their Tellers in Sixteenth-Century France*. Stanford: Stanford University Press, 1987.

Dayton, Cornelia Hughes. *Women Before the Bar: Gender, Law, and Society in Connecticut, 1639–1789*. Chapel Hill: University of North Carolina Press, 1995.

de Bary, William Theodore, and JaHyun Kim Haboush, eds. *The Rise of Neo-Confucianism in Korea*. New York: Columbia University Press, 1985.

de Bary, William Theodore, and Tu Weiming, eds. *Confucianism and Human Rights*. New York: Columbia University Press, 1997.

Desan, Suzanne, and Jeffrey Merrick, eds. *Family, Gender, and Law in Early Modern France*. Philadelphia: Pennsylvania State University Press, 2009.

Deuchler, Martina. "Propagating Female Virtues in Chosŏn Korea." In *Women and Confucian Cultures in Premodern China, Korea, and Japan*, edited by Ko, Haboush, and Piggott, 142–69.

———. "The Practice of Confucianism: Ritual and Order in Chosŏn Dynasty Korea." In *Rethinking Confucianism*, edited by Elman Duncan, and Ooms, 292–334.

———. "Despoilers of the Way—Insulters of the Sages: Controversies over the Classics in Seventeenth-Century Korea." In *Culture and the State in Late Chosŏn Korea*, edited by Haboush and Deuchler, 91–133.

———. *The Confucian Transformation of Korea: A Study of Society and Ideology*. Cambridge: Council on East Asian Studies, Harvard University Press, 1992.

———. "Heaven Does Not Discriminate: A Study of Secondary Sons in Chosŏn Korea." *Journal of Korean Studies* 6 (1988–89): 121–64.

Du, Fangqin, and Susan Mann. "Competing Claims on Womanly Virtue in Late Imperial China." In *Women and Confucian Cultures in Premodern China, Korea, and Japan*, edited by Ko, Haboush, and Piggott, 219–47.

Dudley, Kathryn M. "In the Archive, in the Field: What Kind of Document Is an 'Oral History?'" In *Narrative and Genre*, edited by Mary Chamberlain and Paul Thompson, 160–66. London: Routledge, 1998.

Duncan, John. "The *Naehun* and the Politics of Gender in the Fifteenth-Century." In *Creative Women of Korea*, edited by Kim-Renaud, 26–57.

———. "Examinations and Orthodoxy in Chosŏn Dynasty Korea." In *Rethinking Confucianism*, edited by Elman, Duncan, and Ooms, 65–94.

———. *The Origins of the Chosŏn Dynasty*. Seattle: University of Washington Press, 2000.

Ebrey, Patricia Buckley. *Women and the Family in Chinese History*. New York: Routledge, 2003.

———. *The Inner Quarters: Marriage and the Lives of Chinese Women in the Sung Period*. Berkeley: University of California Press, 1993.

Ebrey, Patricia B., and Rubie S. Watson, eds. *Marriage and Inequality in Chinese Society*. Berkeley: University of California Press, 1991.

Eggert, Marion. "Text and Orality in the Early Reception of Western Learning within the Namin Faction. The Example of Sin Hudam's *Kimunp'yŏn*." In *Space and Location in the Circulation of Knowledge (1400–1800): Korea and Beyond*, edited by Marion Eggert, Felix Siegmund, and Dennis Würthner, Research on Korea Series, 141–59. Frankfurt: Peter Lang International Academic Publishers, 2014.

———. "Translation/Transcoding in a Diglossic Environment: Case Studies in *Sijo* Literature." A paper presented at Association of Korean Studies in Europe in Vienna. July 6–7, 2013.

Elman, Benjamin A. *Civil Examinations and Meritocracy in Late Imperial China*. Cambridge: Harvard University Press, 2013.

———. *A Cultural History of Civil Examinations in Late Imperial China*. Berkeley: University of California Press, 2000.

Elman, Benjamin A., John B. Duncan, and Herman Ooms eds. *Rethinking Confucianism: Past and Present in China, Japan, Korea, and Vietnam*. UCLA Asia Pacific Monograph Series. Berkeley: University of California Press, 2002.

Finn, Margot. "Women, Consumption, and Coverture in England, c. 1760–1860." *Historical Journal* 39, no. 3 (1996): 703–22.

Foucault, Michel. *Discipline and Punish: The Birth of the Prison*. Translated by Alan Sheridan. New York: Vintage Books, 1991.

———. *The History of Sexuality: An Introduction*. Vol. 1. Translated by Robert Hurley. New York: Random House, 1978.

Frevert, Ute. *Emotions in History: Lost and Found*. Budapest: Central European University Press, 2011.

Furth, Charlotte, Judith T. Zeitlin, and Ping-chen Hsiung, eds. *Thinking with Cases: Specialist Knowledge in Chinese Cultural History*. Honolulu: University of Hawai'i Press, 2007.

Geddes, Rick, and Dean Lueck. "The Gains from Self-Ownership and the Expansion of Women's Rights." *American Economic Review* 92, no. 4 (2002): 1079–92.

Gilmartin, Christina K., ed. *Engendering China: Women, Culture, and the State*. Cambridge: Harvard University Press, 1994.

Goody, Jack. *The Interface between the Written and the Oral*. Cambridge: Cambridge University Press, 1993.

Haboush, JaHyun Kim. "Versions and Subversions: Patriarchy and Polygamy in Korean Narratives." In *Women and Confucian Cultures in Premodern China, Korea, and Japan*, edited by Ko, Haboush, and Piggott, 279–303.

———. "Gender and the Politics of Language in Chosŏn Korea." In *Rethinking Confucianism*, edited by Elman, Duncan, and Ooms, 220–57.

———. *The Confucian Kingship in Korea: Yŏngjo and the Politics of Sagacity*. New York: Columbia University Press, 2001.

———. *The Memoirs of Lady Hyegyŏng: The Autobiographical Writings of a Crown Princess of Eighteenth-Century Korea*. Berkeley: University of California Press, 1996.

———. "Filial Emotions and Filial Values: Changing Patterns in the Discourse of Filiality in Late Chosŏn Korea." *Harvard Journal of Asiatic Studies* 55, no.1 (1995): 129–77.

———. "The Confucianization of Korean Society." In *The East Asian Region: Confucian Heritage and Its Modern Adaptation*, edited by Gilbert Rozman, 84–110. Princeton: Princeton University Press, 1991.

Haboush, JaHyun Kim, ed. *Epistolary Korea: Letters in the Communicative Space of the Chosŏn, 1392–1910*. New York: Columbia University Press, 2009.

Haboush, JaHyun Kim, and Martina Deuchler, eds. *Culture and the State in Late Chosŏn Korea*. Cambridge: Harvard University Asia Center, 1999.

Hahm, Pyong-Choon. *The Korean Political Tradition and Law: Essays in Korean Law and Legal History*. Seoul: Hollym Corporation Publishers, 1967.

Hall, John W. "Rule by Status in Tokugawa Japan." *Journal of Japanese Studies* vol. 1, no. 1 (Autumn 1974): 39–49.

Han Ki-ryŏn. "Haep'yŏng Yun ssi ŭi Hanmun sangŏn [Haep'yŏng Yun's classical Chinese petition to the king]." *Yŏsŏng munhak yŏn'gu* [Journal of women's literature] 15 (2006): 383–402.

———. "Paek Kye yangmun sŏnhaengnok ŭi chakka wa kŭ chubyŏn [The writer of a record of good deeds of the Paek and Kye families and her surrounding people]." *Kojŏn munhak yŏn'gu* [Journal of premodern literature] 27 (2005): 329–61.

Han Sang-gwŏn. "Chosŏn sidae sosong kwa woejibu: 1560 nyŏn kyŏngjupu kyŏlsong iban punsŏk" [Litigation and scriveners during the Chosŏn: An analysis of Kyŏngju County's legal case in 1560]. *Yŏksa wa hyŏnsil* [History and reality], vol. 69 (2008): 255–92.

———. "Sejongdae ch'idoron kwa taemyŏngnyul: Chŏldo sambŏmja ch'ŏbŏrŭl tullŏssan nonbyŏn ŭl chungsim ŭro [Sejong's theory about the treatment of thieves and the Great Ming Code: Focusing on the debate over the issue of punishing third-time offenders in robbery or theft]." *Yŏksa wa hyŏnsil* [History and reality] 65 (2007): 27–57.

———. "15 segi noryangch'ŏ kyohon chŏngch'aek kwa kyohon silt'ae [A policy of intermarriage between a slave man and commoner woman and its practice in the fifteenth century ]." *Komunsŏ yŏn'gu* [Journal of old documents] 29 (August 2006): 55–87.

———. *Chosŏn hugi sahoe wa sowŏn chedo: Sangŏn/kyŏkjaeng yŏn'gu* [Late Chosŏn society and the petition system: A study of written and verbal petitions to the king]. Seoul: Ilchogak, 1996.

Han U-gŭn. "Sinmun'go ŭi sŏlch'i wa kŭ silchejŏk hyonŭng e taehayŏ [The establishment of the petition drum and its effectiveness]." In *Tugye Yi Pyŏngdo paksa hwangap kinyŏm nonch'ong* [Festschrift in commemoration of the sixtieth birthday of Dr. Tugye Yi Pyŏngdo], 357–408. Seoul: Ilchogak, 1956.

Han'guk komunsŏ hakhoe, ed. *Chosŏn ŭi ilsang, pŏpchŏng e sŏda: Sosong* [Everyday life of the Chosŏn, turning to courts: Lawsuits]. Seoul: Yŏksa Pip'yŏngsa, 2013.

———. *Chosŏn sidae saenghwalsa* [History of life in the Chosŏn]. 2 vols. Seoul: Yŏksa Pip'yŏngsa, 2002.

Hara Takeshi. *Chikso wa wanggwŏn* [Direct appeals and kingship]. Translated by Kim Ik-han and Kim Min-ch'ŏl. Seoul: Chisik Sanŏpsa, 2000.

Hartman, Saidiya V. *Scenes of Subjection: Terror, Slavery, and Self-Making in Nineteenth-Century America.* New York: Oxford University Press, 1997.

Hatoyama Hideo. *Nihon minpōsōron* [An introduction to the Japanese Civil Code]. Tokyo: Iwanami shoten, 1930.

Heerma van Voss, Lex, ed. *Petitions in Social History.* Cambridge: Cambridge University Press, 2002.

Hegel, Robert E., comp. and trans. *True Crimes in Eighteenth-Century China: Twenty Case Histories.* Seattle: University of Washington Press, 2009.

Hegel, Robert E., and Katherine Carlitz, eds. *Writing and Law in Late Imperial China: Crime, Conflict, and Judgment.* Seattle: University of Washington Press, 2007.

Higginson, Stephen A. "A Short History of the Right to Petition Government for the Redress of Grievances." *Yale Law Journal* 96, no.1 (1986): 142–66.

Hiraki Makoto. "Jūshichi-hachi seiki ni okeru doryōsai shosei no kizoku ni tsuite [On the reversion to slave status of the offspring of male slaves and commoner wives in the eighteenth and nineteenth centuries]." *Chōsen Gakuho* [Journal of Chosŏn], no. 61 (1971): 45–76.

Hirsch, Susan. *Pronouncing and Persevering: Gender and the Discourses of Disputing in an Islamic Court.* Chicago: University of Chicago Press, 1998.

Hodgkiss, Anita. "Petitioning and the Empowerment of Theory of Practice." *Yale Law Journal* 96, no. 3 (1987): 569–92.

Hoff, Joan. *Law, Gender, and Injustice: A Legal History of US Women.* New York: New York University Press, 1991.

Hong Sŭng-gi. *Koryŏ kwijok sahoe wa nobi* [Aristocratic society and slaves in Koryŏ]. Sŏgang Taehakkyo Inmun Kwahak Yŏn'guso Inmun Yŏn'gu Chŏn'gan, vol. 24. Seoul: Ilchogak, 1983.

Hong Ŭn-jin. "Kurye munhwa Yu ssi ka ŭi Han'gŭl soji e taehayŏ [Vernacular Korean petition of Kurye Yu]." *Komunsŏ yŏn'gu* [Journal of old documents]13 (1998): 111–43.

Howell, George. *Geographies of Identity in Nineteenth-Century Japan*. Berkeley: University of California Press, 2005.

Hsu, Dau-lin. "Crime and Cosmic Order." *Harvard Journal of Asiatic Studies* 30 (1970): 111–25.

Huang, Philip C. C. *Code, Custom, and Legal Practice in China: The Qing and the Republic Compared*. Stanford: Stanford University Press, 2001.

———. *Civil Justice in China: Representation and Practice in the Qing*. Stanford: Stanford University Press, 1996.

*Hŭmhyul chŏnch'ik* [Codes for the Treatment of Prisoners]. 1778. Seoul: Kyujanggak Collection, *yuk* no. 3225.

Hunt, Alan, and Gary Wickham. *Foucault and Law: Towards a Sociology of Law as Governance*. Chicago: Pluto Press, 1994.

Hwang, Kyung-Moon. *Beyond Birth: Social Status in the Emergence of Modern Korea*. Cambridge: Harvard University Asia Center, 2004.

*Hyojong sillok* (Veritable records of King Hyojong). In *Chosŏn wangjo sillok*.

*Hyŏnjong sillok* (Veritable records of King Hyŏnjong). In *Chosŏn wangjo sillok*.

*Ilsŏngnok* [Records of daily reflections]. Edited by Kyujanggak Institute of Seoul National University. Seoul: Seoul Taehakkyo Kyujanggak, 1982–96.

Im Hyŏng-t'aek. "Charyo haejae: Kim ssi puin ŭi Kungmun sangŏn [Interpretation of sources: Madam Kim's vernacular Korean script petition presented to the king]." *Minjok munhaksa yŏn'gu* [Journal of Korean literary history] 25 (2004): 358–84.

Im Sang-hyŏk. "1583 nyŏn Kim Hyŏp Ko Kyŏnggi sosong esŏ nat'ananŭn pŏpche wa sahoesang [Law and society reflected in the lawsuit between Kim Hyŏp and Ko Kyŏnggi in 1583]." *Komunsŏ yŏn'gu* [Journal of old documents] 43 (2013): 131–55.

———. "Sosong kip'i ŭi munhwa chŏnt'ong e taehan chaego wa Han'guk sahoe [A reconsideration of the tradition of anti-litigation culture and Korean society]." *Pŏp kwa sahoe* [Law and society] 24 (2003): 145–60.

———. "Chosŏn chŏn'gi minsa sosong kwa sosong iron ŭi chŏn'gae [Civil litigation in the early Chosŏn dynasty and the development of litigation theories]." PhD dissertation, Seoul National University, 2000.

*Injo sillok* (Veritable records of King Injo). In *Chosŏn wangjo sillok*.

James, Susan. *Passion and Action: The Emotions in Seventeenth-Century Philosophy*. Oxford: Clarendon Press, 1997.

Jean-Klein, Iris. "Mothercraft, Statecraft, and Subjectivity in the Palestinian Intifada." *American Ethnologist* 27, no. 1 (2000): 100–27.

Jiang, Yonglin. *The Mandate of Heaven and the Great Ming Code*. Seattle: University of Washington Press, 2011.

Joseph, Suad. "Brother/Sister Relationships: Connectivity, Love, and Power in the Reproduction of Patriarchy in Lebanon." *American Ethnologist* 21, no. 1 (1994): 50–73.

———. "Gender and Relationality among Arab Families in Lebanon." *Feminist Studies* 19, no. 3 (1993): 465–86.

Kahn, Paul W. *The Cultural Study of Law.* Chicago: University of Chicago Press, 2000.

Kallander, George L. *Salvation through Dissent: Tonghak Heterodoxy and Early Modern Korea.* Honolulu: University of Hawai'i Press, 2013.

Kalton, Michael. "The Writings of Kwŏn Kŭn: The Context and Shape of Early Yi Dynasty Neo-Confucianism." In *Rise of Neo-Confucianism in Korea*, edited by de Bary and Haboush, 89–123.

Kalton, Michael, ed. *The Four-Seven Debate: An Annotated Translation of the Most Famous Controversy in Korean Neo-Confucian Thought.* New York: State University of New York Press, 1994.

Karasawa, Yasuhiko. "From Oral Testimony to Written Records in Qing Legal Cases." In *Thinking with Cases*, edited by Furth, Zeitlin, and Hsiung, 101–22.

———. "Between Oral and Written Cultures: Buddhist Monks in Qing Legal Plaints." In *Writing and Law in Late Imperial China*, edited by Hegel and Carlitz, 64–80.

Karlsson, Anders. "Law and the Body in Chosŏn Korea: Statecraft and the Negotiation of Ideology." *The Review of Korean Studies* 16, no. 1 (2013): 7–45.

———. "Famine Relief, Social Order, and State Performance in Late Chosŏn Korea." *The Journal of Korean Studies* 12, no. 1 (2007): 113–41.

———. "Royal Compassion and Disaster Relief in Chosŏn Korea." *Seoul Journal of Korean Studies* 20, no. 1 (2007): 71–98.

———. "Central Power, Local Society, and Rural Unrest in Nineteenth-Century Korea: An Attempt at Comparative Local History." *Sungkyun Journal of East Asian Studies* 6, no. 2 (2006): 207–38.

Kelly, Joan. *Women, History, and Theory.* Chicago: University of Chicago Press, 1984.

Kendall, Laurel, and Mark Peterson, eds. *Korean Women: View from the Inner Room.* New Haven, CT: East Rock Press, 1983.

Kim Chin-myŏng. "Kabujang tamnon kwa yŏsŏng ŭi ŏgap: Naehunsŏ mit Ŭiryesŏ ŭi punsŏk ŭl chungshim ŭro [Patriarchal discourse and the oppression of women: An analysis of the *Naehun* and *Ŭirye*]." *Asea yŏsŏng yŏn'gu* [Journal of Asian women] 33 (December 1994): 61–94.

Kim Chŏng-guk. *Kyŏngminp'yŏn* [Compendium to warn people]. Translated by Chŏng Hohun. Seoul: Acanet, 2012.

Kim Ho. *Chŏng Yagyong, Chosŏn ŭi chŏngŭi rŭl malhada* [Chŏng Yagyong's talk of justice in Chosŏn Korea]. Seoul: BM Sŏng'andang, 2013.

———. "Hŭmhŭm sinsŏ ŭi il koch'al [A study of new writings on circumspection in judicial decisions]." *Chosŏn sidaesa hakpo* [Journal of Chosŏn history] 54 (2010): 233–65.

———. "Kyujanggak sojang 'kŏman' ŭi kich'ojŏk kŏmt'o [A preliminary examination of inquest records in the Kyujanggak archive]." *Chosŏn sidae sahakbo* [Historical journal of Chosŏn period] 4 (1998): 155–230.

Kim, Jisoo M. "Women's Legal Voice: Language, Power, and Gender Performativity in Late Chosŏn Korea," *Journal of Asian Studies* vol. 74, no. 3 (2015): 667–86.

———. "Law and Emotion: Tension between Filiality and Fidelity in a Property Dispute of Early Chosŏn Korea." *Tongbang hakji* [Journal of Eastern studies] 162 (June 2013): 203–39.

———. "Crossing the Boundary of Inner Quarters: Elite Women's Petitioning Activity in Late Chosŏn Korea." In *Korean Studies Forum*, edited by Hyuk-Rae Kim, vol. 4, 221–43. Seoul: Yonsei University Press, 2010.

———. "Individual Petitions: Petitions by Women in the Chosŏn." In *Epistolary Korea*, edited by Haboush, 68–76.

Kim, Joy S. "Representing Slavery: Class and Status in Late Chosŏn Korea." PhD dissertation, Columbia University, 2004.

Kim, Jungwon. "'You Must Avenge on My Behalf': Widow Chastity and Honour in Nineteenth-Century Korea." *Gender and History* 26, no. 1 (2014): 128–46.

———. "Negotiating Virtue and the Lives of Women in Late Chosŏn Korea." PhD dissertation, Harvard University, 2007.

Kim Ki-ch'un. *Chosŏn sidae hyŏngjŏn* [Penal code of the Chosŏn dynasty]. Seoul: Samyŏngsa, 1990.

Kim Ki-hyŏng. "Kubi sŏrhwa e nat'anan kwabu ŭi hyŏngsang kwa ŭimi [Characteristics and meanings of widows represented in oral narratives]." *Han'guk minsokhak* [Journal of Korean folk studies] 26 (1994): 25–53.

Kim Kyŏng-mi, ed. *Han'guk ŭi kyubang munhwa* [The Kyubang culture of Korea]. Seoul: Pakijŏng, 2005.

Kim Kyŏng-suk. "Chosŏn hugi yŏsŏng ŭi chŏngso hwaldong [Women's petitioning activity in the late Chosŏn]." *Han'guk munhwa* [Korean culture] 36 (December 2005): 89–123.

———. "18, 19 segi sajokch'ŭng ŭi punsan taerip kwa sansong [Conflict and the dispersion of elite lineages in the eighteenth and nineteenth centuries through grave-site lawsuits]." *Han'guk hakpo* [Journal of Korean studies] 28, no. 4 (2002): 59–102.

———. "Chosŏn hugi sansong kwa sahoe kaldŭng yŏn'gu [A study of grave-site lawsuits in the late Chosŏn and social conflicts]." PhD dissertation, Seoul National University, 2002.

Kim, Marie Seong-Hak. *Law and Custom in Korea: Comparative History*. New York: Cambridge University Press, 2012.

———. "Law and Custom under the Chosŏn Dynasty and Colonial Korea: A Comparative Perspective." *Journal of Asian Studies* 66, no. 4 (2007): 1067–97.

Kim, Michael. "Literary Production, Circulating Libraries, and Private Publishing: The Popular Vernacular Fiction Texts in the Late Chosŏn Dynasty." *The Journal of Korean Studies* 9, no. 1 (Fall 2004): 1–31.

Kim, Myeong-Seok. "What *Ceyin zhi xin* (Compassion/Familial Affection) Really is." *Dao* 9 (2010): 407–25.

———. "An Inquiry into the Development of the Ethical Theory of Emotions in the Analects and the Mencius." PhD dissertation, University of Michigan, 2008.

Kim Pyŏng-hwa. *Han'guk sabŏpsa* [Korean legal history]. Seoul: Ilchogak, 1979.

Kim-Renaud, Young-Key, ed. *Creative Women of Korea*. New York: M. E. Sharpe,
2004.

Kim Sŏn-gyŏng. "Chosŏn hugi yŏsŏng ŭi sŏng kamsi wa ch'ŏbŏl [Female sexuality,
surveillance, and punishment in the late Chosŏn]." *Yŏksa yŏn'gu* [Journal of history]
8 (December 2000): 57–100.

———. "Chosŏn hugi sansong kwa sallim soyugwŏn ŭi silt'ae [Grave-site lawsuits
and the realities of forest-land ownership in the late Chosŏn]". *Tongbang hakji*
[Journal of Eastern studies] 77–79 (June 1993): 497–535.

Kim Sŏng-u. *Chosŏn chunggi kukka wa sajok* [The state and the ruling elite in the
middle of the Chosŏn]. Seoul: Yŏksa Pip'yŏngsa, 2001.

Kim, Sun Joo. *Voice from the North: Resurrecting Regional Identity through the Life
and Work of Yi Sihang* (1672–1736). Stanford: Stanford University Press, 2013.

———. "Fragmented: The *T'ongch'ŏng* Movements by Marginalized Status Groups in
Late Chosŏn Korea." *Harvard Journal of Asiatic Studies* 68, no. 1 (2008): 135–68.

———. *Marginality and Subversion in Korea: The Hong Kyŏngnae Rebellion of 1812*.
Seattle: University of Washington Press, 2007.

Kim, Sun Joo, ed. *The Northern Region of Korea: History, Identity, and Culture*.
Seattle: Center for Korean Studies, University of Washington Press, 2010.

Kim, Sun Joo, and Jungwon Kim, comp. and trans. *Wrongful Deaths: Selected
Inquest Records from Nineteenth-Century Korea*. Seattle: University of Washington Press, 2014.

Kim Tu-hŏn. *Han'guk kajok chedo yŏngu* [A study on the Korean family system].
Seoul: Seoul Taehakkyo Ch'ulp'anbu, 1969.

———. "Chosŏn ch'ŏpchesa sogo [Brief thoughts on the concubinage system of the
Chosŏn]." *Chindan hakpo* [Journal of Chindan] 11 (December 1939): 43–93.

Kim Yong-kyŏng. "Pyŏnghae Hwang ssiga Wansan Yi ssi ŭi yuŏn mit soji [Will and
petition of Wansan Madam Yi from the Pyŏnghae Hwang lineage]". *Munhŏn
kwa haesŏk* [Sources and interpretation] 14 (2001): 76–87.

Kim Yong-mu. "Chosŏn hugi sansong yŏn'gu–Kwangsan Kim ssi Puan Kim ssi
Kamun ŭi sansong soji rŭl chungsim ŭro [A study of gravesite dispute in the late
Chosŏn: Focusing on the petitions of gravesite dispute of Kwangsan Kim lineage
and Puan Kim lineage]." MA thesis, Kyemyong University, 1986.

Kim Yong-sŏp. *Chosŏn hugi nongŏpsa yŏn'gu* [A study on the history of agriculture
in the late Chosŏn dynasty]. Seoul: Ilchogak, 1970–71.

Kim Young-min, and Michael Pettid, eds. *Women and Confucianism in Chosŏn
Korea: New Perspectives*. Albany: SUNY Press, 2011.

Kim Yunbo. *Hyŏngjŏng toch'ŏp* [Painting collection of penal affairs]. Reprint, *Kyegan
Misul* [Kyegan art] 39 (Fall 1986): 113–22.

King, Ross. "Western Protestant Missionaries and the Origins of Korean Language
Modernization." *Journal of International and Area Studies* 11, no. 3 (2004): 7–38.

———. "Nationalism and Language Reform in Korea: The *Questione della Lingua*
in Precolonial Korea." In *Nationalism and the Construction of Korean Identity*,
edited by Hyung-Il Pai and Timothy R. Tangherlini, 33–72. Berkeley: Institute of
East Asian Studies, University of California, 1998.

Kleinman, Arthur, Veena Das, and Margaret Lock, eds. *Social Suffering*. Berkeley: University of California Press, 1997.

Ko, Dorothy. *Teachers of the Inner Chambers: Women and Culture in Seventeenth-Century China*. Stanford: Stanford University Press, 1994.

Ko, Dorothy, JaHyun Kim Haboush, and Joan Piggott, eds. *Women and Confucian Cultures in Premodern China, Korea, and Japan*. Berkeley: University of California Press, 2003.

Ko Sŏk-kyu ed., *Amhaeng ŏsa ran muŏsinga* [What is a special emissary?]. Seoul: Pakyichŏng, 1999.

*Komunsŏ* [Old documents]. Vols. 16–26. Collected by the Kyujanggak Institute of Seoul National University.

*Komunsŏ chipsŏng* [Compilation volume of the old documents]. 76 vols. Collected by the Academy of Korean Studies.

Koo, Jeong-Woo. "The Origins of the Public Sphere and Civil Society: Private Academies and Petitions in Korea, 1506–1800." *Social Science History* 31, no. 3 (2007): 381–409.

*Koryŏsa* [History of Koryŏ]. Seoul: Asea munhwasa, 1972.

Kuehn, Thomas. *Law, Family, and Women: Toward a Legal Anthropology of Renaissance Italy*. Chicago: University of Chicago Press, 1991.

*Kyŏngguk taejŏn* [Great code of administration]. Seoul: Ilchisa, 1978.

Lansing, Carol. *Passion and Order: Restraint of Grief in the Medieval Italian Communes*. Ithaca: Cornell University Press, 2008.

Larsen, Kirk W. *Tradition, Treaties, and Trade: Qing Imperialism and Chosŏn Korea, 1850–1910*. Cambridge: Harvard University Asia Center, 2008.

Lean, Eugenia. *Public Passions: The Trial of Shi Jianqiao and the Rise of Popular Sympathy in Republican China*. Berkeley: University of California Press, 2007.

Ledyard, Gary. "Kollumba Kang Wansuk: An Early Catholic Activist and Martyr." In *Christianity in Korea*, edited by Robert Buswell, 38–71. Honolulu: University of Hawai'i Press, 2005.

Lee, Peter H. et al., eds. *Sources of Korean Tradition*. Vol. 2, *From the Sixteenth to the Twentieth Centuries*. New York: Columbia University Press, 2000.

———. *Sources of Korean Tradition*. Vol. 1, *From Early Times through the Sixteenth Century*. New York: Columbia University Press, 1997.

Legge, James. *The Chinese Classics: With a Translation, Critical and Exegetical Notes, Prolegomena, and Copious Indexes*. 5 vols. Hong Kong: Hong Kong University Press, 1960.

Levine, David P. *Self-Seeking and the Pursuit of Justice*. Aldershot: Ashgate, 1997.

Liu, Lydia H., ed. *Tokens of Exchange*. Durham, NC: Duke University Press, 1999.

Macauley, Melissa. *Social Power and Legal Culture: Litigation Masters in Late Imperial China*. Stanford: Stanford University Press, 1998.

Mann, Susan L. *Gender and Sexuality in Modern Chinese History*. Cambridge: Cambridge University Press, 2011.

———. "Grooming a Daughter for Marriage: Brides and Wives in the Mid-Qing Period." In *Chinese Femininities, Chinese Masculinities*, edited by Susan Brownell and Jeffrey N. Wasserstrom, 93–119. Berkeley: University of California Press, 2002.

———. *Precious Records: Women in China's Long Eighteenth Century.* Stanford: Stanford University Press, 1997.

Mann, Susan, and Yu-Yin Cheng, eds. *Under Confucian Eyes: Writings on Gender in Chinese History.* Berkeley: University of California Press, 2001.

Mark, Gregory A. "The Vestigial Constitution: The History and Signification of the Right to Petition." *Fordham Law Review* 66 (1998): 2153–231.

Mattielli, Sandra. *Virtues in Conflict: Tradition and the Korean Woman Today.* Seoul: Sawhwa and the Royal Asiatic Society, 1977.

McKnight, Brian E., ed., *Law and the State in Traditional East Asia: Six Studies on the Sources of East Asian Law.* Honolulu: University of Hawai'i Press, 1987.

Meijer, M. J. *The Introduction of Modern Criminal Law in China.* Batavia [Jakarta]: University of Indonesia Sinological Institute, 1949.

Merry, Sally E. *Getting Justice and Getting Even.* Chicago: Chicago University Press, 1990.

Mertz, E. "Legal Language: Pragmatics, Poetics, and Social Power." *Annual Review of Anthropology* 23 (1994): 435–55.

Messick, Brinkley. "Evidence: From Memory to Archive." *Islamic Law and Society* 9, no. 2 (2002): 231–70.

———. "Indexing the Self: Intent and Expression in Islamic Legal Acts." *Islamic Law and Society* 8, no. 2 (2001): 151–78.

———. "Written Identities: Legal Subjects in an Islamic State." *History of Religions* 38, no. 1 (1998): 25–51.

———. *The Calligraphic State: Textual Domination and History in a Muslim Society.* Berkeley: University of California Press, 1996.

Mir-Hosseni, Ziba. *Marriage on Trial: A Study of Family Law.* New York: I. B. Tauris, 1993.

Moore, Erin P. *Gender, Law, and Resistance in India.* Tucson: University of Arizona Press, 1998.

Mühlahn, Klaus. *Criminal Justice in China: A History.* Cambridge: Harvard University Press, 2009.

Mun Suk-cha. *Chosŏn sidae chaesan sangsok kwa kajok* [Inheritance and family in the Chosŏn period]. Seoul: Kyŏngin Munhwasa, 2005.

Munro, Donald. *The Concept of Man in Early China.* Stanford: Stanford University Press, 1969.

*Myŏngjong sillok* (Veritable records of King Myŏngjong). In *Chosŏn wangjo sillok.*

Nader, L., ed. *Law in Culture and Society.* Berkeley and Los Angeles: University of California Press, 1997.

Nicholson, Linda J. *Gender and History: The Limits of Social Theory in the Age of the Family.* New York: Columbia University Press, 1986.

Nubola, Cecilia. "Supplications in the Italian States." In *Petitions in Social History,* edited by Heerma van Voss, 35–56.

Nussbaum, Martha C. *Hiding from Humanity: Disgust, Shame, and the Law.* Princeton: Princeton University Press, 2004.

———. *Upheavals of Thought: The Intelligence of Emotions*. Cambridge: Cambridge University Press, 2001.

Ocko, Jonathan. "I'll Take It All the Way to Beijing: Capital Appeals in the Qing." *Journal of Asian Studies* 47, no. 2 (1998): 291–315.

Ooms, Herman. *Tokugawa Village Practice: Class, Status, Power, Law*. Berkeley: University of California Press, 1996.

Orchard, Christopher. "The Rhetoric of Corporeality and the Political Subject: Containing the Dissenting Female Body in Civil War England." In *Women as Sites of Culture*, edited by Shifrin, 9–24.

Pae Kyŏng-suk. *Han'guk yŏsŏng sapŏpsa* [History of private law concerning Korean women]. Seoul: Inha Taehakkyo Ch'ulp'anpu, 1988.

Pak Chae-u. "Koryŏ hugi soji ŭi ch'ŏri chŏlch'a wa iban palgŭp [An issuance of endorsement and the petitioning procedure in the late Koryŏ]." In *Komunsŏ yŏn'gu* [Journal of old documents] 29 (August 2006): 1–24.

Pak Hŭng-su. "Toryanghyŏng chedo [Weights and measures]." In *Han'guksa* [History of Korea], edited by Kuksa P'yŏnch'an Wiwŏnhoe, 24: 599–625. Seoul: Kuksa P'yŏnch'an Wiwŏnhoe, 1994.

Pak Pyŏng-ho. *Kŭnse ŭi pŏp kwa pŏp sasang* [Early modern law and legal thought]. Seoul: Chinwŏn, 1996.

———. "Ilcheha ŭi kajok chŏngch'aek kwa kwansŭp pŏp hyŏngsŏng kwajŏng [Family policy and the formation of family customary law under the period of Japanese occupation]." *Seoul taehakkyo pŏphak* [Legal studies of Seoul National University] 33 (1992): 1–17.

———. *Han'guk Pŏpchesa ko* [Thoughts on Korean legal history]. Seoul: Pŏmmunsa, 1974.

———. *Chŏnt'ongjŏk pŏpch'egye wa pŏp ŭisik* [The traditional Korean legal system and legal consciousness]. Seoul: Han'guk Munhwa Yŏn'guso, 1972.

Palais, James B. *Confucian Statecraft and Korean Institutions: Yu Hyŏngwŏn and the Late Chosŏn Dynasty*. Seattle: University of Washington Press, 1996.

———. "A Search for Korean Uniqueness." *Harvard Journal of Asiatic Studies* 55, no. 2 (1995): 409–25.

———. *Politics and Policy in Traditional Korea*. Cambridge: Council on East Asian Studies, Harvard University, 1991.

———. "Confucianism and the Aristocratic/Bureaucratic Balance in Korea." *Harvard Journal of Asiatic Studies* 44, no. 2 (1984): 427–68.

Park, Eugene Y. *A Family of No Prominence: The Descendants of Pak Tokhwa and the Birth of Modern Korea*. Stanford: Stanford University Press, 2014.

———. *Between Dream and Reality: The Military Examination in Late Chosŏn Korea, 1600–1894*. Cambridge: Harvard University Asia Center, 2007.

Pasco, Allan H. "Literature as Historical Archive." *New Literary History* 35, no. 3 (2004): 373–94.

Perkins, Judith. *The Suffering Self: Pain and Narrative in the Early Christian Era*. New York: Routledge, 1995.

Peterson, Mark A. *Korean Adoption and Inheritance: Case Studies in the Creation of a Classic Confucian Society*. Ithaca: Cornell University Press, 1996.

———. "Women without Sons: A Measure of Social Change in Yi Dynasty Korea." In Kendall and Peterson, *Korean Women*, 33–44.

Pettid, Michael. *Unyŏng-jŏn: A Love Affair at the Royal Palace of Chosŏn Korea.* Introduction and annotations by Michael J. Pettid. Translated by Michael J. Pettid and Kil Cha. Berkeley: Institute of East Asian Studies, University of California, 2009.

*Pibyŏnsa tŭngnok* [Record of the Border Defense Command]. 28 vols. Seoul: Kuksa P'yŏnch'an Wiwŏnhoe, 1982.

Plamper, Jan. "The History of Emotions: An Interview with William Reddy, Barbara Rosenwein, and Peter Stearns." *History and Theory* 49, no. 2 (2010): 237–65.

Poovey, Mary. *Making a Social Body: British Cultural Formation, 1830–1864.* Chicago: University of Chicago Press, 1995.

———. *Uneven Developments: The Ideological Work of Gender in Mid-Victorian England.* Chicago: University of Chicago Press, 1988.

*Puan minchang ch'ibuch'aek* [A record book on the petitions of Puan county]. Translated by Kim Sŏn-kyŏng. Seoul: Puan Munhwawŏn, 2008.

Rawls, John. *Justice as Fairness: A Restatement.* Cambridge: Harvard University Press, 2001.

———. *A Theory of Justice.* Rev. ed. Cambridge: Harvard University Press, 1999.

Reddy, William M. *The Navigation of Feeling: A Framework for the History of Emotions.* Cambridge: Cambridge University Press, 2001.

Reeve, L. J. "The Legal Status of the Petition of the Right." *The Historical Journal* 29, no. 2 (1986): 257–77.

Roberts, Luke S. "The Petition Box in Eighteenth-Century Tosa." *Journal of Japanese Studies* 20, no. 2 (1994): 423–58.

Roberts, Rodney C. "Justice and Rectification: A Taxonomy of Justice." In *Injustice and Rectification*, edited by Rodney C. Roberts, 7–30. New York: Peter Lang, 2002.

Robinson, Kenneth R. "From Raiders to Traders: Border Security and Border Control in Early Chosŏn, 1392–1450." *Korean Studies* 16 (1992): 94–115.

Rockhill, W. Woodville. "Notes on Some of the Laws, Customs, and Superstitions of Korea." *American Anthropologist* 4, no. 2 (1891): 177–88.

Rosen, Deborah A. *Courts and Commerce: Gender, Law, and the Market Economy in Colonial New York.* Columbus: Ohio State University Press, 1997.

Rosenwein, Barbara H. *Emotional Communities in the Early Middle Ages.* Ithaca: Cornell University Press, 2006.

———. "Worrying about Emotions in History." *American Historical Review* 107, no. 3 (2002): 821–45.

Rosenwein, Barbara H., ed. *Anger's Past: The Social Uses of an Emotion in the Middle Ages.* Ithaca: Cornell University Press, 1998.

Ruberg, Willemijn, and Kristine Steenbergh, eds. *Sexed Sentiments: Interdisciplinary Perspectives on Gender and Emotion.* New York: Rodopi, 2011.

Salem, Ellen. "Slavery in Medieval Korea." PhD dissertation, Columbia University, 1978.

Santangelo, Paolo. *Sentimental Education in Chinese History: An Interdisciplinary Textual Research on Ming and Qing Sources.* Leiden: Brill, 2003.

Scarry, Elaine. *The Body in Pain: The Making and Unmaking of the World.* Oxford: Oxford University Press, 1985.

Scott, Joan W. "Unanswered Questions." *American Historical Review* 113, no. 5 (2008): 1422–30.

*Sejo sillok* (Veritable records of King Sejo). In *Chosŏn wangjo sillok.*

*Sejong sillok* (Veritable records of King Sejong). In *Chosŏn wangjo sillok.*

Shaw, William. "The Neo-Confucian Revolution of Values in Early Yi Korea: Its Implications for Korean Legal Thought." In *Law and the State in Traditional East Asia: Six Studies on the Sources of East Asian Law,* edited by Brian E. McKnight, 149–72. Honolulu: University of Hawai'i Press, 1987.

———. *Legal Norms in a Confucian State.* Korea Research Monograph 5. Berkeley: Institute of East Asian Studies, University of California, 1981.

———. "Traditional Korean Law and Its Relation to China." In *Essays on China's Legal Tradition,* edited by Jerome Alan Cohen, R. Randle Edwards, and Fu-mei Chang Chen, 302–26. Princeton: Princeton University Press, 1980.

Shifrin, Susan, ed. *Women as Sites of Culture: Women's Roles in Cultural Formation from the Renaissance to the Twentieth Century.* Burlington, VT: Ashgate, 2002.

*Shihō seido enkaku zufu* [Paintings related to the evolution of the legal system]. Keijō [Seoul]: Chōsen Sōtokufu Hōmukyoku Kōkeika, 1937.

Shikata Hiroshi. "Richō jinkō kansuru mibun kaikyubetsuteki kansatsu [Observations on the status and class of the Yi dynasty population]." In *Chosōn keizai no kenkyū* [Studies on the Korean economy]. Seoul: Keijō Teikoku Daigaku Hogakukai, 1938.

Shin, Susan. "The Social Structure of Kŭmhwa County in the Late Seventeenth Century." *Occasional Papers on Korea* 1 (April 1974): 9–35.

Shklar, Judith N. *The Faces of Injustice.* New Haven: Yale University Press, 1990.

Shrank, Roger, and Robert P. Abelson, eds. *Scripts, Plans, Goals and Understanding: An Inquiry into Human Knowledge Structure.* Hillsdale, NJ: L. Erlbaum Associates, distributed by the Halsted Press Division of John Wiley and Sons, 1977.

Shultz, Edward J. *Generals and Scholars: Military Rule in Medieval Korea.* Honolulu: University of Hawai'i Press, 2000.

Sim Chae-u. "Chosŏn sidae nŭngji ch'ŏsahyŏng chiphaeng ŭi silsang kwa kŭ t'ŭkjing [The characteristics of the punishment of death by cuts and its execution during the Chosŏn period]." *Sahoe wa yŏksa* [Society and history] 90 (2011): 153–54.

———. *Chosŏn hugi kukka kwŏllyŏk kwa pŏmjoe t'ongje: Simnirok yŏn'gu* [State power and crime control in the late Chosŏn: A study of the *Simnirok*]. Seoul: T'aehaksa, 2009.

———. "Chosŏn malgi hyŏngsa pŏp ch'egye wa tae myŏng ryul ŭi wisang [The structure of penal law and the status of the Great Ming Code in the late Chosŏn]." *Yŏksa wa hyŏnsil* [History and reality] 65 (2007): 122–53.

———. "*Simnirok* yŏn'gu: Chŏngjodae sahyŏng pŏmje ch'ŏbŏl kwa sahoe t'ongje ŭi pyŏnhwa [A study of the *Simnirok*: The change in capital punishment and social control during the Chŏngjo period].” PhD dissertation, Seoul National University, 2005.

———. “Chŏngjo dae hŭmhyul chŏnch’ik ŭi panp’o wa hyŏnggu chŏngbi [The decree of the codes for the treatment of prisoners and preparation of punishment tools during the Chŏngjo period].” *Kyujanggak* 22 (December 1999): 135–53.

*Simnirok* [Records of *simni* (hearings)]. 6 vols. Translated by Pak Ch’ansu and Kim Kibin. Seoul: Minjok Munhwa Ch’ujinhoe, 1998–2007.

*Sinju muwŏllok* [Newly annotated coroner’s guide for the elimination of grievances]. Compiled by Ch’oe Ch’i-ŭn et al., 1438. Translated by Kim Ho. Seoul: Sagyejŏl, 2003.

Smail, Daniel. *The Consumption of Justice: Emotions, Publicity, and Legal Culture in Marseille, 1264–1423*. Ithaca: Cornell University Press, 2003.

Sŏ Il-gyo. *Chosŏn wangjo hyŏngsa chedo ŭi yŏn’gu* [A study of the criminal law institutions of the Chosŏn dynasty]. Seoul: Han’guk Pŏmnyŏng P’yŏnch’anhoe, 1968.

*Sok taejŏn* [Continuation of the Great Code]. Seoul: Pŏpchech’ŏ, 1965.

Solomon, Robert C. “Justice v. Vengeance: On Law and the Satisfaction of Emotion.” In *The Passions of Law*, edited by Bandes, 123–48.

———. *A Passion for Justice: Emotions and the Origins of the Social Contract*. New York: Addison-Wesley Publishing, 1990.

Sommer, Matthew H. *Sex, Law, and Society in Late Imperial China*. Stanford: Stanford University Press, 2000.

Song, Chun-ho and Chŏn Kyŏng-mok. *Chosŏn sidae Namwŏn Tundŏkpang ŭi Chŏnju Yi ssi wa kŭtŭl ŭi munsŏ* [Chŏnju Yi clan of Tundŏk district of Namwŏn county and their documents during Chosŏn period]. Chŏnbuk: Museum of Chŏnbuk University, 1990.

Song, Sang-hyun. *Introduction to the Law and Legal System of Korea*. Seoul: Kyungmunsa, 1983.

*Sŏngjong sillok* (Veritable records of King Sŏngjong). In *Chosŏn wangjo sillok*.

*Sŏnjo sillok* (Veritable records of King Sŏnjo). In *Chosŏn wangjo sillok*.

Stacey, Robin C. *Dark Speech: The Performance of Law in Early Ireland*. Philadelphia: University of Pennsylvania Press, 2007.

Stearns, Peter N., and C. Z. Stearns, “Emotionology: Clarifying the History of Emotions and Emotional Standards.” *American Historical Review* 90: 813–36.

*Sugyo chimnok Sasong yuch’wi* [Collected edicts and judicial cases]. Seoul: Pŏpchech’o, 1962.

*Sukchong sillok* (Veritable records of King Sukchong). In *Chosŏn wangjo sillok*.

*Sŭngjŏngwŏn ilgi* [Records of the Royal Secretariat]. 126 vols. Edited by Kuksa P’yŏnch’an Wiwŏnhoe [National Institute of Korean History]. Seoul: T’angudang, 1961–77.

Swift, Helen J. *Gender, Writing, and Performance: Men Defending Women in Late Medieval France, 1440–1538*. Oxford: Oxford University Press, 2008.

Tadao, Sakai. “Yi Yulgok and the Community Compact.” In *Rise of Neo-Confucianism in Korea*, edited by de Bary and Haboush, 328–48.

*Taejŏn t’ongp’yŏn* [Comprehensive Great Code]. 1785. Seoul: Pŏpchech’ŏ, 1963.

*T'aejo sillok* (Veritable records of King T'aejo). In *Chosŏn wangjo sillok.*

*T'aejong sillok* (Veritable records of King T'aejong). In *Chosŏn wangjo sillok.*

*Tae Myŏngnyul chikhae* [Directly interpreted Ming Code]. Seoul: Kyŏngin Munhwasa, 1974.

Theiss, Janet M. "Explaining the Shrew: Narratives of Spousal Violence and the Critique of Masculinity in Eighteenth-Century Criminal Cases." In *Writing and Law in Late Imperial China*, edited by Hegel and Carlitz, 44–63.

———. *Disgraceful Matters: The Politics of Chastity in Eighteenth-Century China.* Berkeley: University of California Press, 2004.

———. "Femininity in Flux: Gendered Virtue and Social Conflict in the Mid-Qing Courtroom." In *Chinese Femininities, Chinese Masculinities*, edited by Susan Brownell and Jeffrey N. Wasserstrom, 47–66. Berkeley: University of California Press, 2002.

To Myŏn-hoe. "1894–1905 nyŏn hyŏngsa chaep'an chedo yŏn'gu [A study of the criminal justice system, 1894–1905]." PhD dissertation, Seoul National University, 1998.

Tucker, Judith E. *Women, Family, and Gender in Islamic Law.* New York: Cambridge University Press, 2008.

———. *In the House of Law: Gender and Islamic Law in Ottoman Syria and Palestine.* Berkeley: University of California Press, 1998.

Vermeersch, Sem. *The Power of the Buddhas: The Politics of Buddhism during the Koryŏ Dynasty (918–1392).* Cambridge: Harvard University Asia Center, 2008.

Wagner, Edward W. "Two Early Genealogies and Women's Status in Early Yi Dynasty Korea." In *Korean Women*, edited by Kendall and Peterson, 23–32.

———. "Social Stratification in Seventeenth-Century Korea: Some Observations from a 1663 Seoul Census Register." *Occasional Papers on Korea* 1 (April 1974): 39–54.

———. *The Literati Purges: Political Conflict in Early Yi Dynasty Korea.* Cambridge: East Asian Research Center, Harvard University, 1974.

Wallace, Kathleen. "Reconstructing Judgment: Emotion and Moral Judgment." *Hypatia* 8, no. 3 (1993): 61–83.

Walraven, Boudewijn. "Popular Religion in a Confucianized Society." In *Culture and the State in Late Chosŏn Korea*, edited by Haboush and Deuchler, 160–98.

Walthall, Anne. "Devoted Wives/Unruly Women: Invisible Presence in the History of Japanese Social Protest." *Signs* 20, no. 1 (1994): 106–36.

———. *Peasant Uprisings in Japan.* Chicago: University of Chicago Press, 1991.

Waltner, Ann. "The Loyalty of Adopted Sons in Ming and Early Qing China." *Modern China* 10, no. 4 (1982): 441–57.

Weisner, Merry E. *Women and Gender in Early Modern Europe.* New York: Cambridge University Press, 2000.

*Wŏn sinbo sugyo chimnok sasong yuch'wi* [Original and supplementary compilation of royal edicts and litigation cases]. Seoul: Pŏpchech'ŏ, 1964.

Yi Chŏng-ok. "Wansan Yi ssi yuŏn ko [A study of Wansan Madam Yi's will]." *Munhak kwa ŏno* [Literature and language] 3 (1982): 165–67.

Yi Chŏng-yŏp. *Kŭnjonaegansŏn* [Selected letters between women during the Chosŏn], 29–33. Seoul: Kukjemunhwagwan, 1948.

Yi Sang-uk. "Ilche ha chŏnt'ong kajok pŏp ŭi waegok [Distortion of traditional family law under Japanese rule]." In *Han'guk pŏpsahak nonch'ong* [An introduction to Korean legal history], 371–99. Seoul: Pagyŏngsa, 1991.

———. "Ilche ha hoju sangsok kwansŭp pŏp ŭi chŏngnip [The establishment of the household headship system during the colonial period]." *Pŏpsahak yŏn'gu* [Journal of legal history] 9 (1988): 23–61.

Yi Sŏng-im. "16 segi yangban kwanryo ŭi woechŏng [Love affairs of *yangban* bureaucrats in sixteenth-century Chosŏn]." *Komunsŏ yŏn'gu* [Journal of old documents] 23 (2003): 21–59.

Yi Sug-in. "Chosŏn yuhak esŏ kamsŏng ŭi munje [The problem of emotions in the Neo- Confucianism of Chosŏn]." *Kukhak yŏn'gu* [Journal of Korean studies] 14 (Spring/Summer 2009): 391–412.

———. "Yugyo ŭi kwangye yullye e taehan yŏsŏngjuŭijŏk haesŏk [A feminist interpretation of relational ethics in Confucianism]." *Hankuk yŏsŏnghak* [Journal of Korean women's studies] 15 no. 1 (1999): 39–69.

Yi T'ae-jin. "Chosŏn sidae 'minbon' ŭisik ŭi pyŏnch'ŏn kwa 18 segi 'minguk' inyŏm ŭi taedu [The evolution of the consciousness of the primacy of people in Chosŏn and the emergence of the state's people ideology in the eighteenth century]." In *Kukka inyŏm kwa taeoe insik, 17–19 segi* [State ideology and foreign consciousness in the seventeenth through nineteenth centuries], 11–46. Han-il Kongdong Yŏn'gu Ch'ongsŏ [A series of joint studies on Korea and Japan]. Seoul: Ayŏn Ch'ulp'ansa, 2002.

———. "King Chŏngjo: Confucianism, Enlightenment, and Absolute Rule." *Korea Journal* 40, no. 4 (2000): 168–201.

*Yŏngjo sillok* (Veritable records of King Yŏngjo). In *Chosŏn wangjo sillok.*

Yoo, Mi-rim. "King Sejong's Leadership and the Politics of Inventing the Korean Alphabet." *The Review of Korean Studies* 9 no. 3 (September 2006): 7–38.

Yu, Jimmy. *Sanctity and Self-Inflicted Violence in Chinese Religions, 1500–1700.* New York: Oxford University Press, 2012.

*Yullye yoram* [Conspectus of laws and precedents]. Seoul: Pŏpchech'ŏ, 1970.

Yun T'ae-sŏng. "Ilche ŭi Han'guk kwansŭp chosa saŏp kwa minsa kwansŭp pŏp [The Japanese campaign of Korean custom investigations and civil customary law]." *Ch'angwŏndae nonmunjip* [Journal of Ch'angwŏn University] 19, no. 1 (1991): 65–108.

*Yusŏp'ilji* [Essential knowledge for scholar-officials and clerks]. 1872. Seoul: Kyujang-gak Collection, *kyu* no. 6700.

Zarinfraf-Shahr, Fariba. "Ottoman Women and the Tradition of Seeking Justice in the Eighteenth Century." In *Women in the Ottoman Empire*, edited by Madeline C. Zilfi, 253–63. New York: Brill, 1997.

Zelin, Madeleine, Jonathan Ocko, and Robert Gardella, eds. *Contract and Property in Early Modern China.* Stanford: Stanford University Press, 2004.

Zorzi, Andrea. "The Judicial System in Florence in the Fourteenth and Fifteenth Centuries." In *Crime, Society, and the Law in Renaissance Italy*, edited by Trevor Dean and K. J. P. Lowe, 40–58. Cambridge: Cambridge University Press, 1994.

## *Index*

Page numbers in italics refer to figures, maps, or tables; names associated with "case" refer to the petitioner.

categories of petitioning in, 105, 109;
*Great Ming Code and*, 160n27; law
against "oppressing commoners as
slaves," 99; magistrate protection,
alteration of, 39, 126–27, 129
corporal punishment. *See* torture and
corporal punishment
cosmology, legal, 32–34
counties as administrative divisions,
160n24. *See also* death by magistrate
abuse, petitions on; family matters
and women's personal grievances,
local petitions on; magistrates
county courts, *29*
credit and debt: Hwang (commoner
woman) case, 95–96; Sŏ (commoner
woman) case, 94–95
cross-subjective self-enactment, 105
currency, paper, 163n9
customary law, 9, 23, 156n20

Damasio, Antonio, 11
Davis, Natalie Z., 15–16
death by magistrate abuse, petitions on:
about, 126–27; burden of representation and, 123; Kim (commoner
woman; magistrate abuse case), 121,
147; Konsaeng case, 127–30; Madam
Song case, 130–35; pain of the dead,
123; spirits of the wrongfully dead,
124; wife of Chŏng Chun case, 136;
wife of Yi Chinsin case, 135–36; wives
of three brothers case, 136–37
death penalty cases, 118–19
debt. *See* credit and debt
delayed cases as *wŏn* source, 34
diglossia, 54–57, 62–63, 165n48
"Diglossia and the Linguistic Culture of
Chosŏn Korea" (panel), 165n48
districts as administrative divisions,
160n24
divorce, 179n1
*Doctrine of the Mean*, 22
documents: endorsement documents

(*iban*), 34; forging of, 160n19; importance of, 26; land document endorsement requests, 92–93
drought and cosmic order, 33, 34

Eggert, Marion, 165n48
emotion: *chŏng* (emotion, feeling, or sentiment), 10; cognitive turn in study
of, 10; of contagion, 108; emotives
and performativity of, 10–11; hostile
emotions expressed in public, 74;
law as interrelated with, 7; navigated
from family members to petitioners,
120; negative emotions released from
body, 169n8; pain and anger, gendering of, 76–77, 79; Western vs. Chosŏn
understanding of, 10. See also *wŏn*
equality, 14, 36, 154
equilibrium, 10, 22, 124
*Essential Knowledge for Scholar-Officials
and Clerks* (Yusŏp'ilji), 78–79, 170n13
Europe, medieval, 12, 74, 150–51, 157n38
execution practices, 124, 167n69

factionalism in Chosŏn dynasty, 66–72
"fairness" across social statuses, 36
false and distorted statements, 114, 116,
118
family grievances and petitions to
capital on behalf of family members: broadening of "grievance"
to include, 49; cases not adher-
ing to the four categories, 107,
110–13; Chin (commoner woman)
case, 118; circumstances of capital
petitioning, 106–7; cross-subjective
self-enactment, connectivity, and,
105; false statements and distor-
tions or exaggerations in, 114, 116,
118; filial piety rhetoric in, 114–16;
four new categories of petitioning,
104–6, 109–10; Kang (commoner
woman; attempted rape case), 115;
Kang (commoner woman; false

family grievances (*cont.*)
statement case), 115–16; Kim (commoner woman, wife of Yi Tŏksin) case, 114; Kim (commoner woman, wife of Yun Tong'il) case, 116; Kim Sŏngnyŏn case, 117–18; Madam An case, 118; Min (commoner woman) case, 118; mother of Kalju case, 110; multiple patterns within family relationships and, 112–13; Neo-Confucian construction of family and, 109; O (commoner woman, wife of Im Ch'ŏbŏn) case, 115; Pak (commoner woman; imprisoned husband case), 118; Pak (commoner woman, wife of Yi Ch'ŏnbong) case, 116; pardonable crimes and, 115; pardon or vidication appeals, 119; representation, issue of, 107; shared pain and, 122–23; slave of Cho Chŏngnip case, 110; sociality of pain and, 107–8; son of Hyodŏk case, 110; son of Pak Chŏsaeng case, 109–10; sons representing fathers, 109–10; state's concern with verifying facts, 104; statistics, 111–12, *112*, 172n4, 173n24; virtues of filial piety, fidelity, and loyalty and, 105–6, 114; wife of Ch'oi Kŭmgang case, 110; wives representing husbands, 106, 110, 112, 113–19; Yi (commoner woman, wife of Chŏng Yakp'il) case, 103–4; Yi (commoner woman, wife of Yi Myŏnggyu) case, 114–15; Yŏnni (slave woman) case, 116–17; Yun Kukkyŏng case, 110–11
family matters and women's personal grievances, local petitions on: ancestral rites and lineage, 90–92; beginning and ending language in, 79; Ch'ajŏng (slave) case, 93; Chŏng (commoner woman, wife of Kim Manbok) case, 81–87, *83–86*; concerns and strategies of elite vs. nonelite women, 89–90; Confucianization of Korean society and, 88–89; Confucian narrative of female virtue and, 87–88, 89; credit and debt petitions, 94–96; *Essential Knowledge for Scholar-Officials and Clerks* as guidance text, 78–79; gender subjectivity and, 75, 76–77, 87, 93; gravesite disputes, 79–87; Hwang (commoner woman) case, 95–96; incapable husbands and, 76, 87, 169n6; Kim (commoner woman, wife of Chŏng Poksam), 100–101; Kim (commoner woman; oppressing commoners as slaves case), 99–100; land document endorsement requests, 92–93; Madam Chŏng case, 90–92; Madam O case, 92–93; marriage issues, 96–99; Nam (commoner woman) case, 92; Pak (commoner woman; land document case), 93; personal-family grievances, blurring of, 75–76; pity narratives and, 75–76, 82, 89–90, 93, 96; scriveners and crafting the narrative, 77–78; seniority strategy, 94; Sŏ (commoner woman) case, 94–95; social status and slavery issues, 99–101; Song (commoner woman) case, 96–99; Yi Ch'igwan case, 79–81
family structure in Koryŏ vs. Chosŏn dynasty, 88
"fictional" elements, 15–16
fidelity virtue, 105–6
filial piety and duty: daughters and, 173n24; as narrative strategy, 106; to parents-in-law, 98–99; as pillar of Confucian ethics, 105–6; rhetoric of, 114–16; women and, 91–92
Four Beginnings, 10, 156n27
Four-Seven Debate, 10–11

gender: emotions, gendering of, 76–77; female subjectivities constructed through familial relations, 75;

hereditary status system and, 13;
hierarchy of, in *Japanese Civil Code*,
151; legal narrative, gendering of,
78–87; linguistic practice and gender
identity, 57, 73; linguistic practices
and gender norms, 78; narratives of
entwined femininity and masculinity, 87; as organizing element in
Chosŏn society, 13; Qing shift from
status to gender performance, 14;
statements of gender in petitions,
78–79; two-tiered representation of
nonelite women, 93. *See also* men
and masculinity; women
geomancy, 80
gong striking for petitions: custom of,
53; petition drum, transition from,
44–45; Yi (commoner woman, wife
of Chŏng Yakp'il) case, 103
*gongŭi* (righteousness or public justice), 8
governors in judicial system, 27
gravesite disputes (*sansong*): about, 80,
160n19; Chŏng (commoner woman,
wife of Kim Manbok) case, 81–87,
83–86; Kwŏn Chinsŏng vs. Chŏng
brothers, 130; Yi Ch'igwan case,
79–81
*Great Code of Administration*
(Kyŏngguk taejŏn): about, 29; on
corporal punishment, 128–29; magistrates, protection of, 39, 126, 129;
statute of "Appealing grievances"
(*Sowŏn*), 31, 161n31
*Great Ming Code*, 27–29, 161n27
grievance: broadening of meaning of,
49, 53–54; socioeconomic, 53–54; of
*somin* ("small people"), 125; unjust
deaths of family members and, 123.
*See also specific types of grievance*

Haboush, JaHyun Kim, 164n32
Hall, John W., 157n41
Han Sang-gwŏn, 134, 159n61, 165n43,
169n11, 176n51, 177n55

Han U-gŭn, 31
harmony. *See* social order and harmony
Ha Yun, 30, 34
heavenly principle (*ch'ŏlli*), 32–34
hereditary status system: abolition of,
151; freedom and protection within
status boundaries, 13–14; gender
norms and, 13; intermarriage and
offspring social status rules, 138–40;
social mobility and, 137–38. *See also*
social status
Hŏ Ch'ae, 142–43
Hŏ Chip, 45
Hŏ Cho, 37–39
Hŏ Kyŏng, 142–46
homicide case petitions: son of Hŏ
Kyŏng, 142–46; state reluctance
to execute and, 124; statistics on
influence of, 146; as type, 107; Yi
(commoner woman, wife of Chŏng
Yakp'il) case, 103–4
Hong Chungbo, 111
Honggon, 117
Hong Kyŏngnae Rebellion (1812), 150
human feeling (*injŏng*), in legal cosmol-
ogy, 32–34
*Hunmin Chŏngŭm* (Korean alphabet),
54–55
husbands, incapable, 76, 87, 169n6
Hwang (commoner woman), 74, 95–96
Hwang Ch'iryong, 94
Hwang Honggon, 116–17
Hwang Yŏil, 63
Hyodŏk and son, 110
Hyŏnjong, King, 90, 140–41

*idu* (clerk's writing), 165n46
Im, Madam, 57–62
Im Ch'ŏbŏn, 115
Im Hyŏng-t'aek, 72, 167n66
Imjin War, 14, 167n73
imprisonment: *Codes for the Treatment of
Prisoners*, 133–34; death penalty and,
118–19; wife visiting imprisoned hus-

Kwŏn Chunghwa, 139
Kwŏn Kiŏn, 176n41
Kyejŏng, 127
*kyŏkchaeng. See* oral petitions
Kyŏngjong, King, 66–72, 168n74

land dispute cases: Ch'ajŏng (slave),
    93; Madam O, 92–93; Malgŭm
    (slave), 3–4, 5, 6–7; Nam (com-
    moner woman), 92; Pak (commoner
    woman), 93; Song (commoner
    woman), 97–99
language. *See* linguistic practices
law, emotion as interrelated with, 7
legal capacity to petition: empowerment
    to accuse sons-in-law but not hus-
    bands, 99; Japanese colonial period
    and, 151–52; *minbon* philosophy and,
    26; misinterpretation of, by scholars
    of post-Liberation period, 152–53;
    slaves and, 4; women recognized as
    legal subjects, 6
legal codes, 27–29, 160n27
legal culture, 8, 73
legal history, Korean, 8–9
legal knowledge, petitions to gain, 57,
    61–62
legal system: as integral part of adminis-
    trative system, 26; judicial institu-
    tions, 26–27; private law, lack of,
    23–24
lineal succession and lineage grievances,
    59, 90–92
linguistic practices: acknowledgment
    of Korean-script petitions, 56–57; at
    beginning and ending of petitions,
    79; diglossia, 54–57, 62–63; gender,
    specification of, 78–79; and gender
    identity, performance of, 57, 73;
    gender norms and, 78; *idu* (clerk's
    writing), 165n46; invention of
    Korean alphabet, 54–55; scriveners,
    16–17, 47–48, 158n50; textualization
    of language, 17; transcription, 46;

written vernacular Korean vs. classi-
    cal Chinese, 46–47
literacy and illiteracy, 16–17, 48, 166n50
literati purge of 1721–22 (*Sinim Sahwa*),
    66–69
litigations, numbers of, 22, 24
litigators punished for petty grievances
    or lawsuits, 35
lowborn (*ch'ŏnmin*), 14–15, 155n8
loyalty virtue, 114

Maeng Sasŏng, 139
magistrates: Capital Magistracy
    (Hansŏngbu), 27; in judicial system,
    27; kneeling down to petition before,
    52; prohibition of accusations
    against, 37–39, 126–27, 129. *See also*
    death by magistrate abuse, petitions
    on
magistrates, family-matter petitions to.
    *See* family matters and women's per-
    sonal grievances, local petitions on
magnificent harmony (*t'angp'yŏng*)
    policy, 70
Malgŭm (slave), 3–4, 5, 6–7
Manchu invasion, 14
Mandate of Heaven, 33
map of Korea, 28
marriage: differences for elite vs.
    nonelite women, 96–99; empower-
    ment to accuse sons-in-law but not
    husbands, 99; female subjectivities
    constructed through familial rela-
    tions and, 75; Kim Chŏngguk on,
    103; power dynamics, complication
    of, 106; Song (commoner woman)
    case, 96–99
Marseille, France, 12, 150, 157n38, 179n14
masculinity. *See* men and masculinity
matrifilial succession law (*chongmo pŏp*),
    65, 138
mediation, 23
Meiji Restoration, Japan, 179n7
memorial petitions (*sangso*), 19

men and masculinity: anger emotions
and, 76–77, 79; elite men as *ŭisin*
("I"), 78–79; narrative techniques
and, 77; represented husbands as
dependent on wives, 106; role as son
carried into legal space, 111
Mencius, 10, 22, 156n27
middle people (*chungin*), 155n8
*min* ("people"), 78–79
*minbon* ("people as the basis of the
state"), 26
Min Ch'isin, 136
Min (commoner woman), 118
misfortune vs. injustice, 124–25
misjudgment of lawsuits as *wŏn* source,
34
mothers-in-law empowered to accuse
sons-in-law, 99
murder. *See* homicide case petitions

Nam (commoner woman), 92
narrative and storytelling: fidelity and
piety narratives, 106; pity narratives,
75–76, 82, 89–90, 93, 96; scriveners
and, 47–48, 77–78
natural disasters: cosmic order and, 33,
34; public injustice and, 124–25
Neo-Confucian philosophy: Confucianization of Korean society, 88–89;
equilibrium and harmony, mainte-
nance of, 10; family, construction
of, 109; family members representation and Confucianization, 104–6;
female virtue narrative, 87–88, 89;
fidelity virtue, 105–6, 114; filial piety
virtue, 105–6, 114; the Four-Seven
Debate and, 10–11; gravesite disputes
and, 80; injustice and the wrongfully dead in, 124; loyalty virtue,
114; *minbon* ("people as the basis of
the state"), 26; natural equality and
evaluative inequality in, 36; penal
benevolence and right prudence
(*humhyul*), 35–36; protection within

status boundaries and Neo-Confucian polity, 13–14; ruler's obligations,
27; sovereign legitimacy, 32–33, 125;
spread of, 80
No Han'gŏl, 116
nonelite women. *See under* petition
cases
Noron faction, 66–72, 167n71
Nussbaum, Martha, 11

O (commoner woman, wife of Im
Ch'ŏbŏn), 115
O, Madam, 92–93
Ocko, Jonathan, 163n3
Office of the Censor General, 161n34
Office of the Inspector General, 27, 31,
70, 161n34
Oh Kŭmnok, 31
*oksong* (criminal suits), 26
Ooms, Herman, 159n10
orality and textuality, 16–17
oral petitions (*kyŏkchaeng*): elite
women's use of, in cases of injustice,
134–35; interrogation risked in, 135; as
mode, 42, 45; pre-textual mode and
textualization of, 17; process of, 48;
terminology and, 19, 163n14; voice
and body of petitioner and, 48–49
order. *See* social order and harmony
O Sangji, 59–62
O Sinnam, 59–60

pain (*t'ong*): blood writing and, 108;
Chŏng (commoner woman, wife of
Kim Manbok) case, 82; of the dead,
123; family grievances and shared
pain, 122–23; as female-associated,
76–77; sociality of, 107–8, 146
Pak (commoner woman, wife of Yi
Ch'ŏnbong), 116
Pak (commoner woman; imprisoned
husband case), 118
Pak (commoner woman; land document
case), 93

Pak Chŏsaeng, 109–10

Pak Kangsaeng, 110

Pak Pyŏng-ho, 9

Pak Sinsaeng, 110

Pak Sŭp, 173n13

palace, royal: kneeling before, 65, 168n80; petition drum vs., 32; sitting or standing before, 42, 45–46; trespassing through gate of, 53

pardonability, 56, 115, 119

pardons, begging for. *See* family grievances and petitions to capital on behalf of family members

patriarchy and patrilineality: Chosŏn shift to, 88–89; fidelity virtue and, 106; ritual rights and, 90–91

performativity of petitioning: beating the petition drum and striking the gong, 44–45; of emotions, 11–12; and grievance, broadening of meaning of, 49, 53–54; kneeling in front of royal palace, 65; legal culture and, 73; orality, textuality and, 16–17; royal procession and, 45–46, 49, *50–51*; theatrical space and, 43–44; trespassing through the palace gate, 53; written and oral modes and, 45–49

personal grievances of women on family matters. *See* family matters and women's personal grievances, local petitions on

petition cases: Ch'ajŏng (slave) case, 93; Chin (commoner woman), 118; Ch'ŏlbi, 56; Chŏng (commoner woman, grandmother of Yungŭm), 141; Chŏng (commoner woman, wife of Sŏng Yongsŏk), 142–43; Chŏng (commoner woman, wife of Kim Manbok) case, 81–87, *83–86*; Hwang (commoner woman), 95–96; Kang (commoner woman; attempted rape case), 115; Kang (commoner woman; false statement case), 115–16; Kim (commoner woman, wife of Chŏng Poksam), 100–101; Kim (commoner woman, wife of Yi Tŏksin), 114; Kim (commoner woman, wife of Yun Tong'il), 116; Kim (commoner woman; magistrate abuse case), 121, 147; Kim (commoner woman; oppressing commoners as slaves case), 99–100; Kim Sŏngnyŏn, 117–18; Konsaeng case, 127–30; Madam An, 118; Madam Cho, 63, 166n55; Madam Chŏng, 90–92; Madam Im, 57–62; Madam Kim, 65–72, 166n54, 167n66, 168nn78–80; Madam O, 92–93; Madam Song case, 130–35; Madam Yi, 63–65, 166n54; Malgŭm (slave), 3–4, 5, 6–7; Min (commoner woman), 118; mother of Kalju, 110; Nam (commoner woman), 92; O (commoner woman, wife of Im Ch'ŏbŏn), 115; Pak (commoner woman, wife of Yi Ch'ŏnbong), 116; Pak (commoner woman; imprisoned husband case), 118; Pak (commoner woman; land document case), 93; slave of Cho Chŏngnip, 110; Sŏ (commoner woman), 94–95; Song (commoner woman), 96–99; son of Hŏ Kyŏng, 142–46; son of Hyodŏk, 110; son of Pak Chŏsaeng case, 109–10; wife of Ch'oi Kŭmgang, 110; wife of Chŏng Chun, 136; wife of Chŏng Chun case, 136; wife of Yi Chinsin, 135–36; wife of Yi Chinsin case, 135–36; wives of three brothers case, 136–37; Yi (commoner woman, wife of Chŏng Yakp'il), 103–4; Yi (commoner woman, wife of Yi Myŏnggyu), 114–15; Yi Ch'igwan, 79–81; Yŏnni (slave woman), 116–17; Yun Kukkyŏng, 110–11

petition drum (*sinmun'go*): in China, 163n3; evolution of petitions out of, 42; installation of, 7, 30, 150;

CPSIA information can be obtained
at www.ICGtesting.com
Printed in the USA
BVHW032051161218
535550BV00004B/8/P